D1559710

PHILOSOPHY IN

C·R·I·S·I·S

MARIO BUNGE

PHILOSOPHY IN
C·R·I·S·I·S

The Need for Reconstruction

 **Prometheus Books**

59 John Glenn Drive
Amherst, New York 14228-2197

THE PROMETHEUS LECTURES

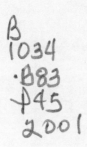
Published 2001 by Prometheus Books

Inquiries should be addressed to
Prometheus Books
59 John Glenn Drive
Amherst, New York 14228–2197
VOICE: 716–691–0133, ext. 207
FAX: 716–564–2711
WWW.PROMETHEUSBOOKS.COM

04 03 02 01 00   5 4 3 2 1

Library of Congress Cataloging-in-Publication Data

Bunge, Mario Augusto.
      Philosophy in crisis : the need for reconstruction / Mario Bunge.
            p. cm. — (Prometheus lecture series)
      Includes bibliographical references and indexes.
      ISBN 1–57392–843–7 (hardcover : alk. paper)
      1. Philosophy. I. Title. II. Series.

B1034.B83 P45 2000
199'.82—dc21

                                                                                00-045844

Printed in the United States of America on acid-free paper

CONTENTS

PREFACE

The consensus seems to be that philosophy is currently at a low ebb. There is even some talk of the death of philosophy. I believe this talk to be silly, for no thinking person can avoid philosophy altogether. Just think of the concepts of reality, truth, and value; or of the principles that the external world is real, that some truths are attainable, and some values objective and cross-cultural. Or think of the negations of these philosophical principles.

What is true is that academic philosophy has become rather stale. It is obsessed with its own past, suspicious of radically new insights, inward-looking, largely removed from worldly concerns, and therefore of hardly any help in tackling most of the issues faced by ordinary people. Hence the word *crisis* in the title of this book. So much for the bad news.

The good news is that philosophy has gone through crises before, which it has eventually overcome. For example, it entered a crisis at the start of the Christian era, at the beginning of the Modern period, and during the Counter-Enlightenment. All three crises were eventually overcome by fresh insights and hard work. In the thirteenth century, Thomas Aquinas overcame for a while the first crisis, mainly by his vindication of reason and his realist epistemology. In the sixteenth century, close contact with the reborn sciences and the newly born ones gave birth to a new, secular, and proscientific worldview. And in the nineteenth century some logicians, prompted by the explosive growth of mathematics, resurrected logic and forged some of the formal tools required to perform exact philosophical analyses.

Every time philosophy seemed to hit a dead end, attempts were made to reconstruct it. Suffice it to mention Cartesianism, Spinozism, Leibnizianism, classical empiricism, Kantianism, Hegelianism, dialectical materialism, pragmatism, phenomenology, logical positivism, and linguistic philosophy. Still, good work has proceeded on the margins of schools and on many limited problems. Beautiful flowers can grow among ruins. Not forests, though.

Good philosophy is worth doing because it is a vantage point for the study of anything, whether concrete things or abstract ideas. Indeed, although it may not see the world, good philosophy helps looking at it—just as bad philosophy blocks the view of ideas and things, in denying that there are any, or in claiming that they can be understood without the help of either reason or experience.

If good philosophy is both valuable and currently in short supply, then it should be reconstructed. Which materials and tools should be used to rebuild philosophy? I suggest that the materials—the substance—are provided by science and technology, as well as by the history of philosophy; and the tools—the form—by logic and mathematics. This is, at least, the kind of philosophy I care for: one capable of tackling interesting philosophical questions in the light of the best available factual knowledge, and with the help of precision tools forged by formal science. A few examples should clarify what I have in mind.

Take for instance the venerable ontological problem of the nature of space and time. There are two main views on these intangibles: the subjectivist and the objectivist ones. Since science and technology treat space and time as real features of the world, the subjectivist view may be discarded as a philosophical extravagance. However, there are two realist conceptions of space and time. One of them states that they are self-existing (absolutist theory), and the other that they constitute the basic structure of being and becoming (relational theory). This is no idle question. Indeed, consider the so-called expansion of the universe. There could be such movement of the universe as a whole only if it were finite, and if space and time were the immutable stage where the cosmic drama is being played out. But if, on the contrary, space and time only exist as relations among things and events, then the universe, even assuming it to be finite, would have nowhere to go. In this case, we should stick to the astronomical evidence, and talk of the mutual recession of the galaxies rather than of the expansion of the universe.

Our next case is the question of the most fruitful approach to the problem of the nature of mind. Currently, the two most fashionable approaches among philosophers are through language and computers. The respective underlying assumptions are that language is the mirror of the mind, and that the latter works like a computer, that is, only with symbols and in accordance with computational rules (algorithms). These assumptions have encouraged the fusion of three fields under the name of *cognitive science*: cognitive psychology of the kind that ignores the brain and its development and evolution, computer science, and linguistics. Neuroscience and evolutionary biology have been excluded from this company, on the tacit traditional assumption that the mind is immaterial, the brain being at most the tool of the self: that which "subserves" or "mediates" the mental functions. I submit that this brainless and pre-evolutionary approach to the problem of mind is wrong: it is far too close to magical thinking, theology, and idealist philosophy to merit being called scientific. Which in turn accounts for its barrenness, particularly by comparison with the spectacular recent findings of cognitive neuroscience, neurolinguistics, and neurology. A major driving hypothesis of these disciplines is that mental processes are brain processes, whence they have evolved along the brain and society. Another is that language is not a separate faculty but initially a by-product, and later on also a partner, of cognition, so that it grows in the socially embedded brain rather than in the mythical immaterial mind.

Take lastly the problem of the nature of values and moral norms. Are all value judgments subjective and therefore beyond truth and error, and are all moral norms bound to particular social groups and times? The affirmative answer is of course that of common sense, as well as that of the relativist philosophers, anthropologists, and sociologists. These students point to the well-known facts that no two societies share exactly the same value system or the same moral code, and that perceptions of what is valuable and just change in time. The obvious rejoinder is that, if this is true, then how to explain that the great majority of people, at all times, have valued life, friendship, loyalty, fairness, reciprocity, good will, knowledge, liberty, peace, and more? And why is it that, at times, some people have risked social standing, liberty, or even life, to defend, promote, or expand such values? For example, what, if not belief in certain basic universal values and norms, motivated or at least justified the American and French revolutionaries? Did they not regard those values and norms as objective and universalizable? In other words, who is right: the relativist or the universalist? Whom should we follow in this matter: the Romantics, Nietzsche, Mussolini, and the postmoderns, or else Descartes, Spinoza, the Enlightenment,

Kant, and Einstein? And how should we seek the correct answer to this question: by shouting, elbowing, and negotiating, or by debating rationally with the help of scientific findings concerning the relevance of certain values and norms to survival, coexistence, welfare, and progress? And why should we prefer either of the alternative approaches? Are there any good conceptual or practical reasons for either? These are typically philosophical questions. However, any answer to them is bound to be socially valuable or disvaluable, in addition to being intellectually satisfying or unsatisfactory.

So much for a random sample of philosophical questions that deserve being discussed in a clear manner, with the help of some formal tools, and in the light of the available scientific knowledge—rather than carelessly and in compliance with superstition. More will be found in this book. Reading it should resemble walking up a gentle ramp. Indeed, I start with a popular subject, namely the impact of the information revolution, and advance slowly up to a diagnosis and treatment of the ills of current philosophy. Along the way, the central topics of the book are displayed and discussed: philosophical materialism, skepticism, realism, scientism, systemism, humanist ethics, and their rivals. Although these may sound like heady subjects, they are actually involved in many a scientific, technological, political, and even everyday-life discussion. So much so, that most of the illustrations in the text are drawn from these fields. Which is purported to show that philosophy is not a luxury but a necessity in the modern world.

Most of the philosophical terms occurring in this book are elucidated in my *Dictionary of Philosophy* (Bunge 1999a). And those interested in further aspects of my philosophy are advised to look up Martin Mahner's *Scientific Realism: Selected Essays of Mario Bunge* (Mahner 2001).

I am grateful to my children, Carlos and Silvia, as well as to my coworker Martin Mahner, for a number of critical remarks. I also thank Paul Kurtz, Champion of Secular Humanism and *Malleus Impostoribus*, for having invited me to contribute this volume to the Prometheus Lecture Series. Last, but not least, I am indebted to Mary A. Read for her superb copyediting.

Mario Bunge
Department of Philosophy
McGill University
Montréal

1

HUMANISM IN THE INFORMATION REVOLUTION

I t is a commonplace that we are going through a technological revolution as radical as the ones initiated by the steam engine, electric power, telecommunications, the internal-combustion engine, and the pill: namely, the information revolution. This revolution has changed not only the way information diffuses through society. It has also changed social relations and activities, in particular the very mode of production, circulation, and utilization of knowledge.

For example, whereas in the past the scholar's alter ego was the library, and the laboratory the experimentalist's, now every worker in the knowledge industry has an additional alter ego: his computer—a genuine *Doppelgänger* in the case of the laptop. And these momentous changes in work style are not confined to cultural activities: Millions of people in nearly all walks of life have now vastly enriched their social circles, their cultural resources, and their influence thanks to the computer, e-mail, and the worldwide web. All this has become commonplace and even object of worship.

We have become used to looking only at the positive aspects of this particular revolution, such as nearly instant spread of information, cuts in mindless toiling, and commercial transactions through the Internet. However, history should have taught us that every technological innovation is bound to harm some people while benefiting others. One reason is that not everyone is as nimble, well-situated, or well-heeled as to make the most of any new sophisticated means. Another is that the worldwide web is threatening privacy. Just think of those uncounted well-meaning people whose messages clutter our screens because they are anxious to share their priceless information and original insights with the rest of us.

The information revolution is, then, just as ambivalent as the previous technological revolutions. Such ambivalence poses no problems to the believers in the inevitability and desirability of all technological advancement. But it should pose a problem to anyone concerned about the unforeseen and sometimes perverse consequences of human actions. In particular, secular humanists should face the possible ambivalence of the current information revolution. However, before tackling this problem we should clarify the idea of secular humanism and dispel a popular misunderstanding about it.

1.1 ❖ SECULAR HUMANISM IS A WHOLE WORLDVIEW

Secular humanism is widely believed to be a purely negative doctrine that boils down to the denial of the supernatural. This is not so, as any fair sample of the humanist literature will show (see, e.g. , Kurtz 1973; Storer 1980; Lamont 1982; Kurtz 1988; Bunge 1989). Indeed, secular humanism is a positive and broad worldview. It is roughly the worldview held by the members of the eighteenth-century Enlightenment, which inspired the American and French Revolutions, as well as the ensuing progressive cultural changes and social reforms.

In my opinion, the trademark of secular humanism is concern for the lot of humankind. This formula may be spelled out into the following seven theses.

1. Cosmological: Whatever exists is either natural or man-made. Put negatively: There is nothing supernatural in the real world.

2. Anthropological: The individual differences among people pale by comparison with the common features that make us all members of the same species. Put negatively: There are neither supermen nor master races.

3. Axiological: Although different human groups may care for different values, there are many basic universal values, such as well-being, honesty, loyalty, solidarity, fairness, security, peace, and knowledge, that are worth working or even fighting for. Put negatively: Radical axiological relativism is false and harmful.

4. Epistemological: It is possible and desirable to find out the truth about the world and ourselves with the sole help of experience, reason, imagination,

criticism, and action. Put negatively: Radical skepticism and epistemological relativism are false and noxious.

5. Moral: We should seek salvation in this world, the only real one, through work and thought rather than prayer or war, and we should enjoy living, as well as trying to help others live, instead of damning them.

6. Social: Liberty, equality, solidarity, and expertise in the management of the commonwealth.

7. Political: While defending the freedom from and to religious worship and political allegiance, we should work for the attainment or maintenance of a secular state, as well as for a fully democratic social order free from unjustified inequalities and avoidable technical bunglings.

Not all humanists assign the same value to all seven components. Typically, whereas some humanists stress the intellectual components, others emphasize the social ones. Which is just as well, for it is evidence that, far from being a sect or party, secular humanism is a broad umbrella covering social activists as well as freethinkers of various hues.

1.2 ❖ RELIGIOUS HUMANISM AND ANTISOCIAL FREETHINKING

The humanist worldview is acceptable in part to believers in the supernatural, so long as they are tolerant of nonbelievers, and are willing to do something to improve the state of the world. By contrast, an atheist or agnostic indifferent to his fellow humans hardly deserves being called a humanist, because the mark of humanism is concern for the lot of humankind. Let me give a couple of examples.

Some years ago I shared a summer course in Spain with the Jesuit philosopher Ignacio Ellacuría. He taught the spiritualist and unscientific philosophy of his fellow Basque, Xavier Zubiri, whereas I taught my own materialist and science-based philosophy. Knowing each other's views, we hardly spoke to each other, until I learned that he was the rector of the Universidad de El Salvador, a well-known center of resistance against the savage military dictatorship that at the time ruled the Republic of El Salvador. He spoke to me with amazing and moving passion of the sufferings of the *campesinos* and the unselfishness and heroism of the *guerrilleros*. A couple of years later, Ellacuría and five of his colleagues were murdered by a death squad in the service of the dozen families that own the best land of the country and control its government. He and his fellow martyrs were religious humanists. Who is more entitled to a place in the humanist pantheon: the priest and idealist philosopher who died for the poor and oppressed, or the materialist and scientistic professor who leads a sheltered life in a peaceful country? I hope to be at the height of the Reverend Ellacuría, so that I may be forgiven for not having risked my life fighting for human rights, and he for having taught an obscurantist philosophy.

Arthur Schopenhauer is reputed to have been the first atheist among German philosophers. However, this does not make him a secular humanist, for he was a misogynist, preached pessimism, and was utterly unconcerned with the plight of the downtrodden. Friedrich Nietzsche too was an unbeliever, but he wrote against reason and science, did not appreciate compassion, and held the "herd" in contempt. Therefore he does not belong in the Humanist pantheon either. Likewise, Sigmund Freud debunked religion, but exaggerated the force of instinct, regarded women as intellectually and morally inferior to men, and held aggressiveness to be inborn. Above all, Freud invented psychoanalysis, one of the greatest intellectual swindles, as well as commercial successes, of all times. This alone disqualifies him as a humanist. Last example: The late Ayn Rand, a popular novelist, homespun philosopher, and early neoliberal ideologue, was an outspoken if shallow atheist, rationalist, and materialist. But I submit that she was not a humanist because she preached "rational egoism" along with "savage capitalism." Moreover, she was a fascist sympathizer about whom Mussolini had a movie made.

Secular humanism teaches not only naturalism and rationalism: it also endorses the wise slogan of the French Revolution: *Liberté, égalité, fraternité* (Liberty, equality, fraternity). This slogan is wise because the three values it proclaims hang together like the sides of a triangle. Indeed, liberty is only possible among equals; equality can exist only where there is freedom to defend it; and every social system, from the family to the nation, requires a modicum of solidarity. (More in chapter 9.)

In conclusion, there are two kinds of humanism: secular and religious. True, the latter is only half-humanistic, for it is centered in fictitious superhuman individuals. But both kinds of humanism share a capital principle: that of solidarity, which in turn presupposes that we are all basically equal, deserving equally to enjoy life, and equally obliged to help others. Hence, with regard to humanism, there are four kinds of people: secular and progressive, secular and regressive, religious and progressive, and religious and regressive. This is why two coalitions are always possible in social and political activities regardless of religious beliefs: the progressive and the reactionary ones.

1.3 ❖ HUMANISTS FACE THE INFORMATION REVOLUTION

What has the above got to do with the information revolution that is changing everyday life in the industrialized countries? Much, because the humanist, whether secular or religious, has something to say about technological innovations, since some of these are beneficial, others noxious, and still others either ambivalent or indifferent. I have just suggested a thesis that will be rejected by technophiles as well as technophobes. My thesis is that technology, unlike basic science but like ideology, is seldom morally neutral and therefore socially impartial.

Obviously, there are beneficial technologies, such as the ones used in manufacturing kitchen utensils and efficient pharmaceuticals. It is equally evident that there are evil technologies, such as those of mass murder and the manipulation of public opinion. And there are also double-edged technologies, such as those employed in the manufacture of TV sets, the organization of firms, or the design of legal codes or public policies. Indeed, TV may entertain and educate, or it may habituate us to violence, vulgarity, and passivity. Management science can enhance consumer and worker satisfaction, or it can aim at utility maximization at the cost of quality product or worker well-being. The legal craft can defend or condemn the innocent, and it can enforce or weaken an unjust law. And a piece of public policy may benefit the rich or the poor, everyone, or no one.

Because technology, unlike basic science, is rarely neutral, it is only natural that most people should be either tecnophiles or technophobes. However, most technophobes have no qualms about using high-tech artifacts, and some technophiles worship technologies they do not understand. An example of inconsistent technophobia is the irrationalist who writes his nonsense on a word processor. And a case of blind technophily is that of the Saudi Bedouin whom my friend Dan A. Seni caught in the act of kneeling and bowing in front of a computer—the Westerner's newest potent and inscrutable deity.

Information technology is ambivalent, because it concerns only the processing and transmission of messages, not their content or meaning. An information net may diffuse knowledge or propaganda, poems or insults, calls to compassion or to violence. Because of this ambivalence, humanists have something to do and say about the information revolution: We have to find out what is good and what is bad about the information revolution, as well as what is true and what is false about the strident info-hype.

1.4 ❖ INFORMATION AND KNOWLEDGE

The enormous role that information plays in industrial societies has given rise to the myth that the universe is made of bits rather than matter. The well-known physicist John Archibald Wheeler has compresssed this myth into the formula "Its from bits." An instant's reflection suffices to puncture this idealist extravagance. In fact, an information system, such as the Internet, is constituted by human beings (or else automata) who operate artifacts such as coders, signals, transmitters, receivers, and decoders. These are all material things or processes in them. Not even signals are stuff-free: in fact, every signal rides on some material process, such as a radio wave.

In other words, it is not true that the world is immaterial or in the process of dematerialization—or, as some popular authors put it, that bits are replacing atoms. We eat and drink and breathe atoms, not bits. And when we get sick we call a physician, not an information expert. What is true is that e-mail is replacing snail-mail. But the electromagnetic signal that propagates along a net is just as material as the letter and the mailman who carries it. The information revolution is a huge technological innovation with an ever stronger social impact, but it does not require any basic changes in worldview: Today's world is just as material and changeable as yesterday's. The main difference with yesterday's is that it is more closely knit—more of a system.

We may laugh at the superstitious Bedouin of my friend Dan's story, while forgetting that similar characters are at the helm of many a powerful modern organization. What else is the politician or civil servant who proposes to swamp schools with computers, in preference to recycling teachers and motivating students, upgrading labs and workshops, restocking libraries, updating curricula—and perhaps serving breakfast as well? What if not a superstitious Bedouin is the science administrator who prioritizes the research projects involving intensive use of computers regardless of the importance and originality of the research problems?

All these modern Bedouins equate information with knowledge, and research with information retrieval or its diffusion. But information or message is not the same as knowledge. Martin Heidegger's sentences "The world worlds," "Language speaks," and "Time is the ripening of temporality," convey no knowledge at all: they are empty strings of symbols. And original research does not consist in retrieving or even processing information, but in formulating new problems and trying to solve them. In particular, the information revolution is the child of a number of findings of basic or disinterested research projects, from pure mathematics to quantum theory, which is the basis of solid-state physics.

Computers are certainly helping find and spread new knowledge, but they cannot replace live, well-educated, curious, disciplined, and strongly motivated brains. This is so only because computers are designed and built by people to help answer questions, not to find, invent, or evaluate problems. And problems happen to be the fountains of research. Moreover, a computer program can only tackle well-posed problems with the help of some algorithm or instruction. It is helpless in the face of an ill-posed problem, or of a well-posed problem for which no algorithm is known (or for which it is known that no algorithm is possible). In particular, computers are helpless in the face of inverse problems, such as guessing the intentions of a person from her behavior, because such problems have at best multiple solutions—as many as the number of educated guesses the observer can come up with. (More on inverse problems in chapter 5.) Nor can there be algorithms for designing new algorithms, or even for repairing unexpected bugs. So much so, that no computer has detected, let alone debugged, the so-called Millennium Bug, that is, the inability of millions of computer clocks to recognize the year 2000.

In general, there are no rules for inventing new ideas, in particular new rules. (If there were, we would be spared hundreds of papers promising that the computers of the next generation will be creative.) Only a living brain, and a well-appointed one at that, can invent radically new ideas, in particular problems, analogies, high-level principles, and algorithms. Computers can just combine or unpack known ideas, only provided they are supplied with the suitable rules of combination or inference. Moreover, computers cannot understand the symbols they process if these happen to refer to items in their surrounding, because the latter contains only a power outlet, a typist, and perhaps other computers. Any reference to atoms or stars, the weather or politics, friends or business, is wasted on a computer.

Furthermore, computers work to rule in all the senses of the word. They are neither curious nor doubtful, neither imaginative nor adventurous; they neither cut corners nor understand incomplete sentences, let alone metaphors; and they can neither craft projects nor evaluate empirical findings or plans. For a word processor, the proverbial sentences "Dog bites man" and "Man bites dog" have the same value (quantity of information), since they have the same number of bits. Likewise, a computer is incapable of ranking research projects. Consequently, it may lend its alleged authority to any wrong-headed project—such as that of creating "artificial life" in the guise of computer programs that mimic selected aspects of living processes.

We all would like to know more and, at the same time, to receive less information. In fact, the problem of a worker in today's knowledge industry is not the scarcity of information but its excess. The same holds for professionals: just think of a physician or an executive, constantly bombarded by information that is at best irrelevant. In order to learn anything we need time. And to make time we must use information filters allowing us to ignore most of the information aimed at us. We must ignore much to learn a little. And to craft such filters we need a naturalistic, comprehensive, deep, and up-to-date worldview. Secular humanism should help here, if only because of its skepticism concerning the supernatural and the paranormal.

In sum, the new information artifacts facilitate the processing and communication of knowledge but do not produce it. In particular, computers neither explore the external world—except occasionally by proxy—nor invent theories capable of explaining or predicting any facts. Hence, they replace neither the explorer nor the inventor, or even the doubter. Nor do they replace the competent and dedicated teacher capable of stimulating curiosity and transmitting enthusiasm for learning. A good teacher can help shape an inquisitive and creative brain. By contrast, the most an electronic device can do is to supply some valuable information and carry out some routine tasks. A powerful algorithm can help solve problems of a particular kind far quicker than a legion of living brains, but it is not a multipurpose organ like a normal brain. It is neither insightful nor creative, or even critical: it must accept obediently almost anything it is fed. It is unable to improvise in the face of unforeseen situations. Last, but not least, no electronic device is capable of autonomous moral judgment. And this point is of particular interest to humanists, whether secular or religious.

1.5 ❖ THE INFORMATION HIGHWAY

The Internet is daily making more converts than any political parties and churches, including Islam. The fervor of some of its users is such, that there is already talk of info addiction (or web alcoholism), on a par with drug addiction. Kimberley Young, a researcher with the University of Pittsburgh, examined Internet addicts. She found that they spend as many hours sitting in front of the screen at home as at work, and that they tend to isolate themselves from their relatives and friends. Besides, when deprived of access to the Net, they exhibit a withdrawal syndrome similar to that experienced by drug addicts.

Fortunately, info addicts are and will always constitute a small minority, and this for two reasons: restricted usefulness and excessive cost. The former is that the vast majority of the tasks we accomplish in daily life do not require the use of computers: think of learning to walk and respect other people, showering and getting dressed, cooking a meal and hammering a nail, greeting a neighbor and imagining a scene, playing ball and attending a party, planning an outing and discussing the day's news, daydreaming and listening to music. The second reason that the Internet is and will remain an elite tool is that access to it involves an expenditure greater than the yearly income of most people in the Third World—where four out of five people happen to live. In particular, the Internet does not reach the shantytowns, which are inhabited by more than a billion people.

However, undoubtedly the lives of an increasing number of people in the First World revolve around the information network. Some of them do not feel alive unless they send at least ten e-mails a day and do not spend some hours surfing the Net or retransmitting trivial information. How to explain this new fad? There are several motives. First, the Net procures a huge quantity of information at a low price: it is the most universal and cheapest of encyclopedias. Second, using the Net confers prestige, it is chic and a sign of youthfulness: those off-line are rustics or fossils. Third, using the Net is more comfortable than visiting museums; attending concerts, plays, or lectures; browsing in libraries, traveling, or teaching one's children. Fourth, anyone can produce his own home page to exhibit his wisdom or sense of humor, or else to relieve himself or bore others with impunity. Fifth, networking allows anyone to make many acquaintances overnight and without commitment. Sixth, the Net is a refuge from job problems and domestic worries.

This is why compulsive networking, like obsessive TV watching, can function as an electronic surrogate of religious worship. "Our Net in Cyberspace, hallowed be thy name. Your kingdom come. Thy will be done on earth as it is in Cyberspace. Give us this day our daily bits."

The info zealots assure us that the info highway is leading to a more equal, cohesive, democratic, and better-educated society. Is it? In fact, only minimally. To begin with, the e-network draws no difference between genuine and counterfeit knowledge. Information technology deals exclusively with information, regardless of content, relevance, value, truth, and fairness. This is why there are such things as info overload and info crime, from swindle to organized pedophily.

Anyone can publish anything they like on their home page. There are no gatekeepers here because there are no standards, and because the decision to publish is left to the user, without consultation with peers. Consequently, intellectual anarchy in the Net is total: Anything goes, fact or fancy, meaningful message or gobbledygook, system or stray item, jewel or junk. Cyberspace is the cultural relativist's paradise. By the same token, it has become an obstacle to serious education, since many students prefer accessing the dubious popularization items easily found on the Web, to painstaking search in the library. Because of such utter freedom of expression, the Internet will never displace carefully refereed academic journals and books. Supplement, yes: substitute, no.

Nor is screen watching as inspiring as good old reading printed stuff. Even a high priest of the newest cult admits that "[i]nteractive multimedia leaves [sic] very little to the imagination. . . . By contrast, the written word sparks images and evokes metaphors that get much of their meaning from the reader's imagination and experiences" (Negroponte 1996, 8).

In short, the information highway leads to no definite place. Traveling along it one may learn almost anything except manual skills, judgment, and good habits; one may communicate with other members of the elite; and, above all, one may escape for a while the petty miseries of everyday life—by dint of unloading them unto others. But for the great majority of people it does not meet any basic needs, for most of us do not work in the knowledge industry. Moreover, the global net will always remain inaccessible to those most in need of it: the shipwrecks of society, that is, the people without relatives, friends, or connections, particularly the jobless and the homeless—or simply the illiterate. And these happen to constitute 21 percent of the American adult population, and 22 percent of its British counterpart. The downtrodden could use the Internet to look for employment or friendship, or at least to relieve boredom. But they cannot read, let alone type, and in any case they could not afford it.

1.6 ❖ TOWARD THE VIRTUAL SOCIETY?

A new utopia was born in the 1980s: that of the electronic or virtual society, cybersociety, or network society (see, e.g., Castells 1996). This was to be a society in which face-to-face human relations would be replaced with screen-to-screen communication. We would all move from physical space to cyberspace. Nature, space, and time would be superseded. People would stop meeting in offices, corridors, markets, cafés, clubs, town halls, or even homes. Offices would work without paper. Classrooms, laboratories, and workshops would become computer rooms. Libraries would be dismantled. Sports would be displaced by computer games. Cities would be razed. Money would disappear, and the Internet would become the global shopping mall. Maybe even family relations would pass through the screen. For example, spouses would communicate with one another only through computers, and virtual love would displace carnal love. Is any of this consistent with what we know about the human need for natural resources, physical contact, and face-to-face dialogue?

It was also prophesied that the generalized use of computers will abolish poverty, and that the Internet will perfect democracy—again, because only information would count, and information is now universally available. Is it really? Let us see. Undoubtedly, the information revolution is expanding cultural democracy, that is, popular access to cultural goods—as well as to cultural junk. However, the people with access to the Internet are and will always be a minority because information, even when worthless, is far from free. Indeed, access to it calls for money and a modicum of education. Consequently, in the end, the Internet introduces one more social chasm: that between those who are on-line and those, the overwhelming majority, who remain off-line. Thus the polarization between the plugged and the unplugged adds to the earlier polarizations—those between haves and have-nots, white and dark, believers and infidels, etc. Thus, the information revolution further disempowers rather than empowers the underdog. Hence, it is false that the information revolution is enhancing economic and political democracy (see Menzies 1995; Hurwitz 1999).

The idea underlying the cybersociety utopia is that communication is the only, or at least the main, social bond. This myth was born in the 1960s. For example, the late Karl Deutsch (1966), a distinguished Harvard professor of social science, defined a people as a body of individuals able to communicate with one another over long distances and about a variety of subjects. Likewise, the late German sociologist Niklas Luhmann (1984), who strongly influenced Jürgen Habermas's "theory of communicative action," held that social systems consist of communications and nothing but communications. But if this were true then all the mail, telephone, and e-mail users would constitute a people. For better or for worse, a people is united by a variety of bonds: telecommunication is only one of them. Networking is no substitute for child rearing, nursing, playing, farming, construction, manufacturing, transportation, policing, investigating, or face-to-face socializing. It only alters the way these and others activities are carried out.

Clifford Stoll, an astronomer, the inventor of a predecessor of the Internet, and a frequent user of this medium, is anything but a technophobe. However, in his *Silicon Oil Snake* (1995, 58) he warns against the new fad. He holds that computer networks are double-edged tools. While they facilitate access to mountains of useful information, they also "isolate us from one another and cheapen the meaning of actual experience. They work against literacy and creativity. They undercut our schools and libraries."

The scientific community is the one exception to this rule. Indeed, the Internet has enormously facilitated the daily work of the researchers in every science, in strengthening their cooperation. This has been possible because the disinterested search for truth, unlike that of economic or political power, is ruled by a unique ethos (Merton 1968). This ethos includes the free sharing of information, and the right and duty to practice constructive criticism. Basic scientists are committed to truth as well as to both epistemic communism and organized skepticism. Alas, this moral code does not work in the market—nor, indeed, in any community other than that of basic scientists. So, the ideal cybersociety is inhabited only by scientists. However, all of them continue to meet face-to-face in the traditional venues, from offices and labs to seminars and congresses.

In short, the virtual or electronic society is just as impossible as the novelist Italo Calvino's imaginary cities. True, the e-market is doing astonishingly well, and it is likely to continue to increase its market share. But society is much more than the market, because the exchange of goods and services is only one of the many social relations. Besides, whereas the market is not a self-regulating system, democracy is. The most that the cyberfundamentalists can hope to accomplish by way of social transformation is to divert public attention from tragic social issues—as when a once-powerful American politician proposed giving out laptops to the homeless, so they could start their own businesses from their favorite sidewalks.

CONCLUSION

Every biological and social advance seems to exact a price. For example, we pay for bipedalism with back pain; for big brains, with high energy consumption; for visual acuity, with optical illusions; for decrease in manual labor and walking, with obesity; for sensitivity to social conflict, with stress; for knowledge, with its misuse; for greater individual freedom, with less solidarity; for democracy, with bureaucracy; for easier access to information, with less time to digest it—and so on and so forth. In short, progress tends to be ambivalent. Hence, every proposed major technological advancement should be weighed and discussed before being adopted. This is what the Office of Technological Assessment of the U.S. Congress is expected to be all about.

Secular humanists do not oppose all technological advancement. We applaud all useful innovations, and we do not believe that machines can dominate people, or that technology marches on inexorably by itself. But, because of the ambivalence of technology—as opposed to the univalence of basic science—we do not embrace new technologies before examining their foreseeable social consequences. And we try to get prepared for their unforeseen perverse effects.

In particular, knowing as we do that technological progress is likely to eliminate jobs, it would be only fair that part of the savings deriving from the use of computers be used to shorten the workweek. Because we know that the e-network tightens some social bonds while weakening or even severing others, we must advocate prudence in its use. We must, among other things, prevent it from further invading privacy. Knowing as we do that social issues do not go away by stepping into virtual reality, we should urge that they remain on the political agenda. And, because we know that information is at best a means to learning, and at worst an obstacle to it, we should prevent the replacement of debates, labs, workshops, libraries, and gyms with computer work. Let us distribute stickers to be placed on all computer terminals: "This extremely valuable tool has bad side-effects. It may weaken human bonds, blunt imagination and criticism, and give back ache. Dose it with intelligence, moderation, and social responsibility."

In sum, blind technophily is just as foolish and dangerous as blanket technophobia. For this reason, we should advocate a symbiosis of technology with humanism. In short,

HUMANISM − TECHNOLOGY = SOCIAL STAGNATION,

TECHNOLOGY − HUMANISM = SOCIAL DECLINE,

TECHNOLOGY + HUMANISM = SOCIAL PROGRESS.

2

TEN COSMOLOGICAL
PARADIGMS

I shall take the word "cosmology" in its broadest sense, as synonymous with "worldview" or *Weltanschauung*. In this sense, a cosmology is a synoptic view of the cosmos—not just of nature, but also of persons, society, and perhaps more. In other words, a cosmology is the branch of ontology that inquires into the basic constituents and patterns of the universe.

A cosmology may be coarse or refined, sketchy or detailed, fuzzy or clear. It may be magical or naturalistic, religious or secular, spiritualist, materialist, or dualist. And a cosmology may be ordinary or science-oriented, barren or fertile—and so on. Moreover, cosmologies are not the private property of philosophers and theologians. In fact, every human being has some cosmology or other, usually tacit rather than explicit: he needs it to navigate in the world. And ethologists assure us that every animal has a representation or model of his immediate surrounding, which allows it to survive in it. The difference between the cosmologies imagined by intellectuals and those held by others is that the former are explicit and therefore subject to analysis, criticism, and correction.

There are many kinds of cosmology, but every reasonably comprehensive cosmology must contain answers to such basic questions as: Does God exist? If so, does He still tamper with the world? Did the world have an origin, and will it end, or is it eternal? What is the stuff of the cosmos? Does everything happen for a higher purpose? What are space and time? What are laws? Are there lawless events? What are causation, chance, and purpose? Is radical novelty possible? Is the cosmos flat or organized in layers? What is life? What is mind? What is a human being? What is society? What holds things together? And what takes things asunder?

Every cosmology discharges both a conceptual and a practical function. Its conceptual function is that of providing a framework where every fact and every idea may fit: a whole where every part "makes sense" or coheres with the rest. The practical function of a cosmology is to provide guidance in life: to help formulate goals, choose means, design plans, and evaluate all that. While I submit that moral and political philosophy make no sense except within an explicit and consistent cosmology, in this paper I shall only be concerned with the conceptual aspect of the question.

I shall first outline ten influential cosmological paradigms: holism, which views the world as an animal; hierarchism, which regards it like a stratified society; tychism, that sees the cosmos as the ultimate casino; dynamicism, which views the world as a river without banks; dialectics, that holds it to be ruled by conflict; atomism, the metaphor for which is the cloud; mechanism, according to which the cosmos is a clock; sacralism, that views the world as the ultimate temple; textualism, which regards the world as a book; and systemism, for which the cosmos is the system of all systems.

I shall examine the main characteristics of these ten paradigms, and shall evaluate them in the light of contemporary science and philosophy. In these I shall find strong reasons for preferring the systemic paradigm. Finally, I shall examine the consequences of this choice for the problems of reduction and of the unity of human knowledge.

2.1 ❖ SKETCH OF TEN PARADIGMS

I now sketch the ten paradigms listed previously. Let us begin with holism, or organicism, the view that the cosmos is an animal or like an animal. The focus of this cosmology is the so-called organic whole. Wholes are said to be "more than the sum of their parts." Moreover, wholes are held to be unknowable by analysis. The hierarchical cosmological model conceives of the world by analogy with a pyramidal social organization. The superior beings are on top, and the inferior ones below, and the former rule the latter in a chainlike fashion. This arrangement is eternal: the pyramid or ladder has always been there and it won't change. Only the position of an individual being in the ladder may change.

Next comes tychism or probabilism. According to this paradigm, anything is possible, and all changes are random. Causality and purposiveness are illusory. At most, causation is a limit value of probability, namely when it equals one.

Dynamicism postulates that everything is in a state of flux. It does not commit itself as to the stuff the world is "made" of. Moreover, extreme dynamicism claims that there is no substance: that concrete things are bundles of processes, such as signals.

Dialectics, a special version of dynamicism, holds that contradiction rules the world: everything is a unity of opposites, and all relations are conflictive. Cooperation is either nonexisting or unnatural. The cosmos is the ultimate battlefield.

The atomistic cosmology views the cosmos as a huge gaseous body. Ultimately there are only atoms moving forever in the void. Atoms of different kinds combine into complex things, such as people—social atoms. In turn, complex things constitute aggregates. By contrast to hierarchism, atomism is a sort of democratic cosmology. Things do not differ by rank or value, but only by their complexity.

Mechanism asserts that every complex concrete thing, including the world as a whole, is a machine. Its epistemological concomitant is of course the thesis that mechanics is necessary and sufficient to understand the world.

According to sacralism, the cosmos is dedicated to worshiping one or more inscrutable deities. Every human action is or ought to be an act of submission to the higher powers, and nature is man's servant, hence ultimately a tool of the supernatural.

Textualism asserts that every existent is a text or discourse. Hence semiotics or the science of signs, or perhaps hermeneutics or the art of interpretation, is the all-encompassing discipline: to understand is to interpret.

Finally, systemism postulates that every thing and every idea is either a system or a component of some system. It fosters the systemic or nonsectoral approach to conceptual and practical problems, which in turn favors the integration of the various research fields.

Let us now proceed to take a closer look at these ten cosmologies.

2.2 ❖ HOLISM: THE COSMIC ANIMAL

Holism is one of the earliest cosmologies. It boils down to the ideas that the world is a *plenum*, all the parts of which are held tightly together, and that the part is subordinated to the whole. Holism comes in two versions: static and dynamic. Parmenides' block universe exemplifies static holism, whereas animism exemplifies dynamic holism.

According to animism, every thing is alive or animated to some degree, and the cosmos itself is an animal or like one. Plato attributed this idea to Timaeus. He made Timaeus say that the world "is a living creature endowed with soul and intelligence by the providence of God" (*Timaeus* 30). But of course the idea is much older: it is found in many primitive and archaic cosmogonies.

However, animism is only one version of holism. Thinkers as diverse as Parmenides, Aristotle, the Stoics, Ibn Khaldûn, Pascal, Goethe, Hegel, Comte, Marx, Engels, and Durkheim were holists of sorts. They stressed the interconnectedness of all things and the subordination of the part to the whole, but they were not animists.

Nowadays holism has few defenders. It is found mainly among social scientists. Thus, there is still some talk about collective memories, the will of the people, and ideas being produced by entire social groups rather than by brains. Holism is still alive even among those methodological individualists who unwittingly invoke wholes such as the market and "the situation," which they do not bother to analyze. This holistic contamination is obvious in the assumptions that every agent acts in accordance to the situation he finds himself in, and that two social agents interact through the market rather than face to face. This strange symbiosis of individualism and holism that is sometimes passed off as individualism I call *individholism* (Bunge 1996a).

The epistemological concomitant of holism is intuitionism, according to which we can grasp a whole only as such and by insight and instantly, rather than through painstaking analysis. An intuitive idea behind this antianalytic attitude is that dissection kills, so that an examination of the *disjecta membra* cannot teach us anything about an organic whole. We shall argue in a moment that this argument is far from compelling.

According to holism, "A whole is more than the sum of its parts." This sentence is imprecise and has therefore been much maligned by analytic philosophers. Yet, its meaning is clear. It means that a whole has properties that its parts or components lack. These properties may be called "emergent" or "systemic." They characterize a system as a whole. Obvious physical examples of emergent properties are the center of mass, density, temperature, and conductivity of a body. Biological examples include: life starts and ends at the cell level; and the units of selection are whole organisms rather than their genomes alone. Social examples are: a factory's organization, a government's stability, a nation's history.

Modern natural and social science employ the notions of whole and emergence, and in this regard they have vindicated holism. But they have not adopted the thesis that the whole determines the part. Rather, the interactions of the parts determine the whole, which in turn constrains the behavior of the part.

The weakest component of holism is its antianalytic stand, for analysis, conceptual or empirical, is inherent in all sciences, technologies, and humanities. Moreover, it is only by analyzing a whole into its interacting parts that we can explain what holds it together, what threatens to break it down, and how we might improve on it. Think, for example, of a chemical system, a soccer team, or a symphony.

2.3 ❖ HIERARCHISM: THE COSMIC LADDER

The cosmos has often been viewed in the image of a stratified society: as a ladder from the higher to the lower beings. This model is a sort of inverted evolutionary worldview, for it assumes that the ladder is static, and that the higher beings dominate the lower ones and have not evolved from the lower ones.

This cosmology was rather popular throughout the Middle Ages. It is first found full-fledged in Dionysius the Pseudoareopagite's Neoplatonic forgery. Nine centuries later it reappears in Dante's *Divina commedia*. The idea of *scala naturae* bore fruit in eighteenth-century biology, where it inspired the early evolutionist speculations of Buffon's and Bonnet's (Lovejoy 1953). And it was later transmogrified into present-day ideas about the level structure of the world, widespread among biologists. So, it was not a total loss.

2.4 ❖ TYCHISM: THE WORLD CASINO

Tychism, or probabilism, is a modern view—just as modern as the concept of probability. At first sight, tychism is supported by the many scientific theories where probability plays a central role, as well as by the very existence of accidental or random errors of measurement. However, even such theories "prohibit" the occurrence of certain conceptually possible events, in particular all those that contradict the laws of nature. Besides, any statement of the form "The probability that event C be followed by event E is such and such" involves the concepts of cause and effect. Consequently, contrary to popular view, causation has not been extruded from modern science.

Besides, there are plenty of nonprobabilistic branches of science and technology. Hence, it is not true that every possible event can be assigned a probability. For example, since elevators, trains, planes, and cars do not work at random, it is mistaken to assign a probability to the event of any of them arriving first. Likewise, rational choice theory, so fashionable nowadays in social studies, is mistaken in assigning a probability to every outcome of an action—unless the action happens to involve a game of chance or random choices. Probability is not a disguise of ignorance: it is a real feature of some things, but not all. The only way to ascertain whether a process is random is to construct a probabilistic model of it, and to test it empirically. (Much the same holds for "chaos.")

In short, tychism holds only a grain of truth: the cosmos is not the Great Casino. Chance is an objective mode of becoming, but so is causation. Moreover, the two intertwine, as when a myriad of random microevents aggregate into a causal process, or when a random external shock diverts a causal line.

2.5 ❖ DYNAMICISM: THE GRAND RIVER

The devise of dynamicism is of course Heraclitus's *Panta rhei*, that is, everything is in a state of flux. Its heuristic metaphor is the river or, more abstractly, the so-called arrow of time. It is a river without source or sink: an unending sequence of beginnings and ends, where every end coincides with a new start.

Dynamicism comes in two strengths: radical and moderate. According to the former, as represented by Alfred North Whitehead, concrete things are only bundles of processes. This, the central thesis of his process metaphysics, is logically untenable. Indeed, the notion of a process presupposes that of a thing, because a process is defined as a sequence of changes in a thing.

On the other hand, a moderate version of dynamicism is inescapable. The universe is restless. Rest, not change, is illusory. For example, your chair looks stationary but it is actually moving with the planet. Moreover, the chair is at rest relative to our planet only because the latter reacts against the former's weight with an equal and opposite force. Because everything is subject to change, all the factual (or empirical) sciences study only changeable things, and all the technologies design alterations in existing things or even wholly new things. In short, the universe is indeed like a river, though not pure flux: what "flows" (changes) incessantly is stuff (matter) of some kind or other—physical, living, social, or artifactual.

It is all very well to sing the praises of change, but it is equallly important to realize that in every change there is something constant, such as a permanent property or an invariant pattern. For example, the life of an organism depends on its ability to maintain a fairly constant internal milieu. As well, reaction is just as important as action. In particular, inhibition is as important as excitation, and the human brain is not just a detector of external stimuli: it is also a buffer against environmental variation. In sum, dynamicism should not be exaggerated to the point of denying the invariant features of change.

2.6 ❖ DIALECTICS: UNIVERSAL CONFLAGRATION

The dialectical ontology is a particular case of dynamicism. It was first hinted at by Heraclitus, then articulated by Hegel, and finally elaborated by Marx, Engels, Lenin, and their followers. Its main principle is that everything is "contradictory" both internally and in its relation to other things. In other words, everything is a unity of opposites, and it stands in conflicting relation to other things. Moreover, "contradiction" is the source of all change.

Dialectics is attractive for two reasons. First, because conflict is a fact of life. Second, because the concept of contradiction is so fuzzy that nearly everything seems to exemplify it. Positive and negative, attractive and repulsive, up and down, left and right, light and heavy, exploiter and exploited, and so on and so forth, can pass for pairs of dialectical opposites. But, precisely because of its fuzziness, dialectics is more of a wordplay than rigorous ontology.

It may be thought that, with enough ingenuity, dialectics might be exactified. The few attempts to accomplish this have been dismal failures. Moreover, even if the enterprise were feasible, which is doubtful, it would not save dialectics from fatal counterexamples. First, in order for something to be internally "contradictory," it must be complex to begin with. However, most of the elementary "particles," such as quarks, gluons, electrons, and photons, are elementary, that is, simple rather than composite, hence not composed of mutually opposed items.

Second, although conflict is real enough on all levels, so is cooperation. Indeed, for a conflict to arise inside a system, or between two systems, the systems must be in place to begin with. And systems emerge through cooperation, mostly unwitting. For example, an atom might be said to be a "unity of opposites," for it is composed of a positively charged nucleus surrounded by negatively charged electrons. But there is no "struggle of opposites" between these components, which in most cases coexist peacefully. Again, conflict is unavoidable, and sometimes healthy, in or between social systems. But the explicit goal of the participants in social conflicts is to remove the sources of conflict.

The very existence of systems shows that cooperation is or was dominant. It also shows that cooperation—in and among atoms, cells, persons, social systems, or what have you—is just as effective a mechanism of novelty emergence as conflict. There is nothing intrinsically good or bad about either equilibrium or disequilibrium: it all depends on whether the outcome is good or bad. Thus, labor market equilibria are always desirable, whereas political equilibrium is bad if it secures an unfair social order.

In sum, dialectics exhibits only one side of the coin, namely conflict, while blocking the view of the other side, namely cooperation. The practical implication of this, particularly for politics, is obvious: If we value social cohesion and peace, let us keep clear from a cosmology that teaches universal conflagration. (More on dialectics in Bunge 1981.)

2.7 ❖ ATOMISM: THE COSMIC CLOUD

According to ancient Greek and Indian atomism, the world is a collection of atoms, or combinations of atoms, moving in the void. Atomism was perhaps the earliest naturalistic and nonanthropomorphic worldview. It was also the most comprehensive and rational one, for it purported to understand everything, whether physical, chemical, biological, or social, in a rational and secular fashion. Moreover, it purported to understand the perceptible features of the world in terms of invisible but material entities—just like contemporary science.

Admittedly, ancient atomism was qualitative and totally speculative. It only became testable and mathematical after the work of Dalton, Avogadro, and Cannizzaro in chemistry, and Boltzmann and Einstein in physics. And it was not until the beginning of the twentieth century that the atomic hypothesis was experimentally confirmed and incorporated into full-fledged theories. However, this was somewhat of a Pyrrhic victory, for atoms turned out to be divisible after all.

Our view of the basic bricks of the universe is quite different from that of ancient atomism. Indeed, according to quantum physics, the elementary "particles" are not little hard balls but rather fuzzy entities. Moreover, they interact mainly through fields, which are more like tenuous liquids than like swarms of corpuscles. As well, there is no absolute vacuum: even in places where there are neither "particles" nor field quanta, there is a fluctuating electromagnetic field that can act on an incoming piece of matter. "Empty" space is thus never totally empty, and it has physical properties such as polarization. Modern physics has thus vindicated the old principle of plenitude, defended by Aristotle, just as much as atomism. In some respects, our view of the physical universe resembles Descartes's own synthesis of plenism and atomism. However, there are big differences: unlike Descartes's speculations, our theories are both exact and empirically testable.

Another important difference between modern and ancient atomism is that the former does not abide by the principle of ontological individualism, according to which every whole is nothing but the aggregate of its parts. This principle holds to a first approximation provided the parts interact very weakly with one another. Otherwise they constitute a system with new (emergent) properties that cannot be discovered by studying only the separate components. In this case, the interaction is a datum or a hypothesis of a new problem that cannot be solved with the sole help of the solutions describing the previously independent constituents of the system. This new problem must be tackled *da capo*. For example, the orbits of two interacting bodies, such as our planet and the Sun, are not obtained by combining two straight lines, which are the orbits of free bodies. And the three-body problem is not soluble exactly. Thus, individualism fails even in classical mechanics.

(Let us get slightly technical for a moment. Consider two material things, 1 and 2, and call S_1 and S_2 their respective state spaces, that is, the collection of really possible states in which each of them can be while not interacting with one another. The methodological individualist should claim that the state space S of the system made up by things 1 and 2 can be built from S_1 and S_2 and, more specifically, that S is either the union or the cartesian product of S_1 and S_2. But this is false, because the interaction between 1 and 2 generates new states that are neither in S_1 nor in S_2.)

It is well known that atomism spilled over into the human sciences. For example, associationist psychology, from Berkeley to Wundt, was atomistic. Indeed, according to it, all mental processes are combinations of simple sensations or ideas. For a while there was even talk of mental chemistry. (See, e.g., Boring 1950.)

Atomism has been somewhat more successful in the social studies. For example, Adam Smith modeled the economy as an aggregate of producers and consumers acting independently from one another. All contemporary rational-choice theories, starting with neoclassical microeconomics, are atomistic. Indeed, they all claim to explain social facts in a bottom-up fashion, that is, starting from individual valuations, decisions, and actions in a social vacuum or, at most, in a social context that is left unanalyzed. Finally, atomism is strong in moral philosophy. Witness Kantianism, contractarianism, libertarianism, and egoism: all of them start from the fiction of the free, isolated, and self-reliant individual.

We all know that atomism has an important grain of truth. In fact, there are physical atoms. But there are also fields, and without these no atoms would exist or combine. There are also biological "atoms," that is, cells, as well as social "atoms," that is, persons. But, again, none of these is isolated. Every single entity except for the universe as a whole is a component of some system. The free electron or photon, the isolated cell, and the isolated person or nation are so many idealizations or fictions. Still, the connections among things are not always as strong as assumed by holism. If they were, the cosmos would be unanalyzable and science would be impossible, for we would have to know the whole in order to know every single part of it.

Though powerful, atomism is limited. For example, not even quantum mechanics can dispense with macro-objects when describing micro-objects. Indeed, any well-posed problem in quantum mechanics involves the boundary conditions, which are an idealized representation of the macrophysical environment of the thing of interest. (See Bunge 1991.)

The importance of the environment is, if anything, even more obvious in social matters. For example, it is impossible to understand an individual's actions if one overlooks the social systems he is a part of. Moreover, individualism tends to exaggerate the importance and even the value of competition at the expense of cooperation, which leads to justifying uncontrolled markets and aggression.

What holds for social science holds, a fortiori, for moral philosophy. In this field, individualism is radically false, for every moral problem arises from our living in society and being able to engage in prosocial or antisocial behavior. Worse, extreme ethical atomism, that is, egoism, is morally wrong and socially dissolving, in advancing the idea of rights without duties.

Since there is some truth to atomism, as well as to holism, we need a sort of synthesis of the two, whereby both are transformed. Systemism will be shown in section 9 to be such synthesis.

2.8 ❖ MECHANISM: THE COSMIC CLOCK

The seventeenth-century Scientific Revolution viewed the world as a machine, in particular as the maximal clock. Accordingly, cosmology equaled theoretical mechanics—Descartes's imaginary fluid dynamics, or Newton's more realistic particle mechanics.

Mechanism was the first scientific worldview. It generalized the most advanced science of its time, and it directed researchers to investigating the mechanical properties of all things visible. Even the animal body was regarded as merely a complicated machine driven by a pump—the heart. Only the soul was exempted, and this not always.

Interestingly, mechanism comes in two versions: secular and religious. Secular mechanism holds the cosmos to be a self-existing and self-regulating mechanism—a sort of self-winding eternal clock. By contrast, religious mechanism assumes the Clever Watchmaker. Descartes's cosmic clock was perfect, as befits God's creation, so it was in no need of a repairman. Having created matter and endowed it with dynamical laws, the Cartesian God need not busy Himself with the physical universe, and could devote all His attention to spiritual matters—in particular, to fighting the Devil. On the other hand, the Newtonian cosmos was dissipative: there was friction among the wheels of the celestial machine, so God had to give it a push from time to time to keep it going. However, He could relax most of the time.

Mechanism stimulated a prodigious scientific and technological creativity from its inception till the mid-nineteenth century. It began to decline with the birth of field physics and thermodynamics, as well as with the rise of modern chemistry and biology (see, e.g., d'Abro 1939). It was quite dead about 1900. We now understand that mechanics is only one of the chapters of physics. We also realize that relativistic mechanics makes no sense apart from electrodynamics, and that quantum "mechanics" is not quite mechanical, for it does not describe bodies with definite shapes and precise trajectories.

In sum, mechanism has had its day. In its day it showed the way to the scientific exploration of the physical world. Indeed, it taught us that the right approach to problems of knowledge is a combination of reason and experience, namely to invent theories couched in mathematical languages, testing them in the laboratory or the field. Thus, though not explicitly, mechanism called for a synthesis of rationalism and empiricism, which may be called *ratioempiricism* (Bunge 1983).

2.9 ❖ SACRALISM: THE COSMIC TEMPLE

Several religious scriptures, the Book of Genesis among them, teach that the entire cosmos is a temple dedicated to the worship of one or more deities. Of course, there is no shred of evidence for this view. On the other hand, natural catastrophes, the extinction of species, plagues, genetic defects, and wars do not speak highly of either the competence or the benevolence of the high powers in charge.

True, every catastrophe, whether natural or social, could be interpreted as a desecration of the maximal temple. But neither worship nor blasphemy help us understand or effectively control the world around us. Understanding and control are only possible on the basis of a secular cosmology. This is so because the gods are assumed to be inscrutable and indomitable (though perhaps susceptible to bribe).

In short, sacralism is a naive and anachronistic cosmology, and one that blinds us and binds our hands.

2.10 ❖ TEXTUALISM: THE BOOK OF THE WORLD

The thesis of textualism is that the world is an infinite text: *Totus in verba* (Everything into words). To regard the universe as a book, or as a library, would seem to be a librarian's nightmare worthy of Lewis Carroll, Anatole France, Karel Capek, Italo Calvino, or Jorge Luis Borges. Yet this view is implicit in Heidegger's existentialism as well as in contemporary hermeneutic philosophy, deconstructionism, and even in the schools of anthropology and sociology of science that they have inspired.

Indeed, remember Heidegger's famous sentence "*Im Wort, in der Sprache werden und sind erst die Dinge*"(Things become and are only in the word, in language) (Heidegger 1987, 11). His follower, the deconstructionist Jacques Derrida, echoes: "*rien hors le texte*" (there is no outside-the-text). And Steve Woolgar (1986, 186), the constructivist-relativist sociologist of science, admits that the kind of discourse analysis he, Bruno Latour, Karin Knorr-Cetina, and others practice is indebted to post-structuralism, which "is consistent with the position of the idealist wing of ethnomethodology that there is no reality independent of the words (texts, signs, documents, and so on) used to apprehend it.

In other words, reality is constituted in and through discourse." Of course, neither of these authors has bothered to offer even a shred of evidence for their extravagant claim. To worry about evidence and argument would seem to be a typically modern aberration. The so-called postmoderns only make assertions, the more hermetic and groundless the better.

Note that, for the above-mentioned authors, the *liber mundi* (book of the world) is not just a metaphor, as it was for the theologians who held that God had written it with His own hand, or for Galileo when he stated that "The book of nature is written in mathematical characters." Hermeneuticists take textualism literally, not metaphorically.

Textualism is probably the most absurd, dogmatic, barren, and misleading of all versions of idealism. It is therefore the easiest to refute. Indeed, suffice it to note that sane people distinguish between words and their referents, or that atoms, stars, plants, people, societies, and things lack syntactic, semantic, phonological, and stylistic properties. We cannot read or interpret them. This is why we study them experimentally and build mathematical models of them without waiting for the semiotician to tell us what they are or how to handle them.

To be sure, scientists expound and discuss their problems and findings, but their discourses refer mostly to extralinguistic things, not to further texts. For example, they conjecture and test equations of motion of bodies or of propagating fields, not of words. As for the "interpretation" of human behavior, it is not such: instead, it consists in conjecturing (often wrongly) the mental processes that guide behavior. For instance, why did my acquaintance so-and-so fail to return my greeting: because he did not recognize me or, on the contrary, because he recognized me? (More on this in chapter 6.)

Not even our ideas about things can be identified with their linguistic wrappings. In particular, mathematical and scientific theories are not just texts, discourses, languages, or "language games." Theories have logical, mathematical, and semantic properties, not linguistic or literary ones. This is why scientific theories are studied by scientists, logicians, and philosophers, not by general semioticians or linguistic philosophers, let alone by literary critics.

2.11 ❖ SYSTEMISM:
THE SYSTEM OF ALL SYSTEMS

We can learn something from every one of the first seven cosmologies we have examined, but nothing from the eighth and ninth. From holism we learn the theses of the universal interconnectedness of things and of the emergence of new properties, as the corresponding systems get assembled, and of the submergence of some properties as they break down. But the antianalytic or macroreductionist bias of holism is inadmissible, for it goes against the grain of science.

Hierarchism has taught us that the cosmos, far from being flat, has a level structure: that things group into levels of organization. In fact, we ordinarily distinguish at least five such levels: the physical, chemical, biological, social, and technological. We accept this ladder, but we reverse the relation of dependence. In fact, we admit the evolutionary principle that the higher-level things have emerged from the lower ones, not the other way round. To be more precise, we postulate that a system on any given level has components belonging to lower levels. We also postulate that a system on any given level emerges by the assembly (natural or artificial) of things (precursors) on the immediate lower level.

From tychism we retain the thesis that chance is for real, both as accident and as randomness. In fact, we have learned that large collections of accidents have statistical regularities, and that individual events of certain kinds, such as the proverbial radioactive disintegration, are irreducibly random. The insurance industry thrives on the first kind of chance, and quantum physics is about discovering the laws of the second kind.

From dynamicism we learn that all concrete things are changeable. Moreover, we add that mutability defines concreteness or materiality, namely thus: An object is concrete or material if and only if it is changeable. (Ideas, taken in themselves, are unchangeable.) We also add the principle of lawfulness: Everything happens according to some law(s). In the case of social systems we must add social conventions, in particular moral and legal norms of conduct.

Dialectics has taught us to mistrust stillness, for it may hide struggle, and equilibrium, for it may be unstable. It has also taught us that not all strife is bad: some may result in new and better things. However, cooperation is at least just as pervasive and beneficial as conflict. Moreover, both modes of becoming can combine. In particular, competition in one regard may coexist with cooperation in another—something we learn in social life. We have also learned that cut-throat competition can be just as harmful as complicity in crime. To build a good society we need both managed competition and nonstifling cooperation (see Bunge 1998a). In sum, dialectics can teach us something about the dark side of things. But it cannot be accepted whole because it is one-sided and incurably fuzzy.

From atomism we learn that the cosmos is composed of subsystems, every one of which is composed of smaller things. We also learn that things combine to form more complex things, and consequently that, in order to understand anything, we must analyze it into its components. But we combine atomism with the holistic thesis about emergent properties, as well as with the hierarchist thesis about levels. We also add fields to atoms, thus combining atomism with plenism. And on the social level we add nonphysical glues such as biological and social relations, customs, and rules.

Besides, we submit that analysis or microreduction must be supplemented with synthesis or macroreduction. This is because the former shows us the composition of systems, while the latter illuminates their structure. Thus, we know what a school is like if we study its teachers and students; but we do not understand what these people do at school unless we recall that they happen to be members of a school, which is a suprapersonal system.

From mechanism we learn that, to understand a thing, it is not enough to describe it. We must also conjecture what makes it tick, that is, what its inner mechanism is. In other words, explanation proper, unlike description and subsumption, involves premises that describe some mechanism (see Bunge 1999b). However, we do not admit that all mechanisms are mechanical, since field physics, chemistry, biology, and social science disclose nonmechanical mechanisms. Nor do we accept that every mechanism must be causal. In fact, some mechanisms, such as random shuffling, are stochastic. Still others, like those envisaged by statistical mechanics, quantum mechanics, and genetics, involve combinations of randomness with causation.

So much for the first seven cosmologies: every one of them involves some deep insight. By contrast, the eighth and ninth do not teach us anything. The eighth, sacralism, diverts our gaze from real things to fictions, and from the workplace to the temple. As for textualism, or the thesis that everything is a text or discourse, it is not just mistaken but wrongheaded or even insane. Far from helping us explore and understand the world, this thesis is misleading, for it invites us to leave the laboratory and the field for the library—or rather for a mathematics library, since only mathematical texts can be understood without reference to the real world. (Yet, paradoxically all textualists, to a man, are innumerate.)

The systemic cosmology is a sort of synthesis of the first seven cosmologies.

It views the cosmos as the supersystem of all lawfully changeable systems, and our knowledge of it as a supersystem of data, hypotheses, conventions, and methods. More precisely, it postulates that *every concrete thing and every idea is a system or a component of some system*. (See Bunge 1979, 1983, 1992.)

An adequate understanding of systemism calls for an elucidation of the concept of a system. The simplest analysis of the concept of a system involves the concepts of composition, environment, structure, and mechanism. Instant definitions follow. The *composition* of a system is the collection of its parts. The *environment* of a system is the collection of things that act on, or are acted upon, the system's components. The *structure* of a system is the collection of relations (in particular bonds or links) among the system's components, as well as among these and environmental items. (I call the former the *endostructure* and the latter the *exostructure* of the system. The total structure of a system is thus the union of these two sets of relations. By the way, every structure is the structure of something: there are no structures in themselves.) Finally, the *mechanism* of a system is the collection of processes that make it what it is and how it gets transformed.

We can now define the concepts of subsystem and supersystem. A thing is a *subsystem* of another if it is itself a system, and if its composition and structure are included in the composition and structure respectively of the latter, whereas its environment includes that of the more encompassing system. Obviously, the relation of being a *supersystem* of a system is the dual of that of being a subsystem. For example, everyone of us is a system of organs, and these are in turn super-systems of the component cells. The universe is the maximal concrete system: the system of all concrete systems.

A realistic model of a system of a concrete system should involve all four features mentioned above. In other words, we should model the system s of interest, at any given time, as an ordered quadruple: $m(s) = < C(s), E(s), S(s), M(s)>$. Obviously, as time goes by, some components of this quadruple are bound to change. It is less obvious, but equally true, that, except in microphysics, we do not need to know, nay we cannot get to know, the ultimate components of every system. In most cases, it will suffice to ascertain or conjecture the composition of a system at a given level. (The concept of composition $C_L(s)$ of a system s at level L is defined as the intersection of $C(s)$ with L.) Thus, social scientists are not interested in the cellular composition of his agents. Furthermore, more often than not, their units of analysis are not individuals but social systems, such as households, gangs, business firms, schools, churches, political parties, government departments, or entire nations. And what some historical sociologists call the *world system* is the supersystem of all social systems.

The above analysis of the concept of a system shows clearly what is wrong with the nonsystemic or sectoral approaches. In particular, holism tackles every system as a whole, and refuses to analyze it into its composition, environment, structure, and mechanism. Atomism refuses to admit the very existence of systems over and above its components, and consequently it overlooks systemic or emergent properties, notably structure. Environmentalism too overlooks the internal structure of systems, and is therefore led to ignore the inner sources of change. Structuralism ignores both composition and environment, and therefore it involves the logical fallacy of postulating relations without relata, above them, or prior to them. And descriptivism (in particular behaviorism and functionalism) willfully ignores that which makes a system tick, namely, its mechanism.

Interestingly, half of the cosmologies we have examined—holism, tychism, dynamicism, dialectics, and systemism—are not committed to any assumption concerning the stuff the universe is "made" of: these views are essentially structural—though of course not structuralist. Consequently, they are consistent with idealism as well as with materialism and their hybrids. Therefore, any of them can be adopted by religious believers as well as by unbelievers. (See Bochenski 1990 for the case of systemism.) In particular, systemism is an incomplete cosmology, one that can be used as a scaffold for building several cosmologies. We shall flesh it out in the next chapter, devoted to materialist and emergentist systemism (or systemist and emergentist materialism).

2.12 ❖ EPISTEMOLOGICAL CONSEQUENCES

Ontological systemism has an epistemological counterpart. We shall note only two of the epistemological consequences of the systemic cosmology. One is that reduction, though necessary, is insufficient. The other is the unity of all the fields of scientific, technological, and humanistic research beneath their obvious diversity.

Atomism suggests explaining a system by analyzing it into its parts. That is, the research strategy of atomism is microreduction. For example, we understand a cell by decomposing it into organelles and other components. True, but this understanding is only partial, because the specific function of each organelle in a cell can only be understood in relation to the overall functions of the whole.

For example, the chemistry of a DNA molecule is not enough to understand the regulating functions it performs in a cell. To attain an adequate understanding of the cell we need to combine the top-down or microreduction strategy with the bottom-up or macroreduction one. (See Coleman 1990; Bunge 1991, 1996a.)

Nor is the need for this combination restricted to cell biology. We also need it in physics to explain, e.g., the behavior of electrons inside a solid; in chemistry, to explain the function of a group of atoms in an organic molecule; in psychology, to understand the functions of motivation and emotion in learning, and the function of reason in controlling affect. And we need it in social science, e.g., to understand how individuals modify their social environment, and how the latter shapes their behavior.

In sum, neither macro-micro, or top-down, nor micro-macro, or bottom-up, reduction is sufficient to explain facts. The ticket is to combine analysis with synthesis, microreduction with macroreduction. This combination of both strategies is necessary because wholes happen to be composed of interacting components, and because the behavior of the latter can only be understood in relation with one another and with their contribution to the whole. (Note that epistemology has ontological roots, whence it cannot be developed independently from ontology.)

A second epistemological consequence of the systemist cosmology is this. Since the world is a system, so must be our knowledge of it. In other words, since there are no stray things, our knowledge of the world cannot be a mere aggregate of disjoint bits, but must be a system. Yet, the current fragmentation of knowledge is a well-known if often deplored fact. How can we explain this fragmentation of knowledge, and how can it be remedied?

The fragmentation of science can be explained by the excessive division of scientific labor that began about two centuries ago, and by the concomitant loss of a philosophical perspective. Ours is a culture of specialists, each with his own sectoral vision. As for the recovery of the unity of human knowledge, the neopositivists tried to effect it by reduction. In particular, Ernst Mach assumed that all things are complexes of sensations, so that ultimately all sciences should be reducible to psychology. By contrast, Otto Neurath assumed that all things are physical, so that ultimately all sciences should be reducible to physics. With hindsight it is obvious that both endeavors were bound to fail, because of the level structure of the world and because we can study every level in its own right in addition to investigating its links with adjoining levels. This is why physicists and chemists make no use of psychology, and why sociologists have no use for physics or chemistry.

The unity of science and, indeed, of all knowledge, is desirable and it is feasible through different means. Let us consider three such means. One of them is the building of interdisciplines. An interdiscipline is, of course, a research field that overlaps partially with two or more disciplines, in sharing some of their ideas and methods, and in containing hypotheses bridging the original disciplines. Biophysics, physical chemistry, biochemistry, behavioral genetics, cognitive neuroscience, neuroethology, social psychology, neurolinguistics, biogeography, bioeconomics, socioeconomics, and political sociology are only a few clear cases of interdisciplinarity. (Incidentally, the mere existence of some of them refutes the idealist claim that there is an unbridgeable chasm between the natural and the social sciences.)

Interdisciplinarity is sufficient but not necessary to ensure the unity of science. The use of a single logic and the same basic method in all the sciences made their unity possible even before the emergence of interdisciplines in the mid-nineteenth century. Another powerful interdisciplinary glue is mathematics, which is portable across research fields because, like logic, it has no ontological commitment. What changes from one field to the next is the factual interpretation assigned to mathematical ideas. Thus, the group operation can be interpreted as number addition, the combination of rotations in the plane, the physical juxtaposition of two things, the concatenation of two words, and so on.

A third interdisciplinary glue is philosophy. Indeed, all factual sciences share a number of philosophical concepts, such as those of thing, system, property of a thing, state of a thing, change in the state of a thing, possibility, causation, chance, space, time, law, knowledge, observation, experiment, datum, hypothesis, theory, logical consequence, empirical evidence, plausibility, truth, and error.

There is more: All the factual sciences, whether natural, social, or mixed, share a number of philosophical principles. One of them is that the real world is composed exclusively of concrete things: that there are no ideas detached from things and hovering above things. This is an ontological presupposition of factual science. Other presuppositions of the same kind are that everything happens according to laws (even if we shall never know them all), and that causation and chance are for real. Besides, there are epistemological principles, such as that the world can be known, at least partially and gradually. Another principle of this kinds is that human knowledge, though fallible, is perfectible.

How do we know that all the sciences share the above-mentioned philosophical principles? Certainly not by circulating questionnaires among researchers, for these seldom bother to ferret out the presuppositions of their own work. If we want to uncover these tacit assumptions we must examine the research process in vivo. For instance, if scientists did not hold the principle that the world preexists them, and manages to subsist without them, they would not explore the world, but would instead construct mathematical theories, or just concoct arbitrary stories.

In short, every science is a conceptual system, and is in turn a member of the system of human knowledge. No factual science is independent or self-reliant: every discipline interacts with some other disciplines, and they all have a common logical, mathematical, and philosophical nucleus. Any field that is not so related is nonscientific: strays are bogus. More on this in chapter 8.

Once we realize the systemic character of human knowledge, we can make explicit use of it in our research by adopting the systemic approach. Unlike a sectoral approach, which studies or handles things outside their context, the systemic approach takes context into account. Unlike the atomistic approach, which minimizes or even overlooks structure, the systemic approach takes structure into account. And unlike the holistic approach, that overlooks the inner process (mechanism) that makes the thing what it is, the systemic approach studies mechanism.

The adoption of the systemic approach is theoretically advantageous because every thing, except for the universe as a whole, is connected to some other things. For the same reason, it is practically advantageous as well. In fact, it spares us the costly mistakes incurred by the expert—scientist or technologist, policy maker or manager—who overlooks most of the features of the real system he studies, designs, or steers. For example, an economist will not build a realistic model of an economic system if he only pays attention to either its composition, environment, or structure—in particular, if he overlooks the environmental, political, and cultural constraints.

Because both the world and our knowledge of it are systems, the best specialists are the generalists, that is, the students capable of setting problems in a broad context, of making use of some of the knowledge acquired in other fields, or of foreseeing some of the consequences that their recommendations or actions may have for systems other than the one they are centrally interested in.

CONCLUSION

Let us conclude by pulling together the main ontological and epistemological maxims of systemism. The ontology of systemism may be compressed into the principle that *every concrete thing is either a system or a component of a system*. The epistemological companion of this postulate is: *Every research field is a component of the system of human knowledge*. These two axioms together entail the following theorem: *Studying, designing, or operating concrete things as if they were simple and isolated, and working in a discipline as if it had no relatives worth looking into, can only get us so far—or it may even lead us astray.*

3

MATERIALISM TRIUMPHANT

hilosophical materialism, or naturalism in the broad sense, is the thesis that all existents are material or concrete: that there are no immaterial beings, such as deities, ghosts, and self-existing ideas waiting to be grabbed. Philosophical materialism is unrelated to moral materialism, or the exclusive pursuit of pleasure or profit. So much so that Epicurus, one of the earliest materialist philosophers, lived an extremely austere life. And yet, anyone who is only interested in the so-called pleasures of the flesh is still said to be an Epicurean—whereas those whose main occupation is to accumulate riches tend to favor idealist philosophies, whose central tenet is that there are self-existing ideal objects, starting with values and morals.

There is a whole family of materialist ontologies, from physicalism (or vulgar materialism) to dialectical materialism (the ontology of Marxism). Physicalism holds that all existents are physical entities, whence all the sciences should be reducible to physics. This reductionist program, though initially extremely successful, has not been fulfilled. There is a good reason for this failure, namely, that physics knows nothing of life, mind, artifact, or society. Organisms, artifacts, and societies have (emergent) properties that their components lack, and physicalism refuses to acknowledge emergence: it is radically reductionist.

As for dialectical materialism, although it rightly stresses change, particularly of the qualitative kind, it is marred by Hegelian dialectics. This is a muddled doctrine centered on the theses that every thing is a unity of opposites, and that "contradiction," or the "struggle of opposites," is the source of every change. Dialectical materialists are not fazed by such obvious counterexamples as quanta, which have no parts, and therefore cannot be unities of opposites; nor are they disturbed by the existence of cooperation alongside competition. The particular materialism to be defended here, namely emergentist materialism, is equidistant between physicalism and dialectical materialism: it is hard-nosed like the former, and friendly to novelty like the latter.

Materialism has had a bad press since its inception in ancient Greece and India about twenty-five centuries ago. It has been slandered by idealist philosophers, and it is still conspicuously absent from most university programs of study. And yet there is nothing wrong or esoteric about materialism: it is the philosophy inherent in all the factual sciences and technologies. Indeed, all of them deal solely with concrete things, without invoking any spiritual powers or self-existing ideas. Only mathematicians find it expedient to feign the autonomous existence of ideas—see below.

One of the reasons for the low esteem in which materialism is held is the crude, obsolete popular view of matter as passive. Let us therefore start by examining this view. Later on we shall attempt to show how materialism can be updated to meet contemporary standards of rigor.

3.1 ❖ MATTER INERT?

The most ancient view of matter, and one that still has partisans, is Plato's. According to this view, matter is the passive receptacle of "forms" (properties), which in turn are ideas: only the soul (or mind) is self-moving. This was not Aristotle's view, according to whom the "forms," far from being prior to matter and entering it from the outside, were generated by and in matter itself. In particular the soul, rather than being self-existing and detachable from the body, was to Aristotle the specific form or essence of the living. However, Aristotle's talk of "forms" was so imprecise that it gave rise to two diverging schools. Whereas one of them continued the traditional view of the soul as insubstantial, the other—led by the Philosopher's direct disciple Dicaearchus—denied the existence of the soul. (See, e.g., Calvo Martínez 1978.)

From antiquity onwards, all materialists have held that change is the essence of matter. Even though the ancient materialists regarded the atoms themselves as unalterable, they supposed them to be forever in motion. Epicurus even endowed them with a spontaneous random departure from rectilinear motion (*clinamen*). And even though the eighteenth- and nineteenth-century materialists usually regarded force as extrinsic to matter and the cause of the latter's changes, they held that no bit of matter can be forever free from the action of forces. Materialism, in short, has always been dynamicist (though only occasionally dialectical). The thesis of the passivity of matter is typically non-materialist. In particular, the idea that living matter is distinguished by its being "animated" (inhabited by an *anima* or soul) is nonmaterialist.

The dynamicist conception of matter has also been held by physicists and chemists since Galileo, Descartes, Boyle, and Newton. In particular, Newton's principle of inertia states—in opposition to Aristotle's physics—that, once in motion, a body continues to move by itself unless stopped by an external force. And both the corpuscular and the wave theories of light assumed that light propagates by itself: that it is self-moving. Moreover, light and fields of other kinds set corpuscles in motion when striking them. This is why all the forces that occur in the field equations are those that the fields exert on particles.

(Kant, who could not read Newton's equations for lack of mathematical knowledge, misunderstood Newtonian physics as asserting the Aristotelian view that whatever moves does so under the action of some force. This is why, to account for the stability of the solar system, Kant postulated a universal repulsive force alongside the universal gravitational force. And Voltaire, who did so much for the popularization of Newtonian physics among his Cartesian countrymen, was struck by the pervasiveness of gravitation, but he could not understand it adequately because he, too, was unable to read Newton's equations of motion. So, neither Voltaire nor Kant realized that the inertia of bodies and light refutes the belief that matter is inert, that is, incapable of moving by itself.)

Classical physics, in sum, regards matter—whether of the body genus or the field genus—as essentially active. So much so, that the nucleus of every physical theory since Newton is a set of equations of motion or field equations, as the case may be. These describe, explain, and predict the motion of particles, the flow of fluids, the propagation of fields, or a change of some other kind.

Needless to say, chemistry adopted this dynamicist conception of matter. Indeed, chemistry studies not only the composition and structure of chemical compounds, but also the processes of formation and transformation (in particular dissociation and substitution) of such compounds. This is why chemical reactions constitute the very core of chemistry. Moreover, as is well known, whereas mechanics ignores qualitative transformations, chemistry specializes in them. The same can be said of biology since Darwin, and of social science since Tocqueville and Marx, namely that the former is particularly interested in the transformations of living matter, and the latter in the transformations of social matter.

Contemporary science has, then, stressed the dynamism of matter as well as its unlimited capacity to generate new "forms" or properties—an Aristotelian first. Think of the humble electron which, even in isolation, is attributed not only a translational motion but also a spontaneous trembling motion (*Zitterbewegung*) as well as a spin. Or think of the modest photons and neutrinos, or any other field quanta, traveling relentlessly until scattered or absorbed by some particle. So, even the elementary particles and fields are perpetually changing. A fortiori, all complex material systems are changeable. And, according to quantum electrodynamics, even the vacuum—that is, space itself—fluctuates spontaneously all the time, so that it can exert a force on an excited atom causing its radiative decay. If all this is not enough, think of atoms, molecules, crystals, fluids, cells, multicellular organisms, social systems, entire societies, and artifacts: think of the marvelous variety of their properties, in particular their properties of undergoing or causing change.

From physics to history, science seems to study matter of various kinds and only matter, "inanimate" or alive, in particular thinking matter and social matter. This is surely a far cry from the view of matter offered by the nonmaterialist philosophers, in particular the immaterialist (or idealist) ones, who deny matter altogether. The kind of materialism suggested by contemporary science is dynamical rather than static. It is also pluralistic in the sense that it acknowledges that a material thing can have many more properties than just those mechanics assigns it. More on this below.

True, any sufficiently advanced scientific theory contains some conservation law or other—e.g., theorems of conservation of the total mass, total linear or angular momentum, total energy, or what have you. Such conservation laws have occasionally been interpreted as refuting dynamicism. But this is mistaken, for any conservation formula states the permanence of some property of a material thing of a certain kind amidst change. These properties are constants of the motion or, in general, constants of the transformation of things. (Trivial example: the difference in age between parent and child remains constant as long as both stay alive.)

In sum, science denies the thesis that matter is inert, and supports instead the philosophical generalization that all matter is continually in some process of change or other. To be material is to become (Bunge 2000c).

3.2 ❖ MATTER DEMATERIALIZED?

Another rather widespread opinion is that modern physics has dematerialized matter. (See, e.g., McMullin 1964, in particular the paper by N. R. Hanson.) There are several versions of this view. The oldest of them is that physics has shown matter to be only a set of differential equations, hence an immaterial entity. Sir James Jeans (1930) claimed that this is so because the universe was created by a Pure Mathematician.

This thesis rests on a faulty semantics, according to which a scientific theory is nothing but its mathematical formalism—a thesis first put forward by Pierre Duhem. Every physicist knows this to be false. A set of mathematical formulas must be assigned a set of "correspondence rules," or semantic assumptions, to acquire a physical content, that is, to describe a physical entity. Thus, the formula $F = e_1 e_2 / \varepsilon \, r^2$ is not Coulomb's law of electrostatics unless one adds the semantic assumptions that F represents the interaction between two point particles with electric charges e_1 and e_2, separated by the distance r, and immersed in a medium of dielectric capacity ε.

In sum, a physical theory is a mathematical formalism together with a physical interpretation. And the theory, far from being identical with its referent (a physical entity), represents or describes it (whether accurately or poorly). The same holds in all factual sciences and technologies: the mathematics that occurs in them tells only half of the story. Any precise theory purporting to represent a real entity can be analyzed into a mathematical formalism and its interpretation in factual terms. (In obvious symbols: $T = M \cup I$.) Incidentally, it is scandalous that most semanticists and philosophers of science have ignored the key semantic concepts of reference and representation. (More on this neglect and its repair in chapter 10.)

A second version of the dematerialization thesis is that, after all, every physical entity is a field or is reducible to fields; and that, since fields are immaterial (meaning massless), physical entities are not material either. This view might have been defended a century and a half ago, when the field concept was young and insecure, and seemed to some—the conventionalists—to be just a convenient way of summarizing information concerning actions on or among bodies. But since at that time physics did not regard bodies as being ultimately reducible to fields, the view would have been discarded right away. Ever since Maxwell formulated the classical electromagnetic theory in 1865, Hertz produced electromagnetic waves in 1885, Marconi used them in 1897 for telecommunications, and Einstein divested the theory of the mythical ether in 1905, fields have come a long way. They are not regarded as convenient fictions but as real if subtle entities.

Shortly before the emergence of the quantum theory, matter could have been defined as the union of two genera: bodies (in particular particles), and fields. Since then, we have learned to regard particles as quanta (units) of fields of a kind unknown to classical physics. (For example, electrons are quanta of the electron field.) And we analyze bodies into particles and the fields that hold them together. So, fields have become the basic mode of matter. (This finding might have pleased Aristotle and Descartes.)

A third version of the dematerialization thesis is based on the Copenhagen interpretation of the quantum theory. According to it, this theory is not about independently existing physical entities, but about experimental setups that include experimenters. Every quantum event would then be ultimately the result of arbitrary decisions made by a human subject. The theory, which is a marvel of accuracy, would then concern matter-mind compounds. Moreover, the border between the material and the mental components could be drawn arbitrarily by the experimenter himself, so there would be no objectively or absolutely existent matter. So far the Copenhagen interpretation.

One flaw of this interpretation is that no formula of the theory contains variables describing any properties of human subjects, in particular psychological properties. (Note especially that the total-energy operator does not contain any contributions from the subject: he is assumed to be at arm's length from the object.) Another defect of the interpretation is that any experiment can be automated, so that its outcomes can be printed and read out by the experimenter upon completion, which is a way of guaranteeing the subject's nonintervention in the process. So, the quantum theory does not support at all the thesis that matter has been spiritualized. (For further criticisms, see Bunge 1959, 1973; Popper 1967; Rohrlich 1983.)

Finally, a fourth version of the dematerialization thesis is Alfred N. Whitehead's neo-Hegelian claim that the world is composed of events. This belief is logically untenable. In fact, by definition, an event is a change in the state of some thing or material entity. There are no events in themselves, but only events in some thing or other, be it body or field or any other concrete object. So much so that the simplest analysis of the concept of an event is this: "An event is a pair of states of a thing relative to some reference frame." Physics does not view the world as composed of immaterial events or of unchanging material objects. The universe—the world of physics—is a system of changing things, and of course the most comprehensive system of this kind. (Recall section 2.12.)

In conclusion, the rumor that contemporary physics has dematerialized matter turns out to be false. Rather, as we shall see below, cognitive neuroscience has materialized mind.

3.3 ❖ QUANTA UNREAL?

Materialists equate reality with materiality. More precisely, they assert that, although the predicates "is real" and "is material" have different senses, they apply to the same objects, that is, they are coextensive. But what if there were nothing out there? What if everything were only in our minds or, as the social constructivists claim, what if all the facts that scientists claim to study are nothing but social constructions or conventions? True, Einstein (1949, 81) held that "[p]hysics is an attempt conceptually to grasp reality as it is thought independently of its being observed. In this sense one speaks of 'physical reality.'" But has not experiment refuted Einstein's contention? At least this is what we were told when Alain Aspect and his coworkers (1982) falsified the celebrated if ill-fated Bell inequalities on the separability of initially coupled things.

However, it can be shown (Bunge 1985, 205–19) that this interpretation of the famous experiment is wrong. What failed is not realism but the intuitive hypothesis that the spatial separation between two entangled things must always result in the weakening of the original bond. Indeed, the experiment in question shows that a pair of initially entangled photons that travel in opposite directions continues to be a single nonseparable thing even if they become separated by hundreds of meters. The origin of the mistake lies in Einstein's confusion of realism with classicism, which includes the intuitive hypothesis that spatial separation always weakens interaction.

Another classical assumption that fails in quantum physics is that all the properties of things have sharp values at all times, like age and weight. But this does not hold for the dynamical variables, such as position, momentum, energy, and spin (or intrinsic angular momentum). For example, the three components of the spin of an electron do not commute, hence they have no sharp values at the same time, whence they cannot be measured exactly and simultaneously. The subjectivist view that the experimenter conjures up the electron or its properties when measuring its spin is false. In fact, when setting up his experimental device and when running his experiment, the experimenter counts on the independent existence of electrons endowed with all their properties. He does so when operating an electron gun, an electron detector, or a magnet (characterized by the alignment of the spins of the constituent atoms). What is true is something totally different, namely this. If one of the spin components acquires a sharp value, either naturally or in an experimental situation (e.g., under the action of a magnetic field), the other two components become blurred. Much of microphysical reality is blurred or fuzzy: this is all.

3.4 ❖ LIFE IMMATERIAL?

Vitalism, a descendant of animism, held that life is the immaterial entity (entelechy, *élan vital*) animating organisms, and that the latter are designed so that they can achieve their purpose, which is the preservation of their kind. By contrast, according to materialism, life is a property of material things of special kinds, and purposeful behavior is exclusive to mammals and birds. To be sure, mechanistic materialism denies that there is any qualitative difference between organisms and nonliving things: it holds that the difference is only one in complexity. This kind of materialism is easy prey to vitalism, for a modern factory is no less complex than a cell, and it is plain that biology studies a number of properties and processes unknown to physics and chemistry. So, mechanistic materialism is not the correct answer to vitalism.

A materialist conception of life has got to acknowledge emergence, that is, the fact that systems possess properties absent from their components. In particular, biosystems are capable of maintaining a fairly constant internal milieu; the activities of their various parts are coordinated; they can self-repair to some extent; some of them can reproduce; they cooperate in some respects and compete in others; and they are all subject to evolution. Emergentist materialism has no trouble acknowledging the peculiarities of biosystems. Moreover, unlike holism, emergentist materialism encourages the search for explanations of emergence in terms of lower-level properties and processes. (More on emergence in section 3.12.)

How do vitalism and emergentist materialism fare in modern biology? The answer depends on the kind of textual evidence one selects. Whereas a few texts still favor vitalism, others defend mechanism (or physicalism), while still others tacitly endorse emergentist materialism. In fact, some biologists indulge in vitalistic, in particular teleological expressions, as when they write about "the purpose of organ X," or "the use of process Y," or "the plan (or design) of system Z." To be sure, they dislike being accused of vitalism, so they often substitute the term "teleonomy" for "teleology." But this is just a verbal fig leaf attempting to hide the old and discredited final cause or purpose. So, if one is intent on collecting verbal evidence for teleological thinking among contemporary biologists, she is sure to come up with plenty of it. The question is to ascertain whether such a wealth of vitalistic phrases is a faithful indicator of the vitalistic nature of biology, or is just a relic of ancient biology, or even an indicator of nonscientific upbringing. This question cannot be answered by going over the same texts once again: it can only be answered by examining actual pieces of biological research.

Now, contemporary biology is observational, experimental, and theoretical. Since the concepts of vital force and purpose are theoretical, not empirical, it is useless to look for vitalism in biological observations or experiments. All such empirical operations can accomplish is to manipulate bits of living matter, supply data about them, and check hypotheses that relate properties of living matter of certain kinds—for example, the relation between body mass and metabolic rate, or the mutagenic effects of X rays. The only place where idealist hypotheses might be found is theoretical biology. Let us therefore peek into it.

A number of branches of biology have been rendered theoretical in the modern sense, that is, mathematized. Suffice it to mention population genetics (which embodies a good portion of the theory of evolution), biophysics (in particular the study of flow and diffusion processes), physiology (in particular the study of biocontrol systems), ecology (in particular the study of competition and cooperation processes), and a few others. Every year, hundreds of mathematical models of biosystems are published in the various journals of theoretical (or mathematical) biology. One will look there in vain for theoretical models that incorporate the hypothesis that life is an immaterial principle. Nor is one likely to have ever seen a mathematically correct and empirically successful model including the concept of a goal-directed process. What the recent literature does show, on the other hand, is (a) an increase in the number of explanations of biological properties and processes with the help of physics and chemistry; and (b) an increase in the number of explanations of apparent purpose in terms of either the feedback circuits studied in control theory, or the theory of evolution.

In conclusion, contemporary biology is not vitalistic, even though many biologists do sometimes employ vitalistic turns of phrase. (Remember that language is the clothing of ideas, and some clothes happen to disguise rather than reveal. Hence, although philosophical analysis starts off with language, one must go beyond it if one is to attain any depth and be of any use.) If anything, biology is becoming more and more materialistic in the process of studying living systems and their nonliving components with the help of physics and chemistry—which does not mean that biology has been reduced to these sciences. (More on this in Mahner and Bunge 1997.)

3.5 ❖ MIND IMMATERIAL?

Psychophysical dualism, or the thesis that there are minds alongside bodies, is probably the oldest of all philosophies of mind. It is part and parcel of shamanistic practices and most religions, and was incorporated into philosophy by Plato. Descartes gave it a new twist by expelling all spirits from the body, and turning the latter over to science—though retaining for theology and philosophy the exclusive rights over the soul. Many modern philosophers, as well as a number of scientists in their philosophical moments, have adopted dualism in some guise or other, a few explicitly, most tacitly. Entire schools of thought have endorsed it. One example is psychoanalysis with its talk of immaterial entities, such as the ego, superego, id, and libido, dwelling in the body and exerting psychosomatic influences. Another is anthropological and historical talk of a spiritual superstructure riding on the material infrastructure. However, the fortunes of psychophysical dualism started to decline about half a century ago under the unconcerted action of philosophy, neuroscience, and psychology. Let me explain.

There are two ways of undermining the doctrine of the immateriality of mind—or any other view for that matter. One is to show that it is defective, and the other is to exhibit a superior alternative. Let us sketch the first task now, leaving the second for chapter 4. The most blatant conceptual defect of psychophysical dualism is its imprecision: It does not state clearly what mind is, because it offers neither a theory nor even a definition of mind. All dualism gives us is examples of mental states or events: It does not tell us what is in such states or undergoes such changes—except of course the mind itself, which is a circular procedure.

A second fatal flaw of psychoneural dualism is that it detaches mental states and events from any things that might be in such states or undergo such changes. This way of conceiving of states and events goes against the grain of science. Indeed, in every science, states are states of material entities, and events are changes in such states. Physiological psychology (aka cognitive neuro-science) complies with this condition, whereas psychophysical dualism does not.

A third serious defect of psychoneural dualism is that it is consistent with creationism but not with evolutionary biology. Indeed, if the mind is immaterial, then it is above the vicissitudes of living matter, in particular natural selection. By contrast, according to materialism, the mind evolves alongside its organ—the brain. This is why, when Pope John Paul II finally admitted in 1996 that biological evolution is for real, he exempted the soul from it.

But the worst feature of psychoneural dualism is that it blocks research. This is so because it has a ready answer to all the problems that gather under the mind-body problem umbrella, and refuses to look into the brain to find out about the mind. (Thus, it enforces the separation between psychology and neuroscience, and accordingly it favors verbal psychotherapy over behavior or drug therapy.) By the same token, dualism fosters superstition, in particular belief in telepathy, psychokinesis, clairvoyance, precognition, and the various psychoanalytic immaterial entities.

And yet, the most influential school in cognitive psychology holds that mental processes consist in information-processing, and that in turn information is stuff-free. But we are seldom if ever told what information is. Only one thing is certain: that the notion of information used by psychologists and neuroscientists is ill-defined, and thus totally different from the concept of information defined in the theory of information crafted by Shannon and Weaver for use in telecommunications engineering (see, e.g., Bunge and Ardila 1987; Fotheringhame and Young 1997).

Indeed, information theory deals with signal propagation, not with signal transduction, that is, the transformation of external stimuli into specific (stuff-dependent) processes, such as the chemical reactions that constitute the units of the life processes—e.g., the binding of a neurotransmitter molecule with a receptor on the neuron membrane. No hypergeneral theory, such as information theory, could possibly account for such specific processes: this is an elementary point in methodology. Moreover, the central concept of information theory is the probability that a signal traveling along a noisy channel will reach its target. But neither psychologists nor neuroscientists ever measure such probability. And in any case this exact concept only makes sense with reference to a material information system such as a TV network: there is no such thing as information in and by itself.

Some experts even claim that everything mental is algorithmic: that it proceeds in accordance with precise mathematical rules, such as the rule for long division. This thesis is controversial to say the least. First, it is highly implausible that there are algorithms for such prerational processes as emotions and feelings. Second, there is no indication that it is possible to design algorithms to invent new ideas, in particular new algorithms. However, this is not important in relation with the materialism-dualism controversy. What matters most is that all algorithms, far from being self-existing, are man-made and, moreover, are all "embodied" or "materialized," be it in living brains, on diskettes, or on sheets of paper. (Try to operate your computer with "mental power" alone.) After all, algorithms are rules for combining symbols; and every symbol is a concrete thing, such as this string of marks: 10110001111. (When typing "0" and "1," one enters physical tokens of the numbers zero and one respectively: computers do not know numbers.) No matter, no information processing. Hence, talk of stuff-free information is at best make-believe.

In short, psychophysical dualism is not a scientific theory. Moreover, it is not even a theory proper, that is, a hypothetico-deductive system. It is just part and parcel of ancient magical and religious worldviews: it is a piece of myth and ideology rather than science. No wonder that it is being displaced by the materialist approach, according to which the mind is a set of peculiar brain functions. (More on this in chapter 4.)

3.6 ❖ CULTURE IMMATERIAL?

The idealist philosophies of culture have accustomed us to thinking of culture and cultural objects as immaterial. This view digs an abyss between man and other animals, as well as between the sciences of culture and all the others. It also makes it hard to understand why the culture of a society depends upon, and coevolves along with, its economy and polity. For example, the idealist art historian detaches the author-work pair from the client-public one, and thus cannot explain why some artists get commissions and are exhibited while others, perhaps better ones, do not.

Historical and cultural materialists have criticized cultural idealism, and have tried to show that the material circumstances and activities of man—namely the natural environment, its transformation through work, and the social relations deriving from this activity—determine everything else. (See Engels 1878; Harris 1979.) In particular, the intellectual and artistic culture, as well as the ideology of a society, become epiphenomena referred to collectively as the (ideal) "superstructure" mounted on the economic (material) "infrastructure." Thus, historical and cultural materialism boil down, essentially, to economic determinism. To be sure, this doctrine is often mellowed by adding the footnote that, once formed, the superstructure acquires a momentum of its own and can react back upon the infrastructure. Still, the latter remains the first motor, and the superstructure is taken to be immaterial (or ideal)—a clear if unwitting case of dualism.

I submit that historical and cultural materialism are only half-way materialist (because they include mind-matter dualism); and moreover, that they cannot explain the actual interactions between the culture of a society and the other subsystems of the latter. That historical and cultural materialism are dualistic seems obvious: To a full-blooded materialist there is no such thing as an immaterial (or ideal) entity, whether or not it rides on a material one. And that the thesis of the absolute primacy of the economy over the rest is inadequate, seems obvious when reflecting that a social change may be initiated either in the economy or the culture or the polity, and that some cultural changes—such as the invention and diffusion of art, religion, literacy, reckoning, science, and science-based technology—have had momentous economic and political effects.

A consistent materialist alternative view is this. A human society may be conceived of as a concrete (material) system composed of human beings and their artifacts, such as tools, machines, domestic animals, formal organizations, and documents. This system is in turn analyzable into four major subsystems: the biological, economic, cultural, and political ones. The culture of a society, no matter how primitive, is a system constituted by living persons and such cultural artifacts as carvings and paintings, papyri and computer diskettes, blueprints and maps, musical scores and statistical tables. This system is held together by information links, just as the biological system is integrated by kinship and friendship relations, the economy is kept together by work and trade links, and the polity by management and power relations. Hence, the culture of a society may be regarded as a material system though not as a physical one, for it is characterized by nonphysical (emergent) properties, relations, and processes, such as creating and spreading knowledge, crafting and interpreting symbols, designing artifacts, dancing, sculpting, and worshiping.

A cultural activity is a brain activity of a certain kind—one increasingly assisted by artifacts of various kinds—that influences the way other people think, feel, or act. The product of such activity is called a "cultural object," be it poem or theorem, cooking recipe or medical prescription, plan or diagram, legislative bill or sonata, or what have you. As long as such a "product" remains inside the skull of its creator, it is only a brain process: to count as a cultural object it has got to be communicable to others. Such socialization or objectification need not be permanent, but it must be accessible to other people. A song that is never sung, or a musical score that is never played, may be a thing of beauty (for its creator), but it cannot be a joy forever because it cannot be transmitted and thus enjoyed by others. The most effective way to transform a mental product into a cultural one is of course through "embodiment" (or transubstantiation, to employ a theological term) into a widely accessible cultural artifact such as a carving, clay tablet, diagram, disc, or video—or a social event such as a concert, an art exhibit, or a public lecture.

To be sure, if we wish we may feign that music and poetry, mathematics and philosophy, biology and theology, are ideal (or abstract) objects—provided we realize that they would not exist were it not for their creators and users, all of whom are material (though not physical) systems embedded in a social system. Even the most complete library, art gallery, museum, or laboratory in the world would cease to be a cultural object after a nuclear holocaust, for there would be nobody left to interpret and understand its contents. In other words, World War III would leave no trace of Dilthey's "objective mind" or Popper's equally imaginary "world 3." Not because the nuclear blasts would destroy such a "world"— for only material entities can be dismantled—but because there is no "world 3" to begin with. Cultural artifacts, such as books, pianos, and computers, are only junk unless utilizable by living and well-appointed brains.

This materialist view of culture as a material system composed of brains and cultural artifacts does not debase or desecrate culture: it just disenchants it. By contrast, the view that books, records, paintings, and the like are intrinsically valuable, that is, have an existence and a value of their own even in the absence of people capable of using them, is a crass materialist one, for it turns them into mere merchandise that may be hoarded by selfish collectors. By avoiding reification and abstaining from locating values outside evaluating brains, full-blooded materialists enhance the value of individual human beings, the sole known creators and consumers of cultural goods. Consequently, sophisticated materialism may be regarded as a strand of humanism. (More on the latter in chapter 1.)

In short, culture is not immaterial. If viewed as a process (of creation or diffusion), culture is just as material as motion or chemical reactions, for cultural activities occur in and among ourselves, and we are material systems, if highly evolved ones. And if viewed as a system—the system constituted by producers and consumers of cultural goods—culture is a material thing. In either case culture is no less material than the economy or the polity. And it is not true that culture is always derivative or epiphenomenal: Most economic and political changes in modern society have originated in scientific, technological, or ideological findings or doctrines.

In conclusion, there is no good reason to suppose that culture is immaterial. By contrast, there are advantages—both intellectual and practical—to the thesis that the culture of a society is a material subsystem of the latter, hence one that can be either nurtured or suffocated by the economy or the polity. One of the advantages of this view is that it helps explain the fertile symbiosis between individual brains and cultural artifacts. This is what Merlin Donald (1991) calls the external symbolic storage, that huge artificial expansion of the working (or short-term) memory, which he regards as characteristic of the modern mind.

Another advantage of the materialist conception of culture is that it reminds culture managers that culture cannot be bought: that the only way to promote culture is to help nurture promising brains, let them develop freely, favor their association, and facilitate their access to cultural artifacts such as journals and measuring instruments. This is because cultural works reside in well-nourished and well-connected brains, not in the idealist realm of pure ideas.

However, not all materialists share this view. Crass materialists—in particular utilitarians and economicists—promote junk culture because it either sells or is expected to "help the cause." By contrast, sophisticated materialists are only interested in noting that culture is not immaterial. They do not care about either the content or the form of works of art, science, or the humanities, as long as they are original creations rather than potboilers or merchandise manufactured for sheer profit, naked power, or academic promotion.

Thus, paradoxically, philosophical materialists can be friendly to art, science, or philosophy for their own sake, whereas philosophical idealists may demand that they be put in the service of some "higher" cause or other—as if pure art, science, or philosophy were not high enough. This liberal policy toward disinterested culture pays off handsomely. For instance, we are still moved and instructed by Tolstoy's novels, whereas his "art for the people" manifesto lies just as forgotten as "socialist realism."

3.7 ❖ SCIENCE IS THE STUDY OF MATTER

We may learn a couple of lessons from the above. One is that the concept of matter has changed dramatically over the centuries—or, rather, that there has been a historical sequence of concepts of matter. There is no reason to suppose that the present-day theories of matter are final: after all, matter is what science studies and, as long as people engage in scientific research, they are bound to come up with new facts and new ideas.

However, in order for a set of concepts to be called by a single name, they must share a core meaning: otherwise we are in the presence of ambiguity generating misunderstanding, not just of conceptual change. The historical sequence of concepts of matter complies with this condition: Every member of it includes the idea that all material entities are changeable, at least with regard to place. To put it negatively: At no time in its checkered career has science asserted the absolute unchangeability or permanence of matter.

Another lesson we can derive from the preceding is that, far from retreating from materialism, science is becoming more and more explicitly materialistic. It is doing so not only by shunning immaterial entities (life force, ghosts, disembodied thoughts, collective memories, national destinies, etc.) but also, nay mainly, by studying material entities. Indeed, science investigates physical things like bodies and fields; chemical systems such as batteries and compost heaps; biosystems such as bacteria and brains; and social systems such as business firms and governments. So much so that factual science may be characterized as the study of material things of various kinds with the help of the scientific method and the aim of finding the laws of such things. In other words, scientific research presupposes and also enriches a materialist ontology. It behooves philosophers to unearth, develop, and systematize this ontology. Let us see next how this task can be accomplished.

3.8 ❖ MATERIALISM AND HOW TO KEEP IT UP TO DATE

Philosophical materialism is a family of ontologies, or extremely general doctrines about the world. What all the members of that family have in common is the thesis that everything that exists really is material—or, stated negatively, that immaterial objects such as ideas have no existence independent of material things such as brains. Aside from this common core, materialist ontologies may differ widely. It is only by adding further requirements that a specific materialist ontology can be individuated or built. We choose two such extra conditions: exactness and consistency with contemporary science and technology. Let us look at these conditions, which are the trademarks of scientific philosophy.

So far, materialism has been a rather amorphous body of somewhat vague beliefs. How can one transform such a doctrine into a system of clearly stated hypotheses consistent with contemporary knowledge, in particular logic, mathematics, natural science, social science, and technology? In general, how can one attempt to overhaul any given philosophy? A short answer is this: By substituting exact formulas for metaphors, by weeding out obsolete theses, and incorporating new hypotheses consistent with contemporary science and technology.

Let us deal with exactification first. It consists in replacing vagueness with precision. This goal is attained by using, wherever necessary, the exact and rich languages of logic and mathematics instead of ordinary language, which is necessarily fuzzy and poor because it must serve to communicate people of widely different backgrounds and interests. (The exactness requirement is perhaps Bertrand Russell's most lasting contribution.) This condition disqualifies phenomenology, existentialism, and even linguistic philosophy as rigorous philosophies. It also disqualifies dialectics, which is vague, obscure, and metaphorical, as the worthy mate of materialism. (More in Bunge 1981, chap. 4.) Modern materialism must be logical and scientific, not dialectical.

Here are a few examples of exactification at a very modest level of formalization.

- Example 1. "All events are changes in some material entity (that is, there are no events in themselves)" is exactifiable as "For every event x, there is at least one material object y, and one change of state z of y, such that $x = z$."

- Example 2. "Only material objects can act upon one another" transforms into "For any objects x and y, if x acts on y, or conversely, then x is material and y is material."

- Example 3. "Physical space is a mode of existence of matter" can be exactified into "Physical spatial relations are relations among material objects."

- Example 4. "Life is a form of matter" should be converted into "All organisms are material objects."

- Example 5. "A society is an organic whole" should be transformed into "A society is a system composed of organisms and artifacts bound together by relations of various kinds and degrees."

The above semiformalizations employ only the most modest, albeit the most universal part of mathematics, namely ordinary logic. (For deeper reconstructions of ontological concepts and hypotheses, using more powerful formal tools, see Bunge 1977, 1979.) Therefore, they only exhibit the gross structure of the original statements. However, this often suffices to remove ambiguity or reduce vagueness. For example, the thesis "Change comes from opposition (ontic contradiction)" can be interpreted in several mutually incompatible ways. Two of them are "All change is generated by some opposition" (false), and "Some changes are generated by some oppositions" (trivially true). The whole of classical philosophy, in particular dialectics, is plagued by such ambiguities and obscurities.

Another merit of exactification is that it helps to locate key concepts that should be elucidated in a second stage, such as those of material object, state, event, space, and life. Also, the above examples show clearly that, whereas the first four constitute universal hypotheses, the fifth is a definition. Hence, if we want our ontology to be scientific, we must try and embed the first four statements into theories, and subject the latter to tests, whereas adopting the fifth is a matter of convention, whence only usefulness is the test of its validity.

Almost any philosophy, provided it is not utterly irrationalistic like Heidegger's, or incurably absurd like Hegel's, can be rendered precise and clear, that is, can be reformulated with the help of logical and mathematical concepts. (The apparent exception is ordinary-language philosophy, which rejects this very move. But since linguistic philosophers do not profess to put forth any original substantive philosophical doctrines, they constitute no genuine exception.) Recall for instance the attempts of Alfred N. Whitehead, Bertrand Russell, Rudolf Carnap, and Nelson Goodman to turn phenomenalism into an exact philosophy. They met with success in the sense that their systems did constitute clear elucidations and systematizations of phenomenalism. But the results were shallow and barren as well as at odds with modern science, which is materialist and realist rather than phenomenalist. (If in doubt, try to describe the properties of either an electron or an economy in terms of phenomena, that is, appearances to some observer.)

Formalization then, though necessary for turning an unorganized body of vague theses into a hypothetico-deductive system, is insufficient to overhaul a philosophy. When we say that philosophy Φ is *obsolete*, we intend to state that Φ fails to meet the contemporary standards of exactness, or that Φ is at variance with the relevant contemporary substantive knowledge about the world and human experience. Traditional materialism is a case in point, for it is not only inexact, but in addition has failed to propose precise and up-to-date answers to most of the philosophical questions raised by modern science. However, there is a difference between materialism and other philosophies, namely that its main tenets, however imprecise, are by and large countenanced by contemporary science and technology. Indeed, as argued in the previous sections, science and technology investigate and alter only material (or concrete) objects, and recognize no immaterial ones—except for such objects as concepts, properties, and relations, none of which need be assumed to be self-existing.

So much for exactness as one of the two necessary conditions for updating materialism. Let us next apply the exactness rule and the condition of matching with science to the definition of the concept of matter.

3.9 ❖ DEFINING "MATTER"

The most popular definitions of the concept of matter offered in the past are inadequate. Material entities cannot be identified with massive objects, let alone solid ones, ever since the discovery of massless fields such as the electromagnetic ones. And material objects should not be defined as those that exist independently of the knower, because an objective idealist will assert the autonomous existence of immaterial objects such as ideas. (In other words, Materiality ≠ Objectivity.) In short, whereas the first definition has turned out to be scientifically obsolete, the second has always been philosophically inadequate, in confusing an ontological category with an epistemological one. (See Cornman 1971 for further misconceptions.)

We should take our clue from contemporary science. According to it, all material objects, unlike the ideal ones, are changeable (section 3.1). Even the so-called elementary particles are either unstable or, if long-lived, they can change in various ways, either spontaneously or by virtue of their interactions with other entities (particles or fields). By contrast, a conceptual object, such as the number 1 or the Pythagorean theorem, is not supposed to be in any state, let alone to undergo changes of state. Thus, it makes no sense to ask "How is 1 doing today?" or "What is the equation of motion (or the field equation or the transmutation schema) of the Pythagorean theorem?"

We may then characterize a material object as one that can be in at least two different states, so that it can eventually jump from one to the other. (Actually, even the simplest material entity, such as an electron or a photon, can be at any given time in any of infinitely many different states. Moreover, a photon keeps moving as long as it exists, and the spin of an electron rotates spontaneously around its direction of motion.) That is, if S_f a state space for all material things of kind K, relative to some reference frame f, then the numerosity of the latter is at least 2, and conversely.

It might be objected that disembodied souls, such as those posited by most religions, and the ghosts said to haunt some Scottish castles, are changeable yet immaterial, so they prove the inadequacy of our definition. Not so, for this definition happens to belong to a materialist ontology, which makes no room for disembodied objects, and where mental states are brain states. Besides, there is no evidence for the existence of the ghostly outside the brains of storytellers and religionists.

(We need not go here into the technique for building state spaces, for which see Bunge 1977a, 1979. Suffice it to say that it is a tacit epistemological postulate of contemporary science that, given any thing x of which we know some properties, it is possible [a] to represent each property of x by some mathematical function; and [b] to collect all such functions into a single function, called the *state function* of x, which [c] is assumed to satisfy some law statement. Every value of that function represents a state of x relative to the given reference frame. The collection of such values, compatible with the laws of x, is called the *nomological state space* of x relative to the frame f. As time goes by, the thing moves from one state to another, slowly relative to some frames, fast relative to others. Caution: reference frames should not be mistaken for observers.)

In short, we shall adopt

DEFINITION 1. An object x is a *material object* (or *entity*) if, for every reference frame f: If S_f is a state space for x relative to f, then S_f contains at least two elements. Otherwise, x is an *immaterial object*.

More briefly,

$\mu x =_{df} \forall f$ (If f is a reference frame and S_f is a state space for x relative to f, then $|S_f| \geq 2$)

This definition allows one to partition every set of objects into entities and nonentities. It also allows one to construct

DEFINITION 2. *Matter* is (identical with) the set of all material objects.

In symbols,

$M =_{df} \{x \mid \mu x\}$

Note that this is a set, and thus a concept, not a concrete entity: it is the collection of all past, present, and future material entities. (Or, if preferred, M is the extension of the predicate μ, read "is material.") Hence, if we want to keep within materialism, we cannot say that matter exists—except conceptually of course. We shall assume instead that individual material objects, and only they, exist really. (That such individuals may be simple like photons or complex like families is beside the question.) But this point calls for another section.

3.10 ❖ THE CENTRAL POSTULATE OF MATERIALISM

To state the central assumption of materialism, we need not only the concept of matter but also that of reality for, according to materialism, all and only material objects are real. Here is a simple definition of the predicate "is real":

DEFINITION 3. (a) An object is *objectively real* if it exists independently of all knowers (that is, in their external worlds). (b) An object is *subjectively real* if it exists only as part of a subjective experience of some subjects.

DEFINITION 4. *Reality* is the collection of all real objects.

Note that, since "reality" has been defined as a collection, it is itself unreal, for sets are incapable of influencing anything. (There is nothing wrong with this, for wholes need not possess all the properties of their parts.)

Even assuming that these definitions are adequate, they do not help identify something as objectively real. To do this job we need not a definition but a general criterion of objective reality, that is, a rule helping to decide in any case whether what we perceive, feel, or think exists independently of us. To find such criterion it suffices to watch how experimental scientists go about ascertaining whether or not an object they hypothesize or perceive exists beyond themselves. To do this they ask themselves whether the object in question can either act upon certifiably real things or can be acted upon by them. Hence we lay down the following:

CRITERION An object x is *real* if either (a) there is at least another object y, whose states are (or would be) different in the absence of x ; or (b) every component of x modifies the states of some other components of x.

In other words, for some thing other than the universe to be real, it is sufficient (though not necessary) to influence or be influenced by another object. The first disjunct makes room for subjects (knowers). The second disjunct is needed to make room for the universe as a whole which, though uninfluenced by anything else, is itself composed of real entities.

We are now ready to state the hypothesis shared by all materialist ontologies, vulgar or sophisticated:

POSTULATE 1. An object is real (or exists really) if, and only if,

it is material. (Shorter: All and only material objects are real.)

This assumption bridges Definitions 1 and 3. By virtue of Definitions 2 and 4, Postulate 1 is equivalent to: *Reality is* (identical with) *matter*. Put negatively: Immaterial objects (nonentities) are unreal. In particular, the properties, relations, and changes in either, of material objects are real only in a derivative manner: strictly speaking, they are abstractions. For example, the distances among entities are not real: only spaced things are. Likewise, events in themselves are not real: what is real is the entire changing thing. However, there is no harm in talking about the properties of entities, and their changes, as being real, provided we do not detach them from the things themselves. Thus, social cohesion can be for real, though only as a property of some social systems.

A standard objection to materialism can now be answered. It is that space and time, though surely immaterial, must be reckoned with: for, are not things supposed to exist *in* (regions of) space and time? The materialist answer is the relational theory (or rather family of theories) of space and time adumbrated by the preceding remark. According to them, space-time, far from existing on its own, is the basic network of changing objects, that is, material ones. Hence, instead of saying that material objects exist *in* space and time, we should say that space and time exist vicariously, namely by virtue of the existence (hence change) of material objects. Space and time do not exist independently any more than solidity or motion, life or mind, culture or history. (For a mathematical relational theory of space-time see Bunge 1977a.)

In sum, all the furniture of the real world is material. The "worlds" of mathematics, philosophy, religion, and art are fictitious, and every fiction is a process in some living brain. Ironically, we have come full circle back to Plato, who held that, whereas mundane things are "corruptible" (changeable), ideas are immutable, with the difference that materialists deny Plato's thesis of the autonomous existence of ideas.

3.11 ❖ MATERIAL SYSTEMS

We need next the notion of a system, if only to justify our previous assertion that social systems are just as material as physical ones. As noted in chapter 2, a concrete system may be characterized as a complex object whose components hang together, as a consequence of which the system behaves in some respects as a unit or whole. Every system can be analyzed into its *composition* (or set of parts), *environment* (or set of objects other than the components and related to these), *structure* (or set of relations, in particular connections and actions, among the components and these and environmental items), and *mechanism* (or set of processes peculiar to it, or that make it tick). In short, the simplest model of a system σ at any given time is this: $m(\sigma) = <C(\sigma), E(\sigma), S(\sigma), M(\sigma)>$.

It follows from the above definition of a system, jointly with Postulate 1 and Definition 3, that, if a system is composed of material (real) objects, then it is itself real. More precisely, we derive:

THEOREM 1. A system is real (material) if, and only if, it is composed exclusively of real (material) parts.

This statement may appear to be trivial, but it is not. For one thing, it tells us that systems other than physical or chemical ones, such as organisms and societies, qualify as material. For another, it entails that, at least according to materialism, the "worlds" composed of ideas, such as stories, arguments, and theories, are unreal. What are real are the creators of such ideal "worlds."

Now that we have the notion of a real (material) system, we may as well add the assumption that renders materialism *systemic*, to wit,

POSTULATE 2. Every real (material) object is either a system or a component of a system.

Stated negatively, there are no stray things—except as fictions. The methodological consequence is obvious: Look for relations, in particular links (or couplings or connections) among things. This piece of advice is particularly relevant to counter the individualism fashionable in social studies.

Note the following points. First, our version of materialism is dynamicist, for it identifies materiality with changeability. Given the obscurities of dialectics, nothing would be gained and much would be lost by appending the qualifier "dialectical." Second, Postulate 1 should not be mistaken for nominalism (or vulgar materialism, or reism), that is, the thesis that there are only things, properties being nothing but collections of things, and relations identical with *n*-

tuples of things. True, we deny the independent existence of properties and relations, but assert instead that all things are propertied and related.

Third, neither the materialism postulate nor the accompanying definitions
place any restriction on the kind of matter, that is, on the composition of reality.
In particular, the above does not involve physicalism, or the thesis that every
real object is physical. More on this in the next section. Fourth, Postulate 2, or
the hypothesis of systemicity, should not be mistaken for holism. Indeed, holism
construes systems as wholes opaque to analysis. By contrast, I conceive of a
system as a complex thing with a definite (though changeable) composition,
environment, structure, and mechanism—hence as analyzable.

3.12 ❖ EMERGENCE

Materialism is a kind of substance monism: it asserts that there is only one kind
of stuff, namely matter. (Substance pluralism, on the other hand, holds that there
are multiple substances, e.g., matter, energy, mind, and information.) But materialism need not be property-monistic: that is, it need not assert that all material
objects have a single property, such as spatial extension, energy, or the ability to
join with other things. Materialism need not even assert that all the properties of
material objects are of the same kind, e.g., physical. In particular, Postulate 1 and
the accompanying definitions make room for property pluralism as well as the
emergence hypothesis and conjectures about the level structure of reality.

Since the notions of emergence and level are somewhat tricky, and sound
suspect in many quarters—particularly among the ultra-reductionists—we had
better define them. To this end we need a prior notion occurring in the definition of the concept of a material system, namely that of composition. The composition of a system is, of course, the set of its parts. More precisely, the L-com-
position $C_L(\sigma)$ of a system σ, or composition of σ on level L, is the set of parts,
all of kind L, of σ. (Recall section 2.11.) For example, the atomic composition
of a molecule is the set of its atoms; the neuronal composition of a brain is the
set of its neurons; and the individual composition of a social system is the set of
persons composing it. We are now ready for

DEFINITION 5. Let σ be a system with L-composition $C_L(\sigma)$,
and let P be a property of σ. Then

(i) P is *L-resultant* (or resultant relative to level L) if every L-com-
ponent of σ possesses P;

(ii) otherwise, that is, if P is possessed by no L-component of σ, then P is *L-emergent* (or emergent relative to level L).

For example, mass and energy are resultant properties of any material system. Again, the components of a cell are not alive: life is emergent, not resultant, relative to the cell components. Perception, feeling, and ideation are functions of multicellular neuronal systems, that no individual neuron is known to discharge: they too are emergent. Likewise the social structure, income distribution, and political organization of a society are emergent properties of it.

There is nothing mysterious about emergence if conceived of in the above ontological sense. Emergence becomes mysterious only when characterized epistemologically, namely as whatever property of a system cannot be explained from a knowledge of the components and their relations. But such characterization is incorrect, for one must then be able to state both the thesis of the explainability and that of the essential irrationality of emergence. (Needless to say, I adopt only the former. But we shall not discuss it here because it is an epistemological thesis, not an ontological one.)

Anyone who distrusts emergence should think of this. It is estimated that the going market price of the main elementary components of the human body—that is, carbon, nitrogen, calcium, iron, etc.—is about one dollar. By contrast, the market price of the biomolecules (DNA, RNA, proteins, etc.) of our body is several million dollars, for this is what it would cost to synthesize them. It has been said that this is the price of information. I prefer to say that it is the price of emergent structure.

And now a hypothesis about emergence:

POSTULATE 3. Every system possesses at least one emergent property.

In a sense, this hypothesis is trivial, for every system has a composition and a structure, which differ from those of its components. (Think of a system with three components held together by interactions of a single kind. It can be diagrammed as a triangle with the vertices representing the components, and the sides the interactions. Remove now one component and compare the resulting system with the former.) However, the postulate is useful, for it draws one's attention to emergence, a much-misunderstood and maligned property.

The concept of emergence suggests partitioning the family of materialist ontologies into two subsets. One is the class of ontologies that may be called *emergent materialism*, for they acknowledge emergence (e.g., R. W. Sellars 1922). Its dual or complement is *physicalism* (or mechanism, or reductive materialism).

This is the class of ontologies asserting that, whether on the surface or "at bottom" (or "in the last analysis"), every existent is physical (e.g., Smart 1963; Churchland 1984). In other words, physicalism, also called *eliminative materialism*, rejects the very concept of emergence.

Because of its denial of emergence, physicalism is the most vulnerable member of the materialist family. It is particularly inadequate as a philosophy of mind and a philosophy of social matter since physics can explain neither mental nor social facts. As for naturalism, although it may be construed in a much broader way than physicalism, it fails in refusing to acknowledge the unnatural character of artifacts, from languages to theories, and from computers to courts of law.

The shortcomings of reductive materialism are particularly evident in three of its contemporary forms: human sociobiology, behaviorism, and machinism. Human sociobiology is untenable if only because it fails to account for the variety and variability of institutions and cultures. Indeed, if every bit of social behavior were just a survival mechanism, then all institutions should be cross-cultural, and there should be no life-threatening social practices, such as environmental pollution, unrestricted procreation, and militarism. As for behaviorism, it is, if anything, even more inadequate, because it disregards biology altogether in modeling organisms as empty input-output boxes. Hence, it overlooks the internal sources of action as well as the mental processes without motor outputs—such as daydreaming and hypothesizing. A fortiori, the same holds for machinism, or the view that humans are automata that could be successfully replicated by smart (that is, nonmechanical) roboticians.

It is no coincidence that this view of man, as a sophisticated cockroach that can best be studied in an artificial intelligence laboratory, has been found to be congenial with existentialism, the pseudophilosophy par excellence. Indeed, if reason is debased, cognition is reduced to a survival tool, sociality and all emotions except for fear are ignored, and moral conscience is set aside, then obviously the man-cockroach gap closes. (See Clark 1997 for the cockroach-robotics-existentialism connection.)

In short, the denial of emergence is incompatible with science. Moreover, the poverty of reductive materialism invites an idealist backlash.

74

3.13 ❖ LEVELS AND EVOLUTION

The emergence postulate suggests looking for emergence mechanisms, such as the clumping of like entities and the combination of unlike ones, as well as for developmental and evolutionary processes in the course of which systems of new species emerge. At least the following comprehensive kinds or levels of entity may be distinguished:

Physical level = The set of all physical things.

Chemical level = The set of all chemical systems (wherein chemical reactions occur).

Biological level = The set of all organisms.

Social level = The set of all social systems.

Technical level = The set of all artifacts.

Semiotic level = The set of all symbolic systems.

We shall not dwell on this typology. Suffice it to note the following points. First, the components of every system belonging to a level above the physical one belong to lower levels. (This relation of level precedence serves to refine the concept of a level.) Second, as we climb up the levels pyramid, we gain some (emergent) properties while losing others. For example, the social level is composed of animals but is not an organism itself. Third, the social and technical levels overlap partially, because all formal organizations are artifacts. (This is why the above is a typology rather than a classification.) Fourth, the collection of semiotic systems, such as languages and diagrams, may be regarded as a subset of the technical level, since they are all made tools.

Finally, we lay down a developmental hypothesis:

POSTULATE 4. The systems on every level have emerged in the course of some process of assembly of lower-level entities.

Postulates 3 and 4 jointly entail

THEOREM 2. Every assembly process is accompanied by the emergence of at least one new property.

There is of course an enormous variety of assembly processes, from mere clumping to the formation of neuronal circuits and the merger of social systems, and there may be entirely new types of assembly processes in store. Moreover, while some such processes have been natural, others are man-made: these are the cases of human social systems and artifacts (including living beings selected by man and, perhaps in the near future, synthesized in the laboratory).

In addition to such developmental assembly processes, we must make room for evolutionary processes, that is, unique processes along which absolutely new things emerge. These are things with properties that no thing has possessed before. In biological evolution, such novelties derive from mutation or recombination, selection and adaptation; in cultural evolution, from ideation and social behavior. Much more could be said about evolution on different levels, but we must close now by adding just one last assumption:

POSTULATE 5. Some processes are evolutionary.

Again, this postulate is far from trivial. Indeed, creationists hold that all novelty is a gift of some deity, and physicalists (or mechanistic materialists) maintain that there is never qualitative novelty, but merely rearrangement of preexisting units. The above postulate is distinctive of emergentist materialism. (See Blitz 1992 for the fascinating history of the concept of emergence in relation to the notions of evolution and level.)

3.14 ❖ A NEW MATERIALISM

The above postulates, theorems, and definitions constitute the core of a research project aiming at rebuilding ontology on a scientific basis—one of Charles S. Peirce's unfinished projects. This new ontology is characterized by the joint possession of the following attributes:

(a) *exact*: every concept worth using is exact or exactifiable;

(b) *systematic*: every hypothesis or definition belongs to a hypothetico-deductive system;

(c) *scientific*: every hypothesis worth adopting is consistent with contemporary science—and therefore must stand or fall with the latter;

(d) *materialist*: every entity is material (concrete), and every ideal object is ultimately either a process in some brain or a class of brain processes;

(e) *dynamicist*: every entity is changeable—to be is to become;

(f) *systemist*: every entity is a system or a component of some system;

(g) *emergentist*: every system possesses properties that its components lack;

(h) *evolutionist*: every emergence is a stage in some developmental or evolutionary process.

So much for the new ontology under construction. (For details see Bunge 1977, 1979a, 1980, 1996a.) Because this ontology is supposed to possess all of the attributes listed above, it is hard to find a suitable name for it. "Emergent materialism" might do no better than "exact (or logical) materialism" or "systemic materialism." However, a name is needed for practical purposes. If pressed to choose, we should pick the most comprehensive. This one seems to be *scientific materialism*, for nowadays "scientific" embraces "exact," "systematic," "dynamicist," "systemist," "emergentist," and "evolutionist." Besides, scientific materialism is expected to be not only compatible with science but also friendly and even helpful to it.

To be sure, there is some overlap between scientific materialism and alternative materialist philosophies—otherwise it would not deserve bearing the family name "materialism." However, all the other materialist ontologies lack at least one of the characteristics listed above. In particular, most of the alternatives are inexact (being verbal or metaphorical rather than mathematical and literal); they are unsystematic or fragmentary; they are atomistic rather than systemic, or physicalist (mechanist) rather than emergentist; or they are dogmatic (unchanging and therefore they date quickly) rather than keeping abreast of science and technology.

CONCLUSION

Materialism has triumphed in all the natural sciences, from physics to the life sciences. But immaterialism is still going strong in psychology and social studies. Indeed, there is much brainless psychology left, and some of it is good if necessarily shallow. However, in recent years cognitive neuroscience has become the main producer of psychology. And, in any case, lack of explicit reference to the organ of emotion, cognition, and volition does not imply rejection of psychoneural identity: it only indicates that, to a first approximation, some mental processes can be studied without dipping into their "substrate." Likewise, communications engineers can study some features of information flow without necessarily specifying the nature of signals, transmitters, channels, or detectors. They need to pay attention to the material "substrate" of information flows only when it comes to designing, repairing, or operating information systems.

The social studies are in a predicament similar to psychology: they are still strongly attached to idealism. This is obvious in at least two schools: interpretivism and rational-choice theory. The former claims that social facts have got to be "interpreted" the way texts are, whereas the second school attempts to explain everything social in terms of "rational" deliberations, choices, and decisions. That is, both schools are only concerned with some of the "symbolic" features of individual action. Although both schools admit the existence of material constraints, neither pays any attention to either natural resources or work, and neither focuses on the peculiarities of the social, namely social systems, and any mechanisms other than exchange.

This self-imposed limitation of both schools accounts for their comparative barrenness. Indeed, neither of them has accounted for any important macrosocial facts, such as business cycles, hyperinflation and stagflation, chronic massive unemployment, exploitation and oppression, hunger in the midst of plenty, epidemics in the golden age of medicine, revolution in an age of reform, or superstition in the age of science. In particular, every major economic or political crisis has taken the idealist schools by surprise. In sum, willful ignorance of the stuff that constitutes concrete things is bound to produce at best very limited results.

Finally, what about mathematics? How can materialism account for it? It does not and it need not to, because materialism is only concerned with concrete things, such as mathematicians and mathematical communities. The materialist does not countenance ideas in themselves except as fictions, if only because there is not a shred of evidence for the existence of Plato's Realm of Ideas. Moreover, no idealists would be foolish enough to claim that disembodied mathematical ideas, rather than live mathematicians, can come up with new mathematical ideas. All they would claim is that mathematicians only discover, never invent. But, again, they cannot prove this contention: they will look in vain for the quarry where theorems are waiting to be discovered.

In sum, materialism is not just one more philosophical fantasy: it is inherent in all of the "hard" sciences as well as in technology. Moreover, it is an efficient debunker of unbridled idealistic fantasy. It can even be argued that a field of study of the real world is soft to the extent that it condones the myth that the world is ruled by ideas in themselves. True, some idealist pockets still linger in the "soft" sciences. But they have not gone unchallenged, as will be seen in the next three chapters. Moreover, they all boil down to the claim that ideas and symbols of various kinds are important. But who is to deny that they are? The only philosophical bone of contention is whether ideas and symbols are self-existing and causally efficient, or whether they are invented and used by real brains, whether to cope with real-life issues or for sheer intellectual or aesthetic enjoyment—which leads us to the next chapter.

4

FROM NEURON TO MIND

U ntil the mid-twentieth century there was little communication between neuroscientists and psychologists. Typically, the former were interested only in the various subsystems of the nervous system, whereas most psychologists studied only overt behavior, or learning, or conscious processes. Hardly anyone was interested in the mechanisms whereby neural systems control behavior, much less in the nonmotor and nonsensorial activities of the central nervous system of the higher vertebrates (mammals and birds). Consequently, behavior appeared largely mysterious, and mind nonexistent or at least beyond the reach of the scientific method. In particular, no self-respecting scientist tackled the problem of the nature of self-consciousness, let alone its location in the brain.

The gap is now slowly closing. Neuroscientists are becoming increasingly interested in behavior, memory, perception, ideation, consciousness, and emotion, while some psychologists and ethologists are happily ignoring the paralyzing injunction "Do not neurologize!" Better yet, they are starting to guess on that which controls behavior and does the mentation, while biological psychiatrists are treating mental disorders with increasing success. For example, it has been found that the questions "What is it?" and "Where is it?" are answered by two different systems of neurons. And of course Prozac and its kin have revolutionized the psychiatric practice and are ruining the logotherapy business.

A consequence of the success of the brain-centered approach to the study of mind and behavior is that the old theological and idealist view that detaches mind from matter is in decline. It survives only in functionalist (nonbiological) cognitive psychology, in the philosophy of mind attached to it, and in such verbal vestiges as "X is the neural *correlate* (or *basis*, or substrate) of mental function Y," and "X is the neural system that *mediates* (or *subserves*) mental function Y." What is really meant by these subterfuges is simply "Neural system X performs mental function Y."

The fusion of neuroscience with psychology is thus finally taking place: Cognitive neuroscience, as psychobiology is now often called, is a going concern. Actually, an even more grandiose and useful synthesis is in the making: the research field that could be termed psycho-neuro-endrocrino-immuno-pharmacology (see, e.g., Beaumont, Kenealy, and Rogers 1996; Changeux 1988; Gazzaniga, Ivry, and Mangun 1998; Gazzaniga 2000; Mountcastle 1998; Kosslyn and Koenig 1995; Rugg 1997; Squire and Kosslyn 1998; Wilson and Keil 1999; and the journals *Cognitive Neuropsychology, Journal of Cognitive Neuroscience, Neuropsychologia,* and *Neuropsychology,* as well as *Nature, Science,* and any of the older journals of neuroscience or experimental psychology).

Neuroscientists know that the nervous system is only one of the subsystems of the whole animal—albeit the most complex and interesting of all; and psychologists are realizing that real animals are not black boxes. The great wall between body and mind is being bored from within (subjective experience) and from without (the brain). The same wall is also being scaled on both sides: from perception to concept formation, and from single neuron to whole brain. As the drilling and the scaling proceed, it is being realized that the wall is not in nature but in theology and the idealistic philosophy that continued the theological tradition. They invented the myths of the immaterial, immortal, and inscrutable soul, and of the radical discontinuity between man and the other primates.

Yet, the fusion or merger strategy has so far been sketched only in vague terms. Moreover, there is some confusion as to the credentials required to be regarded as a card-carrying cognitive neuroscientist. For example, scientists who investigate the visual system, or the effects of stress on self-perception and behavior, do not usually regard themselves as cognitive neuroscientists. Such imprecision and confusion originates not only in historical accident and turf division, but also in philosophical sloppiness. Witnesses of the second factor are the expressions "mind/brain" (why not "walk/legs"?); "the brain causes the mind" (do the lungs cause respiration?); "intentionality" instead of "reference"; and "computation," when all that is meant is signal propagation (e.g., along an axon) and transduction (e.g., across a synapse).

Some conceptual precision should be introduced if we want to find out how best to integrate the various approaches, methods, and findings of the many sciences, from biophysics to sociology, concerned with the problem of accounting for behavior and mentation. In the first place, we should tackle the matter of the variety of approaches to this problem, and weigh their comparative advantages.

4.1 ❖ FIVE APPROACHES TO THE STUDY OF HUMANS

The human animal can be studied from different viewpoints: as a physical entity, a chemical system, an organism, a minding animal, and a component of sundry social systems (family, gang, firm, school, etc.). Each of these approaches has its virtues and shortcomings, and each suggests a one-sided view of man.

Approach 1: physical. No doubt, this is the basic approach and one that has proved fertile. But restricting the study of man to physical components and aspects, that is, adopting physicalism (or vulgar materialism), is ignoring whatever physics fails to explain (recall section 3.13). And trying to reduce the supraphysical features of man to physics is quixotic, if only for being impractical. The mere attempt to write down, and even more to solve, the Schrödinger equation for a brain, or even a neuron, is mind-boggling. But even if such tasks were feasible, a number of essential features of life, such as development and evolution, would remain in the dark. And overlooking them amounts to forsaking the understanding of the complexities of the nervous system, as well as the mental and social peculiarities of humans.

Approach 2: chemical. First the chemical theory of heredity, then molecular biology, and finally neurochemistry have shown that biochemistry is just as important a tool as biophysics for understanding the brain. Yet, the successes of the chemical approach should not be exaggerated, if for no other reason than that we still do not have an adequate (quantum-mechanical) understanding of a DNA molecule. In short, chemism is inadequate. At any rate, it is still largely programmatic.

Approach 3: biological. This is of course the right approach to adopt in the life sciences. This platitude bears repetition in view of the fact that alternative approaches are still going strong. (Thus, many psychologists believe that they can afford to ignore biology, particularly neuroscience and evolutionary biology.) And it also goes without saying that the biological approach can and should be combined with the other approaches rather than being adopted to their exclusion. The

81

latter stand, namely biologism, is one-sided, for it tends to overlook the social dimension of human life. In particular, sociobiology may well account for some human features as survival devices acquired by genic change and natural selection. But, by the same token, it cannot account for the unique human features that are dispensable for survival—such as art, myth, and philosophy. A fortiori, sociobiology cannot explain the equally unique human features that threaten survival, such as cut-throat competition, suffocating social bonds, and misleading superstitions. *Homo erectus*, maybe; *Homo sapiens*, no; *Homo stultus*, even less so.

Approach 4: psychological. The proper task of psychology is of course the understanding of behavioral, emotional, cognitive, and volitional patterns. To be sure, all such functions, whether inborn or learned, are biological: they are performed by live organs. Hence, any deep account of the mental is bound to be psychobiological. However, the functions of the nervous systems of complex organisms are different from those of simpler systems, such as the cardiovascular or the digestive ones. For example, the former can think and plan, two functions that are far beyond the capability of all but highly evolved organisms. Yet, such behavioral and mental abilities should not lead to psychologism, that is, the claim that psychology owes nothing to biology—a dogma of behaviorists and psychoanalysts.

Approach 5: sociological. There is no understanding a gregarious social animal apart from ethology and social science. In particular, work, consciousness, and language seem to be products (and in turn modifiers) of social life; so are stress, moral conscience, and organizational ability. However, it would be mistaken to adopt sociologism, or the attempt to explain man in purely sociological terms. For, although sociality has biological and psychological roots, it transcends them. Indeed, unlike invertebrates and lower vertebrates, the higher vertebrates possess social plasticity, that is, the capacity to readjust their patterns of social behavior in the face of internal or external difficulties. Social plasticity is made possible by brain plasticity, which in turn is honed by social life.

So much for the main legitimate, albeit one-sided, approaches to the study of man: the physical, chemical, biological, psychological, and sociological ones. The engineering approach has not been included because animals are not machines: they are alive, have not been designed, and are a product of natural and social evolution. To be sure, there are some functional similarities between man and machine, in particular computers. If there were none, we would not use machines as labor-saving devices. However, no analog is a substitute for the real thing, particularly when it is so superficial that it overlooks the peculiarities of man, such as the ability to invent problems, symbols, concepts, theories, rules, and plans, and the capacity to imagine, set up, reform, and dismantle organizations.

In short, machinism is inadequate and even wrongheaded, and therefore wasteful. This holds in particular for the marvelous electromechanical insects constructed by the robotics experts at MIT and elsewhere. Far from revealing the secrets of life, they use a bit of biological knowledge. And they may reveal more about the engineer's mind than about the physical and chemical mechanisms at work in insects. The same holds, a fortiori, for the computer metaphor of the mind, if only because computers are neither spontaneous nor capable of referring to things in their external world other than their partners in a computer network—not to mention their lack of plasticity (self-rewiring) and their inability to doubt and to experience emotions, feelings, and moral qualms.

To sum up, there are five legitimate and fruitful approaches to the study of man. However, the adoption of any of them to the exclusion of the others, while tempting given the enormity of the task, should be regarded as only a temporary expedient. We should attempt to integrate them, for humans are complex systems exhibiting all five aspects.

4.2 ❖ SEVEN MODELS OF MAN

The understanding of a thing begins and ends with some conceptual model of it. The model is the better, the more accurate, and inclusive. But even rough models can be used to guide—or misguide—research. Every one of the five approaches examined in the last section has given rise to a set of models of man. The technological and religious approaches too have resulted in certain models. Finally, a seventh model is in the making, which brings together all five scientific approaches.

The first or *religious* (or *animistic*) model is that of Plato, Christian theology, and idealist philosophy. According to it, man is a spiritual being who uses his body as a tool during his temporary sojourn on Earth. (As the late Sir John Eccles put it, the self is to the brain what the pianist is to the piano.) Animism has effectively slowed down the merger of neurophysiology with psychology. To be sure, it was demolished by Darwin and by cognitive neuroscience: if the brain has evolved, so must have the mind. (When Pope John Paul II admitted in 1996 that there had been biological evolution, he made it clear that this process did not affect the God-given immaterial soul—as if there could be substantial anatomical changes without concomitant functional changes.) Yet, animism still lingers on among the philosophers, psychologists, and neuroscientists whose philosophy does not concur with contemporary science.

The second or *technological* (or *machinist*) model regards man as a complex information processor, and the nervous system as a computer. According to this model, even a lowly worm computes its every movement, as if it were born with the suitable algorithms. This model has seduced countless neuroscientists, psychologists, and engineers, perhaps because it has the virtues of simplicity and unity. Indeed, it models the nervous system (or else the stuff-free mind) as a system of black boxes connected by arrows that symbolize information flows—where "information" is left undefined. This shallow description creates the illusion of understanding while actually nothing is being understood because no biological mechanisms are being unveiled. (Recall that to understand a thing is to find out the mechanism that makes it tick.)

To be sure, the nervous system is, among other things, an information system; so is the neuro-endocrine-immune supersystem. However, both happen to be biosystems, that is, systems characterized by biological properties. And computer science has no room for such specific properties, not even for specific physical and chemical properties. (As far as computer science is concerned, an information system can be built out of modules of any kind. Only the design and construction of computers calls for a knowledge of materials and their laws.) Furthermore, it is a mistake to regard biosystems as artifacts, for this suggests that the former, too, have been designed to some purpose. Finally, machinism is incompatible with evolutionary biology, for machines are not subject to blind genic mutation, natural selection, or social interaction. And, above all, they do nothing spontaneously and they lack creativity.

The third, or *physicalist*, model presupposes not only that physics is the basic science, which it is, but also that in principle no other science is necessary—which is false. Not even chemistry, the nearest neighbor, is reducible to physics without further ado. First, because chemical systems have peculiar properties, such as lack of inertia, that physics knows nothing about. (A chemical reaction cannot go on forever: it stops once all the reagents have combined.) And second, physical theory, although necessary to understand chemistry, is insufficient: one must add subsidiary assumptions concerning, e.g., chemical composition, structure, and even chemical kinetics, that go beyond physics. (In particular, quantum chemistry adopts the basic rate equation of classical chemical kinetics: it only analyzes the equilibrium constant in quantum-mechanical terms.)

The fourth or *chemicalist* model of a human as a chemical reactor fares much better than the physicalist model because it is richer and, after all, cells are constituted by chemical subsystems. But of course there is more to life than chemistry. In particular, animals equipped with a neuroendocrine system have neural and hormonal control systems in addition to the genetic control system. To be sure, all such control systems are physicochemical; but they happen to regulate biofunctions, such as metabolism, reproduction, self-repair, flight, and defense.

The fifth or *biologistic* model of man claims that "biology is destiny." It is patent in the physicians who overlook the psychological worries and social circumstances of their patients. It also shows up in social Darwinism, the "selfish gene" doctrine, the German *Soziobiologie* that thrived between the two world wars, human sociobiology, and speculative evolutionary psychology. Biologism underlies also the belief, common among mainstream economists, that man is a natural capitalist—whence the transition between state socialism and free-market capitalism should proceed instantly and to the benefit of all.

Although far superior to the preceding model, biologism is deeply flawed in exaggerating the weight of heredity and underrating that of culture, as well as in neglecting the abilities and shortcomings peculiar to humans. In particular, it overlooks the unique mental and social features of human beings, such as their extraordinary versatility, creativity, and social plasticity. The practical consequence is clear, namely, unwillingness to use social means, particularly legislation, education, and mobilization for public causes, to modify behavior and mentation.

Likewise, the sixth or *sociologistic* (or *culturalist*) model of humans exaggerates one aspect of human life at the expense of all others. According to it, we are what society makes of us. This has two undesirable consequences. One is to view society as an undivided whole (rather than as a system of subsystems), and therefore as existing by itself and above individuals. The other consequence is to deny that there are nervous system disorders, and to blame all behavioral and mental disorders on society as a whole. (This is of course the gist of the antipsychiatry movement.) Like psychologism, sociologism ignores biology, and is therefore scientifically inadmissible.

Finally, the seventh or *systemic* model pictures man as a biosystem composed of numerous subsystems, each with its own specific functions, as well as a component of suprabiological (social) systems, such as families and businesses. This view includes whatever is valuable in the previous models. Indeed, the systemic model of humans acknowledges physical and chemical properties as well as biological, psychological, and social ones. In particular, man as a whole, as well as his every component, possesses physical properties such as energy and mass; but from the cell upward all systems have peculiar supraphysical properties, that is, features that physics is not competent to study. Humans and other primates can feel and dream, imagine, plan, and enter into social relations and thus modify other animals' emotions, thoughts, and behavior—all of which lie beyond physics and chemistry although they are rooted to the peculiar physical and chemical properties of living tissue.

In conclusion, there are (at least) seven models of man, or rather kinds of anthropological model. Two of them, the religious and the engineering models, are unscientific, and four are scientific but one-sided, for each of them accounts only for one side of the whole. Only the systemic model brings together whatever is valuable in each of the four one-sided or partial scientific models, by depicting man as a bio-psycho-social being with physical and chemical components.

4.3 ❖ SYSTEMS AND LEVELS

The main postulate of the systemic worldview is that everything is either a system or a component of a system, that is, a thing composed of interconnected things. (Recall sections 2.11 and 3.12.) In particular, a human being is a component of several social systems (family, club, school, firm, etc.), and is in turn composed of a number of subsystems—in particular the nervous system—which are in turn composed of smaller subsystems. This "hierarchical" organization goes up to the world system and down to the cell level and even further, to the level of cellular subsystems (e.g., ribosomes) and their molecular components (see figure 4.1). This being so, to understand the behavior of each module we must understand its components, environment, and structure, as well as the supersystem of which it is a component. One may despair at the complexity of the task, but may take consolation in the fact that the job is being performed by the entire scientific community.

We define a *level of organization* as a collection composed of all the material things characterized by peculiar properties (in particular laws). Examples include the physical, chemical, biological, and social levels. Obviously, each of these levels can be split into a number of sublevels. For example, the biological level can be divided into the cell, organ, system, supersystem, organism, and biopopulation sublevels. (Recall chapter 3.)

The interlevel relation in the level "hierarchy" (or better-level structure) is this. Any thing belonging to a given level is composed of things belonging to lower levels. For example, an organ is composed of cells, which in turn are composed of organelles and other things, and so on down to elementary particles and

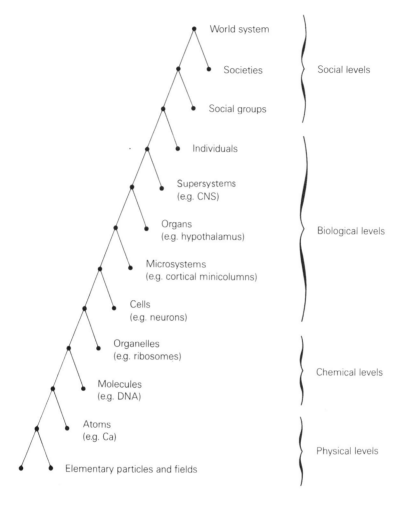

Figure 4.1. Human beings and their subsystems and supersystems.

fields. Similarly, a city is composed of neighborhoods, each of which is composed of households, every one of which is constituted by human beings and domestic animals. The family of levels is thus ordered by the precedence relation defined in that way. (More precisely: Level n *precedes* level $n + 1 =_{df}$ All things in level $n + 1$ are composed of things in level n or lower—if any.) The properties of things of the nth level not possessed by things in the lower levels are said to be the *emergent* properties peculiar to the nth level.

So far, our sketch of the level structure has been static. But we know from studies in various fields, in particular from studies on self-organization, development, and evolution, that the level structure is far from having been given once and for all. In fact, we know that every system has self-assembled (or self-organized) from things on the preceding level. That is, every system on a given level is preceded in time by its components, which are therefore rightly called its *precursors*. For example, the precursors of a molecule are the atoms that combined to form it.

The systems on any given level have some properties in common with their own components, and others that the latter lack: these are their *emergent* properties. For example, an atom has an energy spectrum that its individual components do not possess; likewise, a molecule has an energy spectrum that is not the mere superposition of the spectra of its component atoms; and a neuronal system has a connectivity that is absent from its components. In short, at every level some properties (in particular laws) are gained (or emerge), while others are lost (or submerge). In short, along the developmental and evolutionary processes there is both emergence and submergence of properties.

The methodological morals of the preceding ontological considerations are quite obvious:

1. Identify the level(s) crossed by your object(s) of study.
2. Do not skip levels.
3. Recognize the genealogy of the higher levels.

These injunctions help evaluate research strategies and projects. We may distinguish four main such strategies or methodologies: holism, analysis, synthesis, and the multilevel approach.

Holism advocates the study of every thing as a whole and only on its own level. Examples: the study of the brain as a whole by electroencephalographic means, and the holographic model of memory. *Analysis* (or "top-down" study) is the reduction of the system to its components. Example: the identification of the neurons that make up the simplest of all systems capable of having a mental experience, such as perceiving a sound as a call, or a shape as a letter. *Synthesis* (or "bottom-up" study) is the building up of the whole from its constituents. Example: characterizing the neuronal system that binds the perceptions of the shape, color, texture, and movement of a thing moving in the visual field. Finally, the *multilevel* approach is the study of every system on its own level as well as a component of a supersystem and as composed of lower-level things.

Each of the first three strategies has its virtues and shortcomings. Holism rightly emphasizes that the whole has emergent properties; but, because it refuses to explain them in terms of composition and structure, it borders on irrationalism. The analytic method stresses the importance of the composition of a system, but misses its emergent properties. The synthetic method does not have the defects of the other two methods, but it is not always practicable; for instance, so far biologists have not synthesized a living cell. I submit that the multilevel approach is the best of all for it recommends studying each system on its own level as well as on its adjoining levels. It has rightly been called "the backbone strategy in cognitive neuroscience" (Gazzaniga, Ivry, and Mangun 1998, 11).

The multilevel approach is an eclectic or catch-as-catch-can strategy for it allows one to use whatever approaches, techniques, models, and data may seem promising at the moment. Hence it is integrative though not holistic—an undeniable merit at a time when excessive specialization leads to artificial fragmentation. In particular, it is the one strategy capable of bringing together all the studies in neuroscience and psychology, and thus the one capable of bridging the gap between neuron and mind.

The multilevel strategy has proved its worth in a number of domains. Thus, solid-state physicists build mathematical models of crystal structures (the ion lattice together with the electron cloud) to explain such macrophysical properties as electrical and thermal conductivity. Quantum chemists, even when intent on adopting a purist or *ab initio* (synthetic or bottom-up) approach, make use of whatever knowledge they can get from both classical chemistry and atomic physics. And the neurobiologists who study a particular system, such as Wernicke's area, approach it on at least three levels: as a system of neurons, as a macrosystem with peculiar properties, and as the organ of the formation and understanding of linguistic expressions, as well as a bridge between cognition and motor outputs.

4.4 ❖ SEEKING TO EXPLAIN BEHAVIOR AND MENTATION

The most ancient, popular, and simplistic explanation of behavior is of course the animistic or mentalistic one: it takes the mind for granted and attributes to it the ability to control behavior. It is encapsulated in the popular phrase "mind over matter." The barrenness and untestability of this account drove the behaviorist psychologists to deny the mental, whereas the right attitude should have been to regard the mental as something to be explained rather than as self-evident. Behavioristic psychology attempted to dispense with the mind, and to describe behavior, in particular learning, exclusively in terms of external stimuli. But, because it ignored the nervous system, behaviorism gave a superficial account of behavior—just as superficial as the description of motion offered by pre-Newtonian kinematics, which lacked the concepts of mass, force, and stress.

By contrast, psychobiology, while admitting the valid findings of behaviorism, goes far beyond it in looking into the neural (or neuro-endocrino-immune) mechanisms that "mediate" (actually effect) observable behavior. Thus, it proceeds centrifugally, from the central nervous system to the musculoskeletal system that effects overt behavior. For example, psychobiology attempts to explain voluntary movement in terms of the specific activity of certain neuron assemblies located in the frontal lobes that activate neuron assemblies in the motor strip—and so on, until the peripheral nerves that activate muscles. And, rather than regarding the brain as a mere information processor restricted to transducing (or encoding) external stimuli, neuroscience has learned that the brain is spontaneously (not stimulus-bound) active: that neuronal activity is modulated by environmental stimuli rather than being exclusively and uniquely determined by them. This explains why a neuron's response to a given stimulus is highly dependent on the animal's level of arousal and attention to that stimulus at the time of its presentation. It also explains why we often fight external pressures and why on occasion we come up with original ideas.

Psychobiology is not restricted to the study of behavior: it also studies mentation when it occurs, from emotion, perception, and imagery to deduction and self-consciousness. The strategy is the same in all cases, namely to tackle the data of observation and self-observation as problems; to craft neurophysiological conjectures concerning the mechanisms of behavior and subjective experience; and to check such conjectures by means of further observations, measurements, or experiments. The ultimate goal is of course to organize such conjectures into neat models (or special theories) of the behavioral and mental processes of various kinds—e.g., one for working memory and another for long-term memory, a third for semantic memory, and a fourth for episodic memory. Thus, one would like to know the modus operandi of the smallest neuron assemblies—or psychons, as I call them—capable of feeling fear or anxiety, seeing a picture, recalling an event, thinking up a proposition, or making a decision.

Traditional (mentalistic) psychology was "pure" or untainted by neuroscience, for it dealt with the putatively immaterial soul or mind. Psychobiology, on the other hand, is based on (presupposes) neurophysiology and, indeed, several other branches of biology as well, such as endocrinology, immunology, and evolutionary biology. Besides, it needs social science to help explain some of the higher functions, such as empathy, the sense of fairness, and moral qualms. Thus, psychobiology in effect brings together all the studies relevant to the understanding of behavior and mentation. In other words, it contributes powerfully to the synthesis we are after, the one capable of bridging the gaps between cell and whole animal, between processes at the subcellular level and biological and social processes, and between organ (e.g., the amygdala) and function (e.g., fear).

Is this synthesis a reduction, in particular a reduction of psychology to neuroscience? Yes in one sense, and no in another. Let me dissolve this apparent paradox, which has plagued the philosophy of mind. We must distinguish two aspects of reduction: the ontological and the logical ones. Psychobiology (in particular cognitive neuroscience) is ontologically reductionistic in that it identifies the mental with the neurophysiological. More precisely, it presupposes the so-called identity theory: "Every mental event is a brain event." Indeed, this is the very rationale and program of psychobiology: To identify, analyze, manipulate, and alter the neuronal mechanisms that experience fear or pleasure, perceive or remember, imagine or infer, choose or plan, etc.

However, this ontological reduction has no logical concomitant, at least for the time being. That is, the thesis that the mental is neurophysiological is not accompanied by a deduction of psychology from neuroscience, and this for the following reasons. First, there are too few theories proper (hypothetico-deductive systems) in both fields, and as a consequence there are few intertheoretical bridges. Second, even at lower levels, the derivation of one scientific theory from another usually requires adding premises not contained in the reducing theory. (For example, quantum chemistry requires some classical chemistry, such as chemical kinetics, and it makes use of semiclassical models such as the spoke-and-rod models of molecules.) Third, far from being able to dispense with classical psychology, cognitive neuroscience needs it to supply problems and provide guidance. Thus, the study of perceptual systems is a matter not only for neurophysiology but also for the psychology of perception, which takes into account characteristics of the environment, sometimes even of the social environment. (Recall that perceptual error can be caused by social factors, such as social pressures to conform.) Fourth, there is more to neurobiology than neurophysiology, namely developmental and evolutionary biology. This point deserves some elaboration.

91

Every contemporary adult organism is the outcome of two different processes: an ontogenetic or developmental process, and a multimillion-year evolutionary process. Either way, nature accomplishes the assemblies, coordinations, and substitutions we find hard to conceptualize. Indeed, the processes leading from molecule to cell to fertilized ovum to adult primate are processes of self-assembly (or self-organization), hence integrative. And some of the processes leading from our remote ancestors to ourselves have been processes whereby old components have assumed new functions, whereas in other cases new organs have supplemented old ones. (For a magisterial survey of evolutionary cognitive science see Allman 1999.)

All of this is well known, yet it is apt to be temporarily forgotten by the anatomist, the physiologist, or the psychophysicist, interested as they are in studying short-lasting processes with the help of extremely time-consuming laboratory equipment. The division of scientific labor has reached such an unhealthy extreme that many workers in neuroscience and psychology tend to pay only lip service to studies in development and evolution.

The neglect of development and evolution has had such undesirable consequences as (a) overlooking the biological maturation of the brain, a process that spans the first two decades of human life; (b) exaggerating leaps at the expense of graduality (as is the case with mentalistic psychology, particularly of the information-processing variety, and its refusal to learn from animal psychology); or, conversely, (c) exaggerating evolutionary continuity at the expense of the emergence of qualitative novelty (as in the case of the animal psychologists who claim that human mental abilities differ only in degree from nonhuman ones).

To sum up, behavior and mentation can be explained, always in principle and increasingly in practice as well, with the help of biology (mainly neuroscience, endocrinology, immunology, and evolutionary biology) and social science. The new science of mind and behavior constitutes a synthesis or merger of disciplines rather than the epistemological reduction of psychology to biology advocated by the eliminative materialists: it has enriched psychology instead of impoverishing it. However, this merger has been prompted by the ontological reduction of the behavioral and mental to the neurophysiological. And, in turn, this reduction has been motivated by philosophical materialism as well as by a plethora of sensational scientific and medical findings.

4.5 ❖ TWO SYNTHESES

In the 1960s cognitive psychology underwent a verbal revolution: it adopted the vocabulary, though not the concepts, of information theory—a branch of telecommunications engineering. Cognition was seen as a matter of information flow and processing. Since the accent was on function regardless of organ, the new approach was rightly said to be *functionalist.*

Shortly thereafter, a bunch of psychologists joined forces with linguists and computer scientists. They launched the *cognitive science* movement, which displaced behaviorism almost overnight. The differences between people on the one hand, and computers and robots on the other, were slighted. As a consequence, such subjects as creativity, consciousness, attention, emotion, and development were neglected. Only the algorithmic operations, that is, the routine ones, were deemed of interest. Coincidentally, this is where the research money was: after all, neither the computer industry nor the armed forces could be persuaded to fund research on such subjects as, say, the effect of hormones on birdsong, the process of falling in love, or the socialization mechanisms in childhood.

That a synthesis was necessary had become obvious, because the study of mind and behavior is so complicated that it could no longer fall to a single science. But I submit that cognitive science was the wrong synthesis because it bypassed the brain. A brainless mind is like a planetary system without a star, an economy without work, respiration without lungs, or smiles without facial muscles. Because it ignores the brain, cognitive science can neither account for the neural mechanisms of mental processes, nor help treat neurological and psychiatric disorders. And because cognitive science replaces neurobiology with engineering, it misconceives the task of the science of mind and behavior as that of mimicking rather than understanding them.

All of these misconceptions have a single philosophical source. This is the belief that mental processes are stuff-free, so that they can be "embodied" in machines, or perhaps even in ghosts, as well as in live brains—as such well-known philosophers as Hilary Putnam, Jerry Fodor, and Daniel Dennett have stated again and again. Though archaic, this belief sounds modern when couched in terms of information, computation, and algorithm—particularly since neither of these words is used in psychology, or even in neurobiology, in their strict original senses in information science. No wonder that the computational theory of the mind has been prevalent in cognitive science and in the philosophy of mind since about 1960 (see, e.g., Pinker 1997).

The union of the three above-mentioned research fields has not been particularly fertile. What explains the blooming of cognitive psychology from about
1960 on is that behaviorism had run its course. It refused to investigate the most
interesting questions, and so it became barren and boring. The demise of behaviorism left psychologists free to restate some of the old but still unanswered questions concerning the mind, such as how we experience images or make decisions. Whereas some of them sought the answers in the brain, others sought
them in the computer.

Though it may have benefited artificial intelligence, this second approach has
not advanced psychology, and it does not seem to have affected linguistics. The
main effect of the association of cognitive psychology with cognitive engineering
has been the rewriting of cognitive psychology in Computerese. In turn, this translation has been effected through a systematic misuse of the term "information,"
which is well-defined in telecommunications engineering but not in either psychology or neuroscience (see Bunge and Ardila 1987). To be sure, the functionalist (nonbiological) cognitive psychologists went on making valuable contributions, but they kept describing them in terms of information encoding and processing. There has even been talk of algorithms for emotion, and of designing
creative machines—which sounds like mixing love potions, and inventing rules
for behaving spontaneously or for inventing radically new ideas or artifacts.

Most of the important discoveries about the mind made over the past three
decades came from the partial overlaps between psychology, neurobiology,
endocrinology, immunology, neurology, and psychiatry. In fact, they originated
mostly in neuroscientific laboratories and hospital wards: they fall mostly under
the new rubric of *cognitive neuroscience*. Let the following random sample of key-
words suffice: Agnosia, aggressiveness, Alzheimer's disease, anomia, anxiety,
aphasia, apraxia, blindsight, depression, enkephalin, evolution, fear, obsessive-
compulsive disorder, phantom limb, plasticity, speech disorder, split-brain, stress,
and the smell-sniff and what-where dissociations.

Cognitive neuroscience, born in the mid-nineteenth century and reborn in
the late 1970s, has not only discovered new intriguing facts: it has also started
to explain them in terms of physiological mechanisms. Here are a couple of well-
known yet still partially unsolved cases. Example 1: The shape, color, and movement of visible objects are perceived by three different visual systems. Hence, if
any of these systems becomes anatomically disconnected from the others as a
result of a brain insult, the subject will be unable to "bind" all three properties.
For instance, he will see a moving red patch but won't know its shape. The

search for the neuronal system that performs the binding and the way it works is under way. Example 2: Changes in mood are caused by changes in the concentration of certain neurotransmitters. In particular, depression results from serotonin deficiency, although it may be triggered by external stimuli. This is why the wondrous Prozac works: it increases the number of serotonin molecules at the synapses between neurons by blocking the process of serotonin reuptake (hence depletion) that normally controls that number. Both discoveries are beyond the ken of cognitive science because it ignores the brain—as a consequence of which it is in no position to help mental patients.

Because of its success in fact-finding, in unveiling mechanisms, and in suggesting therapies, psychobiology (in particular cognitive neuroscience) has started to displace cognitive science. Unlike the latter, psychobiology is brain-centered. It thus puts an end to the methodological anomalies of a brainless psychology and a mindless brain science. Indeed, ideally psychobiology is a fusion of neurobiology, psychobiology, endocrinology, immunology, and two branches of medicine, namely neurology and psychiatry. See figure 4.2.

This new synthesis came about from the realization that the said disciplines share a goal: that of attaining a scientific understanding of behavior, ideation, emotion, and mental disorder—which understanding requires unveiling the neural mechanisms of such processes. (Remember that to understand X amounts to finding out what makes X tick, that is, what are the processes peculiar to X, and that maintain or alter X: see Bunge 1999b.)

The goal of the new synthesis has been described as that of "mapping the mind onto the brain." More precisely, the psychobiologists have set themselves two mutually complementary tasks. One is: Given a mental function M, find the neural system(s) that perform M (or whose specific activity is M). The other task is: Given a neural system N, find out which if any mental function(s) N performs, contributes to, or inhibits. (Each problem is the inverse of the other.) Note that I write "N performs M," not that "N subserves (or mediates) N," nor that "N is the substrate (or basis, or correlate) of M." Instead, I write "N does M," just as in "lungs breathe" and "legs walk."

This ambitious goal could not possibly be attained by a single science because the problem is a multilevel one: recall section 4.3. Nor can philosophy be left aside, because it too is interested in the nature of mind, and it can offer valuable suggestions to facilitate the integration of the disciplines that the problem calls for—as well as to avoid pitfalls, such as behaviorism, functionalism, and machinism (in particular computerism). In fact, psychobiologists are working toward carrying out a synthesis that may be pictured as forming a hexagon around materialism. This polygon is replacing the cognitive science triangle centered in idealism. See figure 4.2.

How about such closely related research fields as linguistics and sociology? Linguistics is likely to continue to learn from the emerging conglomerate. But it cannot hope to occupy a central position in it, if only because speech is only one of the mental functions. Besides, part of linguistics is already included in the new synthesis. Indeed, neurolinguistics is the oldest part of cognitive neuroscience, and psycholinguistics is a part of psychology. As for Artificial Intelligence and other "dry" technologies, they had better watch what is going on in the new science of mind because to successfully mimic X one must first get to know something about X.

What about sociology, which some decades ago was, along with psychology, one of the main partners of the now defunct "behavioral science"? Though sociology is central to social science, in the science of mind it performs only an auxiliary function. The reason is that, even though all persons are embedded in social networks, mental processes occur inside skulls, not in society. Society is brainless, hence mindless. It shapes subjective experience and behavior but does not produce them. Moreover, stressing the social environment can lead to the exaggerations of classical behaviorism, Vygotsky's social behaviorism, and the "ecological psychology" of the Gibsons. All of them ignored the brain, as a consequence of which they fall under the so-called hollow organism psychology.

Since the mid-1950s, when the first effective psychotropic drugs were discovered, pharmacology too has become an associate of the new science of mind and behavior. However, it has not been included in the conglomerate because it is an auxiliary discipline. In fact, it is applied biochemistry in the service of the whole of medicine, in particular psychiatry.

Last, but not least, philosophy lies at the very center of the hexagon, sometimes distorting or even blocking the whole view, as in the cases of psychoneural dualism and vulgar materialism; at other times favoring the integration of research fields—the case of emergentist materialism; and at all times interacting with the other disciplines—albeit, with unnecessary time lags, due largely to overspecialization.

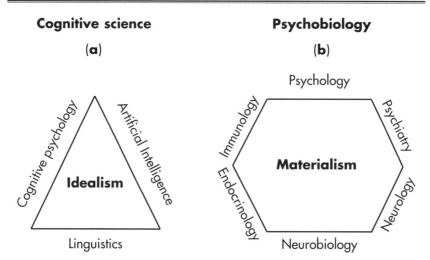

Cognitive science
(a)

Psychobiology
(b)

Figure 4.2 (a) Cognitive science: the brainless synthesis inspired by idealism.
(b) Psychobiology: the brain-centered synthesis stimulated by emergentist materialism.

CONCLUSION

Evidently, whoever wants to make original contributions to knowledge must specialize. But specialization need not, nay must not, exclude the elaboration or use of a comprehensive (philosophical) scheme of things allowing one to locate one's problems, choose the right approach to tackle them, and make use of any relevant scraps of knowledge found in adjoining fields, to the point of integrating erstwhile disparate research fields.

Such integration of formerly disjoint research fields, particularly neurobiology and psychology, has shown its worth in bridging the gap between neuron and mind, as well as in treating some serious mental disorders. (How else can we explain that anxiety, hyperactivity, depression, the obsessive-compulsive disorder, schizophrenia, and other disorders refractory to logotherapy can be alleviated by pills?) This integration has been proceeding successfully for a century and a half—in fact, since the momentous neurolinguistic discoveries of Paul Broca (1861) and Carl Wernicke (1876).

The integration of the various sciences of mind and behavior is being effected despite the resistance put up by the old theological and idealist dogma of psychoneural dualism, as well as by radical reductionism. And the synthesis in question is witness to the intellectual vigor, fertility, and practical usefulness of both materialism and systemism, as well as to the truth of the thesis that science and philosophy overlap partially rather than being disjoint.

Finally, the same synthesis of psychology and neuroscience falsifies the claim that, since science does not know about souls, which are the concern of religion, there is no basic conflict between the two "non-overlapping magisteria" (Gould 1999). Indeed, science does know something about the soul, namely, that it does not exist any more than the phlogiston, the aether, life force, penis envy, collective memory, or the manifest destiny of a certain nation. It also knows that the soul is an invention that began as a naive explanation of certain daily-life events—such as dreams and unexplained phenomena—and ended up by becoming the nucleus of a whole family of ideologies used for social control.

Moreover, it is easy to see that science and religion are mutually exclusive rather than compatible. Indeed, science takes it for granted that the world is material and lawful rather than spiritual and miraculous. This assumption underlies the very endeavor to explore and control the world, at least in part, with the help of mundane technological procedures rather than through religious practices (see, e.g., Mahner and Bunge 1996a, 1996b). By the same token, every success of the scientific and technological endeavors weakens the hold of religion and its secular arm, namely philosophical idealism. Still, this weakening is only conceptual or de jure, not practical or de facto. Indeed, we all know that, contrary to the expectations of the members of the Enlightenment, from Hume, Voltaire, Jefferson, and their followers, religious fervor and religious militancy have been on the rise since the end of World War II. Maybe the sociology and political science of religion can explain this contradiction. However, the social studies are the subject of the next chapter.

5

TWO TRILEMMAS ABOUT SOCIAL MATTER

The social sciences, such as anthropology, sociology, political science, economics, and history, are expected to study social facts with the aim of understanding them. By contrast, the social technologies—such as management science, normative macroeconomics, the law, and urban planning—tackle social issues, such as poverty, violence, and overcrowding, with a view to doing something about them. This division of labor parallels the truth-efficiency, disinterestedness-partiality, and positive science-policy science distinctions. However, this distinction entails no separation. Indeed, many a problem in social science is prompted by practical considerations; and in turn any efficient social policy or program will be prompted and guided by some findings of basic social research.

Whether descriptive or prescriptive, a social study is expected to be objective, that is, to handle social facts as real events that happen outside the knower's brain. Yet, this does not involve ignoring what may be going on inside the brains of the subjects of study, in particular what may motivate their actions or inactions. Although social facts are just as real as physical facts, they cannot be studied in the same way because social facts are ultimately results of actions stimulated or inhibited by personal interests and commitments, perceptions and misperceptions, deliberations and emotions, decisions and plans. It is not that only individuals count in social matters, but that without them nothing social happens.

A social fact is one in which at least two agents are involved whose behavior is partially determined by their ties to other members of the same society, and that may in turn affect third parties. Thus, whereas marriage and divorce are social facts, love is a private matter. Industrial production and trade are social processes, but the choices of producers and consumers, however influenced by social circumstances, are processes in individual brains. Craving power is locked in an individual's brain, but power is a social relation since it consists in the ability to alter other people's behavior, perhaps even against their will. The history of a firm or a community is a social process since it is what all the members of the group do together. By contrast, a life history is not a social process even though it is embedded in history.

All this sounds plain, yet it raises a number of philosophical problems that have been spiritedly debated for over a century. For instance, how should the study of social facts proceed? Bottom-up or synthetically, from individuals to totalities? Top-down or analytically, from social wholes to individual components? Or, alternatively, combining the two approaches? This is what I call the *individualism-holism-systemism trilemma*, which belongs in the ontology of social studies. In other words, the question is whether society is just an aggregate of individuals, a solid bloc, or a system of interconnected individuals.

A second trilemma belongs in the epistemology of social studies. Should social scientists restrict themselves to describing social facts, that is, to gather social data? Or should they, on the contrary, behave like novelists and attempt to guess the "meaning" (purpose) of their subjects' actions? Or, finally, should social students describe objectively social facts and attempt to explain them by unveiling their underlying mechanisms, that is, the processes that maintain or alter the social systems within which individual actions occur? This is what I call the *positivism-idealism-realism trilemma*.

I will argue for systemism in ontology and realism in epistemology. And I will do so by first discussing a few interesting cases and then proposing a few general definitions and principles. (For detailed metatheoretical discussions concerning the social sciences, see Bunge 1996a, 1998b, 1999b.)

5.1 ❖ MICRO-MACRO LINKS

All social facts involve agents who act in some social systems. For example, on leaving home a person chats briefly with a neighbor, then goes to work, and on his way back he stops by a grocery store. In one day he has enacted five roles in so many different social systems: family, neighborhood, transportation network, firm, and grocery store.

Whether banal or important, all social facts occur in social systems. If preferred, they link two levels of organization: the microlevel (system components) and the macrolevel (systems). Such micro-macro links help explain social facts better than exclusive reference to either personal or collective factors. Let us look briefly at a few examples drawn from the social science literature.

Example 1: Roots of the French Revolution. In his epoch-making work *L'ancien régime et la Révolution* (1998 [1856]), Alexis de Tocqueville argues convincingly for the following two-tier causal chain that started with Louis XIV's centralization of the aristocracy in Paris, and culminated in the French revolution of 1789:

Macrolevel	Political centralization	→	Impoverishment & alienation & social fragmentation
	↓		↑
Microlevel	Landlord absenteeism	→	Agricultural stagnation & weakening of social ties

This is my own reading of Tocqueville. I call the above a Boudon-Coleman diagram (Bunge 1996a). It exhibits some of the consequences that a macrosocial event has on individual lives, changes that in turn have aggregate effects.

In the eighteenth century, the typical English aristocrat lived much of the time on his estate and saw personally to it that his land was well cultivated, his tenants paid their rent punctually, and his neighbors observed law and custom. By contrast, from the early seventeenth century on, the typical French nobleman took up a position as a civil servant or a courtier in Versailles and left the management of his land in the hands of a steward. In sum, whereas the typical squire remained at the center of his rural network, his French counterpart marginalized himself.

Tocqueville's point is that landlord absenteeism, originating in the absolute monarch's desire to tame the nobility and construct a powerful central state, destroyed the rural network around the landlord, in addition to impoverishing landlord and peasant alike. To be sure this process, like all other social processes, involves uncounted individual choices, decisions, and actions. But all of these occur within or between social systems, and they reinforce or weaken the bonds that keep these systems together. Action, bond, and context go together. Eliminate either and no social fact remains. Tocqueville was then, in my view, a systemist *avant la lettre*, who combined sociological, economic, politological, and historical analyses.

Example 2: Relation between health, productivity, and economic growth. In his

Nobel Prize lecture, the economic historian Robert W. Fogel (1993) tackled a problem that leaves mainstream economists cold. This is the relation between health, on the one hand, and productivity and economic growth on the other. And yet this problem involves both the micro- and the macrosocial levels, and it lies in the intersection of four disciplines: demography, epidemiology, economics, and socioeconomic policy-making. One of Fogel's many findings is that, at the time of the French Revolution, the average caloric intake of French workers was only 2,000 kcal. That is, they were undernourished, which explains why the average height and weight of men were only 163 cm and 50 kg respectively. The poorest 30 percent of them had no energy to work more than three hours a day. This explains why one out of five inhabitants were beggars. In sum, the French were caught in the infernal causal cycle:

Poverty → Malnutrition →Weakness & ill-health→ Low productivity
and high morbidity → Poverty & short life expectancy

There is more to be learned from these statistics, namely how to shape socioeconomic policies so as to decrease morbidity and at the same time increase productive capacity. A key to such policy-making is the BMI, or body mass index. This indicator is defined as: Weight in kg/square of height in meters, or BMI = W/H^2 for short. The mortality vs. BMI curve turns out to be U-shaped with a minimum at 25 kg/m². That is, the optimal weight is twenty-five times the square of the height. The tall and skinny and the short and obese are equally at risk. If the economists of the International Monetary Fund knew this, they might never recommend cuts in public-health expenditure, not so much out of benevolence but because ill health leads to low productivity.

Example 3: Mechanisms of social inequality. Socioeconomic inequality, in particular income, is the rule everywhere except in primitive societies, where only status or rank differences are found. How do wealth inequalities emerge even within otherwise homogeneous societies: what are its mechanisms? In their bestseller *The Bell Curve*, Richard Herrnstein and Charles Murray (1994) claimed that the root cause of all social disparities are differences in native intelligence, which would in turn originate in racial differences. Using roughly the same data and more, Fischer, Fernández, Jankowski, Lucas, Swidler, and Voss (1996) demolished the Herrnstein-Murray thesis and, with it, their claim that remedial social programs are useless or worse. The key factor in scholastic and economic achievement is economic rather than genetic initial endowment—a factor only in exceptional cases.

The sociologist Charles Tilly (1998) has proposed four main mechanisms of durable "categorical" inequality in modern societies: exploitation, opportunity hoarding, emulation, and adaptation. Exploitation is exemplified by asymmetrical labor contracts, that is, deals between the strong and the weak. Such inequality is particularly pronounced when the state does not protect the employees, and the labor union is nonexistent or lacks clout because of a high unemployment rate. Opportunity hoarding occurs when members of a network get hold of a valuable resource—as when an elite monopolizes the right to enslave or kill, or immigrants from the same region corner the stonemason market. The in-out distinction becomes an upper-lower inequality.

The other two mechanisms, namely emulation and adaptation, occur among subhuman animals too. But among us they result in the emergence or reinforcement of social barriers and the concomitant struggle for power. True, the savanna baboons organize themselves hierarchically, but the alpha male is constantly challenged by rivals, whereas human economic relations are subject to legal, political, and cultural controls that render them durable.

So far we have been concerned with social statics and, in particular, with social mechanisms that maintain social systems. Let us now examine a few examples of social dynamics.

5.2 ❖ SOCIAL DYNAMICS

All social systems change all the time. A social system is bound to change because of changes in either of the following features: composition (e.g., hiring or retiring), environment (e.g., draught or social reform), structure (e.g., promotion or reengineering), or mechanism (e.g., change of a firm from producer to trader or financier). A social system may be said to undergo a revolution if it changes swiftly in all four respects. Let us take a quick look at three quite different cases of current interest.

Example 1: Prison riots. Prison riots may be regarded as social minirevolutions, and they have been studied for at least two centuries to craft and test social theories. After studying a dozen American prison-riot data, Goldstone and Useem (1999) have come to the conclusion that the joint occurrence of at least three of the following five factors are necessary for such events to occur: (a) disorganization of the state, particularly during times of changes of rules; (b) dissension between the warden (prison director) and the correction officers; (c) grievances of the prison inmates about changes seen as unfair; (d) spread of ideologies of protest or rebellion; and (e) punitive actions taken by the prison authorities in response to expressions of grievances.

The inmates' rebellion cannot be understood aside from the prison conditions, which in turn are subject to political, legal, and bureaucratic pressures. Nor can it be understood exclusively in terms of "the situation," as a methodological individualist would claim. We must focus instead on the propagation of the protests and proposals of the ringleaders along the existing prison network. The entire process can be summarized in the following two-step Boudon-Coleman diagram:

Macrolevel	Change in prison regime		Riot	→	Repression or compromise
	↓		↑		↓
Microlevel	Dissatisfaction & protest	→	Individual rebellion	→	Change in inmates' lives

Example 2: Foreign investment and development. Both common sense and the neoliberal (paleocapitalist) gospel say that foreign investment promotes economic development in peripheral countries. However, the statistical analyses of Dixon and Boswell (1996) and Kentor (1998) suggest strongly that this piece of received wisdom is a myth. The real story appears to be this. The initial effect of foreign investments is indeed positive: They create some jobs, transfer technologies, stimulate the consumption of new products, and spread modern ideas, attitudes, and habits—not all of them good, though. However, most of the beneficial effects prove to be only short-lived, as well as marginal by comparison with the permanent perverse effects. Among these the following stand out: unemployment, overurbanization, increase in income inequality, social unrest due to frustrated rising expectations, and, of course, a greater national dependency. Some of the more conspicuous mechanisms are the replacement of traditional agriculture with cash crops, the destruction of traditional industries, the substitution of supermarket chains for family-owned retail stores, the displacement of folklore by international commercial "art," the superficial imitation of everything Western, and corruption of the civil servants and politicians involved in foreign-investment ventures.

Example 3: Technological innovation. This is a clear case of mutual dependence of individual and society because invention is a brain process, whereas diffusion is a social process. (So much so that only a small percentage of patents ever get implemented.) There are two main views on the ultimate sources of technological innovation. Individualists claim that inventors propose and markets dispose. Holists hold, by contrast, that invention is market-driven: that market demands and inventor supplies. (Yet, ironically, all market worshipers espouse individualism.) Each party parades a large collection of favorable examples, and neither bothers about counterexamples. I submit that only a systemic view of the matter attains the whole truth. Let us see why.

Let us begin by noting that there are big inventions and small ones: radical novelties and improvements. Whereas the former are motivated mainly by sheer curiosity and love of tinkering, improvements may also be motivated by profit: these are often commissioned by the technologist's employer with a view to marketing the corresponding products. By contrast, some radically new inventions have created whole new markets. For example, the electrical industry was made possible by electrical engineering, which in turn was the unexpected child of experiments and theories on electromagnetism. In particular, Michael Faraday discovered the principle of electromagnetic induction, which Joseph Henry used to design the electric motor, and Nikola Tesla to design the dynamo. Industry transmuted these and many other bits of scientific and technological knowledge into welfare, wealth, and power.

Necessity is only the mother of small invention: the one that can be improvised or made to order. Big invention requires a protracted and costly R&D process. And, in contradistinction to small inventions, big invention generates desires, some of which develop into necessities. (Think of the railway, electric light, telecommunications, refrigeration, synthetic pharmaceuticals, and the computer.) The market does not create: it only demands and selects—that is, rewards or punishes. Moreover, it usually rewards the follower rather than the pioneer. (The second mouse gets the cheese.) It would be just as silly to underrate the power of the market as to regard it as the fountain of technological ingenuity. What holds for technology holds, with all the more reason, for science, the humanities, and the arts: the market can nurture or smother, and it can diffuse jewel or trash.

Example 4: Neoliberal policies. The countries whose governments implemented neoliberal policies during the last two decades of the twentieth century have undergone deep and presumably irreversible social changes, mostly for the worse. The main inputs have been market deregulation and the starving of the welfare state. The main outputs have been globalization (particularly of the capital market and of American mores), increased social inequality, weaker social cohesion, increased morbidity and mortality rates, deepening of the core-periphery chasm, and often political unrest as well. (See, e.g., Gray 1998 and Soros 1998.) The free-market ideologues designed carefully the causes and foresaw the resulting economic globalization. But, being neither sociologists nor socially sensitive, they failed to foresee the perverse social consequences of their "adjustment" and lower trade-barrier policies, in particular the deterioration of social values. The process can be represented in rough outline by the following Boudon-Coleman diagram:

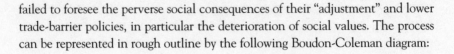

Macrolevel	Neoliberal policies	$\rightarrow$	Decline of social cohesion & political unrest
	$\downarrow$		$\uparrow$
Microlevel	Wage decline & loss of good jobs	$\rightarrow$	Increase of social inequality

So much for social dynamics and, in particular, mechanisms that induce structural changes in social systems. Let us now stipulate a few definitions of some key social-science concepts. This will equip us to hazard a few general principles concerning the nature of social matter in contradistinction to nonsocial matter (section 4) and, later on, the optimal way of studying it (section 5).

5.3 ❖ DEFINITIONS

In the so-called hard sciences, one does not start by defining the key concepts: these are defined implicitly by the general principles in which they occur. (For example, the electric charge concept is tacitly defined by the equations of electrodynamics.) Given the relative theoretical poverty of social science, and the concomitant uncertainty concerning its basic concepts, it will be convenient to start by clarifying some of them in an explicit fashion.

Definition 1: A *social system* is a concrete system composed of animals that (a) share an environment; (b) act directly or indirectly upon other members of the system; and (c) cooperate in some respects with one another while competing in other respects.

Definition 2: A *human social system* is a social system composed by human beings who depend upon their own work or that of others to meet their needs and satisfy their desires.

Families and formal organizations are social systems. By contrast, ethnic groups, crowds, and bands of marauders are not—at least as long as they are not organized to act in a concerted manner.

Definition 3: A human social system is

(a) *natural* or *spontaneous* if it is self-organized, that is, if it emerges spontaneously through reproduction or free association;

(b) *artificial*, or *formal*, or a *formal organization*, if it is formed and maintained in accordance with explicit policies, plans, and rules.

For example, bands of hominids, families, children's gangs, circles of friends, neighborhood soccer teams, and amateur chamber music ensembles are spontaneous social systems. By contrast, business firms, armies, schools, and churches are artificial social systems. Caution: the natural/artificial distinction is purely descriptive: it only refers to the mode of formation of social systems. Once in place, even spontaneous social systems may make use of sophisticated technologies.

Now, human societies, even if primitive, are more than systems: they are supersystems. This fact invites

Definition 4: A *human society* is a system composed of four major subsystems:

(a) the *biological system*, whose members are held together by sexual relations, kinship relations, child rearing, or friendship;

(b) the *economic system*, whose bonds are relations of production and exchange;

(c) the *political system*, whose specific functions are to manage the common goods and control the social activities; and

(d) the *cultural system*, whose members engage in such cultural or moral activities as learning or teaching, informing or recording, discovering or inventing, designing or planning, singing or dancing, counseling or healing, worshiping or debating, and so on.

Villages, neighborhoods, towns, counties, provinces, and nation-states are societies because each of them is composed of biological, economic, political, and cultural systems. By contrast, hospitals, prisons, armies, and transnational corporations, though very complex social systems, are not societies.

Definition 5: A *supersociety* is a system composed of human societies.

For example, the former USSR, the European Union, and the American empire are supersocieties. The Islamic world and Mercosur are emerging supersocieties.

Definition 6: The *world system* is the supersociety composed of all the human societies. The world system was born on October 12, 1492, and it was consolidated in the course of the nineteenth century. The integration process was violent: it was carried out by war, invasion, colonization, and sometimes the destruction of local economies in the name of free trade. Globalization proceeds nowadays sanctified by the same gospel though mostly in a peaceful manner.

Curiously, it took students five centuries to realize the occurrence of the globalization process: so blinding was their focusing on individuals and nation-states. In fact, the first to treat explicitly the world system was the historical sociologist Immanuel Wallerstein (1976). (Regrettably, this correct novel idea was later on used to explain all large-scale social facts in terms of the rank of the nation concerned in the world system—as if the local natural resources, ruling classes, and traditions played always a subordinate role.)

So much for social statics. Let us now introduce three concepts concerning social change.

Definition 7: A human *social process* (or *activity*) is a process in which at least two interacting persons take part.

Marriage and divorce, making friends or enemies, working or playing together, rearing children or debating are examples of social processes. So are exchanging goods, services, or information, as well as organizing and making war.

Social processes come in all sizes. Some engage a few persons, whereas others involve entire nations or even the whole world. The industrialization, urbanization, secularization, and rationalization processes that started in Europe in the seventeenth century began on a local scale and spread eventually throughout most of the world.

Definition 8: A *social movement* is a directed (nonspontaneous) social process occurring in at least one social system, and that draws people who did not originally belong to it.

Movements of social or religious reform, as well as cultural currents such as the Renaissance, the Enlightenment, and the Counter-Enlightenment; and political movements such as feminism, environmentalism, liberalism, socialism, and fascism are examples of social movements.

Definition 9: A *social invention* consists in deliberately setting up a social system of a new kind, or in drastically reorganizing (changing the structure of) existing social systems.

Marriage, slavery, bureaucracy, the state, organized religion, insurance, the university, and all public rites and ceremonies are examples of social inventions.

Social inventions may be the work of leaders, bureaucrats, or social movements. Some of them consist in willed reforms or revolutions. There are also involuntary or quiet social reforms and revolutions, such as those triggered by industrial, political, and cultural innovations, from electric power, agricultural machinery, refrigeration, automobile transportation, the political enfranchisement of women and minorities, and welfare legislation, to the world-wide diffusion of college education, TV, the computer, made in USA pop culture, and the repackaging of conservatism as liberalism.

Regrettably, the concept of radical social change is alien to most social theorizing. In particular, mainstream economics and rational-choice theories take the social context (or institutional framework, or social structure) for granted. And yet, every single social action (or inaction) is not only socially embedded: it also either strengthens or weakens the social context, and thus the very rules of social life. For example, every time someone utters the instruction "Charge it to my credit card," he contributes to the dangerous accumulation of public debt; every time someone abstains from casting his ballot, he erodes democracy; and every sale of a rock music record contributes to the degradation of culture.

Let us now put our definitions to work.

5.4 ❖ PRINCIPLES ABOUT SOCIAL SYSTEMS

We proceed to laying down some basic assumptions (that is, postulates or axioms) about social systems. (Reminder: Postulates are just initial hypotheses, not self-evident truths.) We shall also note some of their logical consequences (corollaries and theorems). The miniature hypothetico-deductive system to be displayed will then be a sort of breviary of systemic sociology.

Postulate 1 Every human being belongs to at least one social system.

Corollary 1 There are no wholly marginal persons.

Even autistic patients, hermits, and prisoners maintain bonds, however weak or ephemeral, with individuals who are fully integrated in social systems. Even the newborn belong to a social system, namely a family or an orphanage. As they grow and develop, children make their way into other social systems, at first as patients and later on as agents. Coming of age is more than menarche or puberty: it is usually identified with full membership in most if not all the major systems of a society.

The previous postulate is the systemic version of the Aristotelian description of the human being as a *zoon politikon*, that is, social animal (usually translated as political animal). And the corollary suggests that marginality comes in degrees; hence also its dual, namely integration, comes in degrees.

Postulate 2 The social systems are held by bonds of various types: biological (including the psychological ones), economic, political, or cultural.

Corollary 2 Social segregation of any kind (sexual, ethnic, economic, political, religious, etc.) weakens social cohesion.

It is mistaken to privilege any type of social ties, such as the biological ones (as is the case with sociobiology), or the relations of production (Marxism), the political relations (liberalism), or those of communication (symbolic interactionism, hermeneutics, and ethnomethodology). All social ties are important and are entangled with one another. What is true is that, in certain processes, one of them may take precedence over others. For instance, a family connection may give rise to a cultural or economic relation, which may in turn originate a political allegiance.

Postulate 3 By virtue of belonging to several social systems, the beliefs, preferences, attitudes, expectations, choices, and actions of every person are socially conditioned as well as innerly motivated.

Corollary 3 Human beings are neither fully autonomous nor fully heteronomous.

That is, both Kantianism and behaviorism are wrong: We are all partly autonomous and partly heteronomous. But of course autonomy is largely dependent upon power. The powerless can hardly afford to exercise their free will.

Postulate 4 Every social system has a specific function (that is, a process or activity that no other social system can perform).

This assumption does not amount to attributing social-systems goals, intentions, or other functions performed by the brain. For example, the specific function of the mail system is to distribute mail: only some of the mail employees have this goal.

The preceding postulate does not imply that all of the functions of a system be beneficial to its components, let alone to society as a whole. As a matter of fact, some social systems, such as standing armies in peacetime, have no known beneficial functions. In others words, the preceding axiom is merely descriptive.

Postulate 5 Every social system, at any time, is engaged in some process—gradual or discontinuous, causal, stochastic, or hybrid.

This hypothesis should reassure those who fear that systemism favors stasis and is therefore conservative. In fact, the axiom does not exclude swift qualitative changes. Moreover, it is just possible that so-called chaotic processes are conspicuous in society. (Caution: there is nothing literally chaotic, that is, lawless, about chaos theory. All "chaotic" means is critical dependence upon initial conditions: a small deviation in these may grow explosively in time.) This is due in part to the fact that, in contradistinction to electrons and photons, persons have memory and purposes. It is also due to the fact that, like with electrons and photons, human life histories are subject to unforeseeable accidents, such as casual encounters with people bound to exert a strong influence on either choices or circumstances. Still, at the time of writing we still do not know of any "chaotic" social processes. And we won't know for sure unless social scientists state, solve, test, and confirm empirically some nonlinear differential (or finite-difference) equations describing social processes.

Postulate 6 The changes of a social system originate in (a) changes in its components or (b) interactions among its components or among these and things in the system's environment.

In other words, whereas sometimes a systemic change originates in individual actions, at other times it is caused by social interactions, and at still other times it is rooted in environmental changes or in new human actions upon the environment. Although this is obvious, it is overlooked by rational-choice theory.

The processes of capture, loss, and substitution may be merely quantitative. By contrast, those of association, dissociation, and reorganization (change in structure) may be qualitative as well.

Postulate 7 All the members of a social system cooperate with one another in certain respects and compete in others.

This assumption combines Marx's thesis on conflict with Durkheim's on solidarity. No concrete system of any kind would emerge or subsist without some cooperation, whether tacit or deliberate. But, once a social system is in place, its members are bound to compete with one another for scarce resources—from food to love—whether internal or external.

Postulate 8 For a system to remain stable (or rather in a stationary state) it is necessary that internal cooperation be stronger than internal conflict.

This axiom cries for definitions of the concepts of stability and of strength of a social bond (centripetal or centrifugal). However, the intuitive concepts will have to do for the moment.

Postulate 9 Whereas competition stimulates initiative and innovation, cooperation favors the efficiency and continuity of the system, and it promotes social cohesion and individual responsibility.

Postulate 10 A social system emerges (spontaneously or by design) if and only if its existence contributes to satisfying some of the needs (real or perceived) or desires of some of its members.

If the needs and desires that motivate the formation of a social system are either imaginary or tiny, the system becomes a burden to its members, who eventually neglect, abandon, or dismantle it. Which takes us to the next assumption:

Postulate 11 A social system disintegrates, spontaneously or by design, if (a) it no longer benefits most of its members, or (b) its conflicts become more intense than its cooperative ties.

Corollary 4 Perfect (unregulated) competition is socially dissolving.

The free-market ideology, which preaches the sovereignty of the market, is socially and morally just as corrosive as any other form of selfishness.

Postulate 12 The efficiency of any social system improves with competition as long as it is not allowed to undo the ties that hold the system together.

Corollary 5 All social systems stagnate or decline if their members cease to either compete or cooperate.

Shorter: A combination of competition with cooperation results in social good health.

Postulate 13 All social inventions benefit some people whereas they harm others.

Corollary 6 Every social invention is resisted, passively or actively, by those who believe, rightly or wrongly, to be harmed by it.

To limit the harm and conflict caused by a given social invention, it is desirable to involve all the stakeholders, as well as to seek the help of experts in the design, planning, and execution of the innovation in question. This suggests that the ideal social order combines integral democracy with social technology.

So much for a bundle of general principles concerning the nature of social systems and their changes. Let us now peek at some general principles concerning the optimal approach to the study of social systems.

5.5 ❖ PRINCIPLES ABOUT THE STUDY OF SOCIAL SYSTEMS

It stands to reason that the proper study of systems of any kind is systemic rather than either individualistic or holistic. That is, the description and explanation of social facts should start by locating these in the social systems where they occur. And the very first thing to do with such systems is to analyze them rather than to either reduce them to their components (individualism) or feign that they are solid blocs (holism). This is why we propose:

Postulate 14 Every social system is to be analyzed into its composition, environment, structure, and mechanism: $m(s) = <C(s), E(s), S(s), M(s)>$.

The composition $C(s)$ is taken on some level or other: that of individuals, households, firms, electoral districts, or what have you. The environment $E(s)$ represented in the model is only the part of the environment of s currently known to be relevant to s; this excludes most of the actual environment. The structure $S(s)$ includes not only the bonds that make a difference to individual behavior, but also the nonbonding relations that may be socially relevant, such as those of being nearer, older, or richer. Finally, the mechanism M(s) includes only the processes that "make the system tick," such as loving and caring in the case of a family, work in a production unit, and learning in a school.

Holists refuse to analyze systems. Individualists focus on composition and environment ("the situation," or "external constraints"). Environmentalists (particularly behaviorists) regard the environment as both the source and the sink of human behavior. Structuralists focus on structure and disregard the rest. And all of them ignore mechanisms, and consequently cannot or will not explain social change. Only systemists join all four aspects. Hence only they can explain what makes people flock into systems, work for them, fight them, reform them, or leave them.

Postulate 15 The social sciences study social systems.

This principle is clear but far from obvious since it goes against the two leading fashions of the day, namely interpretive (*verstehende*) social studies and rational-choice theory. Both schools focus on individuals with total disregard for social systems and social movements, and each of them assumes a one-sided view of man: as *homo symbolicus* and *homo œconomicus* respectively. (More in chapter 6.) However, the fact of the matter is that only biologists and psychologists study individuals. Anthropologists, demographers, sociologists, economists, political scientists, historians, management experts, urban planners, and others study social systems. This is why they are called *social* scientists. By contrast, finance experts study only the financial aspect of the economic system instead of studying the whole system. This may explain why they have failed so far to come up with a true theory of finance. Parallel: a physiologist who, to explain hypertension, were to study only blood instead of the entire cardiovascular system and the other body systems coupled to it.

The above postulate does not question the legitimacy of social studies of individual behavior, as long as it is regarded as being decisively influenced by social circumstances—as is the case with social psychology and economic-behavior research. Only biologists study humans regardless of their social circumstances. Even so, some of them tackle the action of social stressors on the psycho-neuro-endocrino-immune supersystem. Their studies may be placed in biosociology, the emerging intersection of biology and sociology—not to be confused with human sociobiology, or the study of human society as if it were an anthill or, at most, a troop of baboons.

The most analytically minded students of society are naturally drawn to rational-choice models, which focus on individual decisions and assume that these are essentially free and guided mainly by self-interest. Such models work in simple cases, like those of a driver in light traffic and the self-employed professional. In both cases, the agent may be regarded as acting only under external constraints and forces, much as an electron in a magnetic field—with the difference that the agent has a will of his own. But this is not the case of a driver during rush hour: his only rational choice is to go with the traffic flow—that is, to surrender his freedom of choice. Likewise, the worker in a corporation has very little leeway: he is more like a cog in a machine, even if he himself originally designed and assembled the machine. In these cases, only a systemic model can work, because every agent is strongly coupled to every other agent in the system.

These considerations apply in particular to the attempts to reduce any social science, even economics, to the study of individual choice in markets, or to goods and prices, the way Gary Becker (1976) and his fellow "economic imperialists" have proposed. The reason is that all economic activities are embedded in social networks, which are in turn included in society at large. Economic sociology has amply confirmed this view (see Smelser and Swedberg 1994). Hence, economic science is the study of economic systems in their relation to other systems, both economic and noneconomic. Similar considerations hold for sociology, political science, and culturology.

For example, viewing the Parthenon exclusively as a unique work of art—which it is—does not explain why it was erected at great expense to the Athenian taxpayers. This fact is explained by regarding it as being at once a place of worship, a treasury, an act of glorification of Athens, and—like many other monumental constructions—a provider of plenty of jobs, as Plutarch noted. In short, the construction of the Parthenon was a cultural, political, and economic event, whence it should be a subject of interdisciplinary study.

Postulates 14 and 15 jointly imply:

Theorem 1 A scientific study of any social system involves research (both empirical and theoretical) into its composition, environment, structure, and mechanism.

In turn, this theorem and definition 4 jointly imply:

Theorem 2 A scientific study of any human society involves research (both empirical and theoretical) into its biological, economic, political, and cultural subsystems.

Corollary 1 Any purely biological, economic, political, or cultural account of a social system is at best only partially true.

This indicts, in particular, the self-styled economic imperialism, which is the aping of neoclassical microeconomics in all social fields of study.

Corollary 2 No social science is self-reliant.

Axioms 5 and 16 jointly imply:

Theorem 3 The social sciences study social activities (processes).

Corollary 3 The synchronic social studies only provide snapshots of social processes.

So much for the pure or basic social sciences, which seek to account for social facts in the most objective possible way—without however neglecting some of the inner sources of social action, such as empathy and envy. Some of their findings are expected to be used by the corresponding technologies: the sociotechnologies. These design or redesign social systems, and prescribe how to put them together, manage, or reform them. Market research, operations research, finance, normative macroeconomics, and the law are among the sociotechnologies. All of these disciplines are expected to make use of social science findings, rather than to follow either routine or mindless trial and error.

This characterization of the sociotechnologies, together with postulate 14, have the following logical consequences among others:

Theorem 4 The efficient organization of a social system involves the consideration of its composition (e.g., the personnel of a firm), environment (e.g., the appropriate market), structure (as represented by organization graphs), and mechanisms (as represented by, e.g., delivery and work schedules, timetables, and budgets).

Theorem 5. Any efficient and lasting social reform is the product of changing several social features in tandem rather than one by one.

Systemic problems call for systemic solutions. To tackle systemic social issues in a sectoral way is an act of either self-deception or political propaganda. A current example of this kind is the proposal of ending domestic poverty by having the poor plug into the Internet. Another is free trade as the clue to the development of the poor nations. These cure-all recipes remind one of George Berkeley's advocacy of tar water as the universal remedy.

This will have to do as a thumbnail sketch of systemic sociology, the alternative to rational-choice theory, "interpretive" sociology, Marxist economism, and holistic sociology à la Talcott Parsons, Niklas Luhmann, or Jürgen Habermas. (For details see Bunge 1974, 1979, 1995, 1996a, 1998a, 1999b, 2000a.)

CONCLUSION

We started by recalling the two trilemmas in contemporary social studies: the individualism-holism-systemism, or ontological trilemma, and the positivism-idealism-realism, or epistemological one. We then drew a sketch of systemic sociology, which joins the ontological thesis that all social facts occur in social systems, with the methodological norm that all facts should be accounted for in an objective way. The ontological thesis draws the student's attention to the wider social context, as well as to what is peculiar to social facts, namely that they consist in interpersonal connections that generate, maintain, strengthen, or weaken social systems or networks. And the methodological norm demands that the motivations of the agents be embedded in social networks, and be studied in a scientific way rather than from an armchair. However, this subject touches on the next chapter.

6

INTERPRETATION
AND HYPOTHESIS
IN SOCIAL STUDIES

The classical positivists, from Ptolemy in the second century, to Bacon in the seventeenth, and Mach in the nineteenth, equated scientific research with data gathering. Consequently, they regarded hypothesizing and theorizing as merely the economic summarizing of empirical data—never as imaginative torches to illuminate the search for new data, let alone to understand them. The sharp distinction between research and theory, now inconceivable in physics, is still standard in social studies. And even in 1967, when positivism had already run its course, no entry for "hypothesis" was included in the authoritative *Encyclopedia of Philosophy*.

Yet, it is obvious that scientists routinely presuppose, as well as frame and check, plenty of hypotheses. These are nothing but educated guesses that, in breadth or in depth, go beyond or even against common sense and immediate experience. Let the following random sample of counterintuitive scientific ideas suffice to make this point: the principles of inertia and of electromagnetic induction; the atomic theory and the photon hypothesis; the hypothesis of evolution through genic variation and natural selection; the hypothesis that the genetic material is constituted by DNA molecules; the hypothesis that mental processes are brain processes; the hypothesis that the legalization of abortion contributed to the decline in crime; and the hypothesis that all technological advances have unforeseen perverse effects. As Darwin noted, even data gathering is preceded by hypotheses, starting with the hypothesis that what one is looking for may exist and may be relevant to the problem at hand. No hypothesis, no science proper: neither interesting data nor well-grounded explanation. (See, e.g., Herschel 1830; Whewell 1848; Naville 1880; Peirce 1958 (1902); Poincaré 1903; Popper 1959 (1935); Bunge 1998a (1967); Wolpert 1992.)

Idealists claim that, although the above may fit the natural sciences, it does not match the social sciences, which they call "spiritual sciences" (*Geisteswissenschaften*) or "moral sciences." This holds, in particular, for the hermeneutic school, initiated by the neo-Kantian philosopher Wilhelm Dilthey (1883, 1900) and paid lip service to by Max Weber (1913, 1922). The hermeneuticists propose replacing hypothesis and explanation with *Verstehen* (interpretation or comprehension). This thesis is worth discussing not so much because of its merits, as because of its popularity among the so-called humanist (armchair) social scientists, as well as in the postmodernist movement. (See, e.g., Garfinkel 1967; Taylor 1971; Geertz 1973, 1983; Ricoeur 1975; Dallmayr and McCarthy 1977; Mueller-Vollmer 1989.)

6.1 ❖ MEANING, GOAL, FUNCTION, OR INDICATOR?

According to hermeneutics, social facts, unlike the natural ones, have "meanings." Hence they are not to be explained in the manner of natural facts. Instead, they are to be "interpreted" or "comprehended" in the manner of texts rather than being explained in causal terms. Regrettably, the hermeneuticists do not care to elucidate this peculiar concept of meaning. Still, from its context it appears that they mean something like purpose, goal, or function. That is, they seem to use the vulgar sense of "meaning" prevalent in colloquial German and English, as when one says of a given action that it is "meaningful," or "makes sense," because it is conducive to the desired goal or performs the desired function—or else it is "meaningless" in failing to do so. In this sense, the "meaning" of the ancient Egyptian pyramids is that they symbolized the pharaoh's power—or perhaps that their construction was "meant" to provide gainful employment to the farmers in between the periodic floodings of the Nile riverbanks.

In other words, the hermeneuticists do not use the *semantic* concept of meaning, namely sense together with reference (or connotation-cum-denotation) of a predicate or a proposition. (For example, "trade" *denotes* people and *connotes* mutually agreed to change of hands, in contrast to both gift and theft.) As noted above, the hermeneuticists use instead the *vulgar* (or pragmatic, or praxiological) concepts of meaning, which apply not to predicates and propositions but to attitudes, intentions, decisions, and actions. Yet, they equivocate systematically, though unwittingly, in claiming that, because social facts are "meaningful," they are texts or similar to texts. Which is like claiming that culture and horticulture are one because both involve cultivation.

As for "interpretation" or *Verstehen*, in social studies it is supposed to mean grasping the "meaning" (goal) of an action, a custom, or a symbol. Actually, the context suggests that to "interpret" an action or a custom is only to guess its goal or function with the sole help of intuition and of one's preconceived ideas about human nature. For example, whoever believes that all humans are basically selfish will "interpret" every human action as selfish. And if, by contrast, one believes that humans are complex, varied, and somewhat unpredictable— whence they do not behave like automata—he is likely to suspend judgment until a detailed investigation discloses the real motivation of the action in question. But of course such investigation, if scientific, will involve the explicit crafting and checking of precise and scrutable hypotheses. Resorting to "interpretation" is only a license for arbitrary fantasizing.

Take, for instance, the work of Clifford Geertz (1973, 1983), a famous "meanings-and-symbols" ethnographer who does not believe in what he calls "the science thing." Geertz has done fieldwork in Java, Bali, and Morocco. Let us start with his view of the typical Javanese villager—whose occupation and status are not disclosed. It appears that this person's goal in life is to be *alus* (refined) in both *batin* or inner life and *lair* or outward behavior. The former is attained through religious discipline, and the latter through etiquette.

Even a psychoanalytic anthropologist who does not flinch at Freud's fantastic "interpretations" questions Geertz's fantasies about the Balinese cockfight as a drama of status hierarchy: "We must ask: on what grounds does he [Geertz] attribute 'social embarrassment,' 'moral dissatisfaction,' and 'cannibal joy' to the Balinese? to all Balinese men? to any Balinese man in particular?" (Crapanzano 1992, 65).

Even admitting that *alus* (refinement) is a goal of that people, is that their overriding goal rather than meeting their basic needs? A scientifically minded anthropologist would presumably hold that this question can only be answered by watching the behavior of Javanese in times of duress. And he would surmise that amidst a famine, plague, hurricane, or war those people are likely to behave like everyone else: they would sacrifice ceremony to survival. A scientific anthropologist would also wonder how the striving for refinement could possibly explain why the Dutch conquered Java, or why the Javanese eventually fought for independence—only to end up, along with the other Indonesians, by being exploited and oppressed by their own oligarchy. He would hypothesize that symbols and ceremonies do not explain such sea changes. And he might conclude that individual psychology cannot explain macrosocial facts anymore than particle physics can explain the flow of rivers.

Let us now look at Geertz's account of the Balinese. Apparently these people do not need to toil or fight, and they face no pressing social problems. To them, the world is a theater, and life a play with symbols. Their society, and indeed every society, must be represented as "a serious game, a sidewalk drama, or a behavioral text" (Geertz 1983, 23). Thus, every Balinese enacts a role in an eternal play characterized by a spiritual meaning—presumably as witnessed by cock-fighting, widow-burning, and other jolly spectacles. What matters most in his or her life is not to grow rice, prepare for the monsoon, raise a family, get along with neighbors, tackle community problems, or resist the landlord or the colonial administrator. Instead, what matters is to overcome *lek* (stage fright) and avoid the *faux pas* (Geertz 1983, 64). But how do we know that this is a faithful "thick description" free from hypotheses rather than one anthropologist's fantasy? We are not told: after all, if anthropology is a literary genre, testability is irrelevant.

Another original finding of Geertz's concerns the way Moroccans individuate people. We are told that their main means is the *nisba*, a linguistic form that can be roughly translated as attribution or imputation (Geertz 1983, 65 ff). For example, Muhammed will be characterized as a native son of Fez and a member of such and such a tribe, occupation, religious brotherhood, and so on. That is, every Moroccan is individuated as the person who belongs in the intersection of a certain number of social groups. But what is so special about this individuation method that cannot be used by a native of Manhattan? And why should such universal procedure be regarded as a linguistic device rather than as a cognitive one? Since many subhuman animals and all mute humans have the ability to individuate their conspecifics, it must be a prelinguistic operation. And, being universal, it does not help to understand the specifics of life in Morocco.

I submit that these findings of Geertz's fall into either of three categories: trivial, conjectural, and false. This is not to belittle the importance of the so-called symbolic components of any society. But the part is not the whole—particularly if it is minor. After all, *primum vivere, deinde philosophari* (First live, then philosophize). Something similar holds for social conventions: they are rules of social restraint and coexistence (or class submission, as the case may be). Neither symbols nor social conventions can take the place of the central social engine, namely work. An anthropology that ignores the modus vivendi of people is not just idealistic and sectoral: it is unrealistic to the point of frivolity. And someone who advances arbitrary symbolic interpretations of personal experiences and social customs without checking them follows in the steps of Freud's "interpretation" of dreams, which in turn was no better than the dream almanacs popular in an earlier age. (See further criticisms of literary anthropology in Cohen 1974 and Reyna 1994.)

The cult of symbols reminds one of Maximilian, the emperor that the French foisted upon the Mexicans in the 1860s. As the Mexican revolutionaries stormed his Chapultepec palace, Maximilian was busy putting the finishing touches to his etiquette manual. Being interested only in social symbols, he had no inkling of any social issues, and no intimation that he would shortly be facing a firing squad. Moral: Retiring to a world of symbols can be hazardous to your health.

There is yet another sense of "meaning" in use in social studies, namely the one attached to social, economic, and political indicators. Thus, an increase in the number of street riots is said to mean or indicate social malaise or political discontent—much as smoke indicates fire, and fever sickness. In general, an *indicator* is an observable (or even measurable) variable that is assumed (rightly or wrongly) to be related to an unobservable variable in a more or less precise way. This relation is usually (and wrongly) called an "operational definition." I prefer to call it an *indicator hypothesis* (see, e.g., Bunge 1996a, 1998b). Ideally, this is a causal relation representable by a functional dependence.

But social indicators are notoriously ambiguous. That is, most social indicator hypotheses are statistical correlations rather than functional relations. For example, a drop in the price of merchandise may indicate either a decline in the demand for it, or a decrease in its production cost. Likewise, an increase in the number of hospital beds per thousand inhabitants in a given region may indicate either poor health of the population or excellent public health care. Because of such ambiguity, entire batteries of indicators are routinely employed to disclose such unobservables as the level of human development or the state of the economy, the polity, or the culture of a society.

There are two reasons for the ambiguity of most social indicators. One is that they concern disjoint multiple causal relations of the form "C_1 or C_2 or . . .

$C_n \rightarrow E$." (This is reflected in the existence of n significant but not decisive statistical correlations between the n possible causes and the effect.) The second reason for the ambiguity of social indicators is that they are empirical: they are not related in a lawful manner to other variables, the way physical indicators are. In other words, most indicator hypotheses are stray rather than being embedded in theories.

The moral is that the word "meaning" is polysemic and should therefore be used sparingly or not at all in social studies. In some cases it is best replaced with the words "goal" or "function," and in others with the term "indicator." Furthermore, the word in question should always be accompanied by the caution that what is at stake is a clear and testable hypothesis rather than an obscure and infallible intuition. In science, by contrast to literature, intuitions are at best the precursors of hypotheses: they belong in the scaffolding, not in the building.

The following anecdote highlights the dangers of uncontrolled interpretation. In 1983 I was lecturing to a large audience at Ains Shans University in Cairo. Once, in the middle of a lecture, a man stood up, shouted something angrily in Arabic, and left the classroom followed by a good third of the audience. He returned the next day, persuaded by my host that he should discuss his discrepancies with me. It turned out that he was a professor of physics, and had been infuriated by my attempt to show that science and religion are mutually exclusive. He was particularly incensed by my claim that, unlike science, which is forever chasing new truths, every religion is a bunch of dogmas, some false and others untestable. My opponent claimed instead that the Koran contains all that is worth knowing. When I asked him "Even atomic physics?" he replied: "Yes, if properly interpreted." By whom? By those who know. And by which rules? The ones that are laid down by those who know. End of the debate.

6.2 ❖ INTERPRETATION, INFERENCE, OR HYPOTHESIS?

Empirical data are mute: they tell us nothing by themselves. They are raw material to be processed. There are five main views concerning what do with them. I shall call them the hermeneutic, the pseudodeductivist, the inductivist, the deductivist, and the scientific ones. The first is, as we saw, the attempt to grasp directly the intention or the goal behind the data: this is the purported function of *Verstehen*. However, this word is ambiguous. Indeed, the philosopher Dilthey understood it as meaning empathy, or putting oneself in the place of the agent. On the other hand, the sociologist Max Weber understood it as guessing the "significance" (*Sinn, Deutung, Bedeutung*) of an action in the sense of its intention or goal. Moreover, Dilthey took this operation to be subjective, intuitive, and infallible, whereas Weber regarded it as objective, rational, and fallible. The debate over the correct interpretation of "interpretation" has been going on for over a century, but no resolution is in sight—as befits inexact philosophy. (See, e.g., Bianco 1981; Dahrendorf 1987; Bunge 1996a.)

In any case, whether as empathizing or as guessing intention or goal, *Verstehen* concerns only individual actions, not macrosocial events or processes. Hence, it hardly contributes to understanding such macrosocial processes as massive unemployment, inflation, business cycles, or the rise and fall of popular superstitions—not to mention the social consequences of environmental catastrophes. So much for "interpretation." Let us move on to alternative strategies.

What I called the pseudodeductivist strategy consists in claiming that one must make "inferences" or "deductions" from data. For example, paleobiologists, prehistorians, and archaeologists are in the habit of saying that they "infer" or "deduce" the behavior and even the ideas of our remote ancestors from the bones and artifacts they find in archaeological sites—as if there could be a logical calculus leading from data to conjectures (see, e.g., Renfrew and Zubrow 1994). But of course such "inferences" are neither more nor less than conjectures about human behavior. Indeed, a set of empirical data entails hardly anything. (Thus, the datum that a given individual has a certain property P only entails that some individuals possess P. And the datum that all the individuals in a sample of a population are Ps suggests, but does not prove, that every member of the population is a P.)

The archaeologist who attempts to figure out the origin or the possible utilization of an ancient artifact does not *infer* a set of propositions from another in accordance with any rules of inference: what he does is to advance more or less plausible guesses. Moreover, far from trusting his intuition, the way hermeneuticist do, scientists put their hypotheses to the test. For instance, they manufacture replicas of the artifacts and try them out to check whether, in fact, the originals could have performed the hypothesized functions.

In short, in the sciences, whether natural, social, or biosocial, one attempts to account for empirical data in terms of hypotheses. A scientific hypothesis, whether narrow or broad, shallow or deep, may or may not concern the motivations of any actors, it is not exuded by the relevant data, and it is often anything but self-evident. If confirmed, the hypothesis H, together with the pertinent empirical data D, will account for the fact(s) F in question according to the logical schema: H & D ⇒ F. Example: Unemployment breeds criminality. Now, criminality has decreased. Hence, we infer that unemployment must have dropped—as in fact it has done in the United States during the 1990s. (Incidentally, this particular hypothesis is of the mechanismic type: it suggests a mechanism for the change in crime rate. An additional mechanism is the legalization of abortion, since it decreases the number of unwanted and therefore neglected children, who develop into criminals because of anomie and lack of skills [see Bunge 1999b for the role of mechanism in explanation].)

Inductivists claim that there is "logic" for confirming hypotheses or even for constructing them on the basis of empirical data. It would work like this: given a set of data of the form "x is a P," where the variable x ranges over the natural numbers, it is possible to assign a probability to the hypothesis "All the given individuals are Ps." This probability would function like a credence or degree of belief (see, e.g., Carnap 1950). There are at least three objections against this claim. One is that the concept of degree of belief is psychological, not semantic: it is unrelated to truth. Moreover, as Peirce (1958 [1902]: 101) noted a century ago, such "probability" is alien to the mathematical theory of probability. Second, the inductivist procedure is inapplicable to continuous (nondenumerable) variables, such as position and time. Third, as Einstein (1951) noted, the basic (or high-level) scientific hypotheses contain predicates (such as "energy" and "demand elasticity") that do not occur in the empirical data relevant to them. In sum, inductivism does not work, even if we do make low-level inductive generalizations from data, and induce again when confronting the testable consequences of a hypothesis with the pertinent data—as when we "conclude" that the data provide a strong indication that the hypothesis is true.

Deductivism, the fourth view of the role of data in scientific research, rests on the inference rule called *modus tollens*, namely: From A ⇒ B and not-B, infer not-A. Thus, if we guess that A causes B, and fail to observe B, then we infer that A was not the case. So, data serve to falsify hypotheses. Popper and the other deductivists claim that this is *the only* function of observation and experiment: to shoot down hypotheses. But this is obviously false since we are more interested in collecting truths than falsities. And a hypothesis can be regarded as true, at least to some approximation, when it matches a substantial body of empirical evidence. This is why scientists care for confirmation at least as much as for refutation.

True, confirmation is rarely conclusive, whereas falsification is definitive provided the negative evidence is unambiguous. Still, empirical confirmation can be conclusive in the case of existential hypotheses, such as "There are atoms," "There are genes," "There are oligopolies," and "There are political democracies." In such cases, a single favorable example suffices to confirm the hypothesis.

Besides, deductivists and inductivists alike miss an important step in the confirmation process. This consists in checking the compatibility of the new hypothesis with the bulk of antecedent knowledge. Indeed, one does not even bother to design an empirical test of the hypothesis at stake unless it is plausible, that is, consistent with the best available knowledge. I call this the requirement of external consistency (Bunge 1998b [1967], chap. 15). In short, scientists do not abide by pseudodeductivism, inductivism, or deductivism: they use data to check hypotheses as well as to motivate their construction, propose explanations, and make forecasts and hindcasts.

So much for the pseudodeductivist, inductivist, deductivist, and scientific views on the role of empirical data. Let us now return to the hermeneutic school. When intent on studying social matters, the hermeneuticists are bound to hazard hypotheses. This is what they do every time they impute definite motives to their actors. But, as Durkheim (1988 [1894], 188) warned long ago, such imputation is too subjective to be handled objectively, particularly with regard to agents that are too far away in space or time to be interviewed. After all, intentions are imperceptible; different people may engage in the same observable actions for different reasons or driven by different passions; and many a cold calculation has unforeseen consequences, some good and others bad.

Besides, even if we could read intentions off actions, this would only account for individual behavior under given or assumed circumstances, such as institutional constraints. But this is the comparatively easy part of the social scientist's task. As James Coleman (1990) noted, the hard part is going from the microlevel to the macrolevel: that is, to figure out the mechanisms whereby individuals, whether independently or in concert with others, alter social structure. But the interpretivists of either school do not even attempt to solve this problem: they just assume that individual action changes the social world. In other words, they do not solve the problem of figuring out the ways (mechanisms) whereby actions at the microsocial level have a macrosocial impact: the upward micro-macro arrow of the Boudon-Coleman diagrams remains unaccounted for. (Recall chapter 5, sec. 1.) Let us examine two classical examples of such a micro-macro analysis.

Recall first how Tocqueville (1998 [1856], bk. 2, chap. 1) tackled the problem of land tenure in France before the 1789 Revolution. He started by asking himself whether the administrative records supported the widely held hypothesis that land reform had been a result of the Revolution. His investigation showed him that land reform had been in slow progress for some centuries before the Revolution. The farmers had been buying small parcels of land, which they worked much as they pleased, though subject to hundreds of petty, unjust, and therefore hateful restrictions. The serf or tenant in other countries was not a victim to such restrictions because he did not own the parcel he cultivated. For example, he did not have to pay tributes or taxes when buying or selling land or its produce, for only the landowner could engage in such operations.

Tocqueville admits of course that the Revolution did distribute some land, particularly the Church's and the émigré's. But he shows that its main effect was to liberate the farmers from the residual feudal ties. The first people to rebel against the feudal order were the French, not because they suffered the most under it but, on the contrary, because their condition had improved to such a point that they could no longer tolerate the multitude of exactions imposed by the absentee landlords, who rendered no services in return. In short, the Revolution was the sudden and unforeseen culmination of a centuries-long process of transformation of the structure of French society, and had no parallel in the rest of Europe. This transition can be summarized in the following Boudon-Coleman diagram:

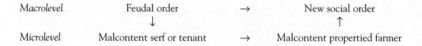

Macrolevel	Feudal order	→	New social order
	↓		↑
Microlevel	Malcontent serf or tenant	→	Malcontent propertied farmer

In the same work (book 2, chap. 9) Tocqueville poses the problem of the origin and consequences of the proverbial French individualism. He traces it back to the successive fragmentations of French society caused jointly by landlord absenteeism and privileges without duties. All the great aristocrats lived in Paris, whereas the small ones remained in the village but—unlike the English squires—exerted no public functions and were thus isolated from the peasants, whom they regarded only as debtors. Similar divisions occurred in the cities among the clergy, the bourgeois, the craftsmen, and the officeholders. It was every small group for itself, all (unwillingly) for the crown, and neither for the public good. The absolute central administration had robbed the French of the very possibility and desire to help one another, to the point that one would have looked in vain for ten men used to acting regularly in common (bk. 3, chap. 8).

The net effect on French society as a whole was such a weakening of the overall social structure that it crumbled without bloodshed in the course of the evening of July 14, 1789. The fragmentation process, which took three centuries, can be summarized in the following three-tier Boudon-Coleman diagram:

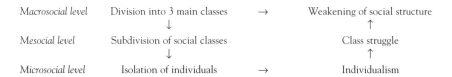

Macrosocial level	Division into 3 main classes	→	Weakening of social structure
	↓		↑
Mesocial level	Subdivision of social classes		Class struggle
	↓		↑
Microsocial level	Isolation of individuals	→	Individualism

Note incidentally that, far from being a methodological individualist of either the hermeneutic or the rational-choice persuasion, Tocqueville may be regarded as a materialist and a systemist *avant la lettre*. Indeed, he stated that the aim of social science is "to understand the general movement of society" (bk. 3, chap. 1). Moreover, Tocqueville not only places individuals in their social classes and in their (rural or urban) networks: he states explicitly (bk. 2, chap. 12) that he talks about classes, for "only these must occupy history." This is exactly what he accomplishes in this work, namely, a superb class analysis. This analysis is superior to the standard Marxist class analysis because it encompasses and interrelates all three artificial subsystems of every society: its economy, polity, and culture.

Clearly, Tocqueville's work is far superior to that of the hermeneuticists. Whether intuitionists or rationalists, the interpretivists miss the very hub of social life because they concentrate on individual actions, with neglect of the bonds that hold the social systems together, and because they prefer bookish speculation to painstaking data gathering and hypotheses testing. This is why they do not explain satisfactorily how the division of labor and social classes have emerged; why agricultural surplus rendered the state possible and necessary; why empires have declined and fallen; why people join mutual-help societies, cooperatives, or labor unions; why some people bother to vote; why so many Americans, though renowned for their individualism, devote much of their time to voluntary work; why the prices of raw materials and foodstuff lag further and further behind those of manufactured goods; why the labor unions are withering in America while they are still going strong elsewhere; why cooperatives flourish in some countries while they languish in others; why NATO is being kept after the end of the Cold War; why globalization has rendered capitalism more fragile instead of strengthening it; or why politicians the world over are failing to face new facts with new ideas. Neither the hermeneuticists nor the rational-choice experts have tackled, let alone solved, these social problems.

In particular, these schools have carefully skirted such serious social pathologies as long-lasting market disequilibria (e.g., chronic unemployment); the increasing income inequality concomitant with growing productivity; the unexpected catastrophic financial crises (in particular stock-market crashes); and the intensification of ethnic conflicts and religious fundamentalism in the age of science. With regard to social pathologies, interpretivism and rational-choice theory look like medicine without sickness, meteorology without storms, and earth science without earthquakes. They are little better than jeux d'esprit. (More in Bunge 1996a, 1998a.)

I submit that the failure of interpretivists and rational-choice theorists alike to even address large-scale social problems stems from their wrong methodological perspective. It derives, in particular, from their focusing on individuals with disregard for social systems, social classes, and social mechanisms, and from their inability to diagnose the kind of problems that social scientists are expected to tackle. However, this subject deserves a new section.

6.3 ❖ WHY SOCIAL-SCIENCE PROBLEMS SEEM INTRACTABLE

Mathematicians class problems into direct and inverse. For example, the task of adding numbers is direct, whereas that of decomposing a number greater than 2 into digits is an inverse problem. Again, whereas deduction from a set of premises is a direct problem, inventing the premises that will entail a given set of theorems is an inverse problem. The existence of an algorithm for solving direct problems of a certain type does not guarantee the existence of an algorithm for solving the corresponding inverse problems, which in general have either multiple solutions or none.

In the sciences of man, from psychology to history, a direct problem looks like this: Given the motivations and circumstances (constraints and stimuli) of a human agent, as well as the behavioral regularities or norms he is expected to follow, find out his behavior. The problem for a social system is parallel, with the difference that the hypothesized personal motivations will be replaced with the hypothesized social mechanism. In either case, the statement of the direct problem may be summarized as follows:

Given motivation or mechanism M and circumstances C, find out behavior B = MC.

(B and C may be construed as column matrices, and M as a rectangular matrix.) Admittedly, this is no easy task, mainly because of the dearth of known mental and social laws. But in principle it is soluble; and, if soluble, it has a single solution.

However, this difficulty is as nothing compared with the corresponding inverse problem. This is the following: Given the agent's observable behavior and circumstances, figure out his intentions. In the case of a social system, we are asked to "infer" (guess) the mechanism, knowing only its behavior and the stimuli that prompted it. Shorter: Given B and C, find out M.

The difficulty in reading intention off behavior and circumstance is high-lighted by the game of poker and its analogs in family life, business, and politics. Each side knows his cards and tries to guess the other's. But success in guessing depends not only on the player's skill but also on his opponent's bluffing ability. In serious real-life "games" the difficulty is compounded by the inconsistencies and inconstancies of every one of us. Indeed, a seasoned social psychologist has found that "almost everybody is of at least two or three minds about almost everything of any real social importance" (Bales 1999, 89).

In our symbols, the inverse problem about the engine of the behavior of persons and social systems reads thus:

Given the circumstances C and the behavior B, figure out the motivation or the mechanism M:

$M = B\ C^{-1}$, *where* C^{-1} *is the inverse of the circumstances matrix.*

But this problem, like all inverse problems, has either multiple solutions or none.

However, this is not the end of the methodological story. Indeed, whereas both direct and inverse problems can be well posed, if seldom well solved, the typical problem in social studies is not even well posed. In fact, because of the poverty of social theory, in most cases the investigator does not know which motivation or mechanism M is likely to mediate between circumstance and behavior. Worse, because of the underdevelopment of social metatheory, he may not even realize that it is always necessary to hypothesize some M or other. Indeed, ordinarily he grapples with *ill-posed* problems of the following types:

Direct: *Given only the circumstances, conjecture the behavior. (Or: given the cause, guess the effect.)*

Inverse: Given only the behavior, conjecture the circumstances. (Or: Given the effect, guess the cause.)

Obviously, something crucial is missing in the very statement of each of these problems: a clue as to how to proceed. They resemble the poster in Edison's research factories: "There must be a better way. Find it!" Clearly, ill-posed problems, that is, incompletely stated ones, are not scientific problems proper. They at most elicit scientific problems. Hence, it is no wonder that they are insoluble except by accident—a name for a lucky guess. This deep flaw in the problematics of social studies goes a long way to explaining their backwardness.

Consider the following examples. Why was there a riot in town X? Why were the crops not collected in territory X? Why did the literacy campaign in X fail? Why did the stock market crash? Why has computerization failed to increase productivity in most industrial sectors (the so-called Solow paradox)? It is impossible to say without further information. But even adding information about the circumstances would be insufficient to find a unique solution to any of these problems, for in every case more than one mechanism might have operated. For instance, a riot may be caused by food shortages, unjustified tax hikes, unequal taxation, police brutality, interethnic hatred, religious fanaticism, or even a wild rumor.

We have just cited a few alternative hypotheses likely to explain a given social fact. Their mere explicit statement is likely to spur the search for the respective circumstances that are to function as further evidence. Having found them, we would then be faced with a set of alternatives to be investigated:

$B = M_1C$, $B = M_2C$, . . ., $B = M_nC$, where M_i, with $i = 1, 2, . . ., n$, is the ith hypothesis about the motivation, mechanism, or means that mediates between circumstance C and behavior B.

The goal of the investigation is to find out which one of these n hypotheses (or "interpretations") is the truest and deepest. To refuse to frame explicit and reasonably detailed mechanismic hypotheses is like restricting the study of human metabolism to observing people eating and excreting. And to refuse to check any mechanismic hypotheses against data is to exhibit arrogance.

To put it in pictorial terms, the social scientist is faced with a number of alternative boxes mediating the output B to the input C:

$$C \to M_1 \to B, \qquad C \to M_2 \to B , . . ., \qquad C \to M_n \to B,$$

where C and B are observable in principle but not necessarily in fact. Typically, the chronicler records B but, not having had advance notice that B would be important, he paid scant notice to C when it happened. So, he is likely to have missed some of the most important factors involved in the production of the outcome B. One does not collect facts unless one suspects they may be of interest.

In sum, the vast majority of social-science problems are inverse, on top of which they are not even well posed. These peculiar features of social-science problematics are seldom if ever noticed, which is a sad comment on the state of social metatheory.

6.4 ❖ BASIC SIMILARITY BETWEEN *VERSTEHEN* AND RATIONAL-CHOICE THEORY

As we saw earlier, in social studies two outwardly very different methods have been proposed to solve problems: "interpretation" (*Verstehen*) and rational choice. The former consists in guessing the agent's motivation in each particular case, and the latter in assuming that everyone always behaves "rationally," that is, in their own best interests. Both procedures are a priori: they are not usually checked by further observation, much less experiment. Hence, they are methodologically far less different than usually presumed.

Indeed, these methods are alternative versions of "interpretation": intuitionist and rationalist respectively. In the former case, the observer proceeds case by case, always relying solely on his preconceived notions, common sense, and intuition. By contrast, the rational-choice theorist assumes the same rule for all cases, namely, that all persons, in all societies and in all circumstances, behave as utility maximizers.

In other words, whereas the interpretivist makes up a particular story in each case, the rational-choice theorist uses the same story in all cases. The methodological difference may be characterized as case-interpretivism and rule-interpretivism respectively—by analogy with the two versions of utilitarianism. The schools in question may also be called "local apriorism" and "universal apriorism" respectively.

The only important difference between these schools is that, whereas Dilthey's followers see people as symbol manipulators, rational-choice theorists regard them as rational utility maximizers. Seen in this light, the difference between the two schools turns out to be negligible. So much so, that an eminent proponent of the rational-choice approach describes strategic analysis, which he calls "vicarious problem solving," in exactly the same manner as Dilthey (1959 [1883]) one century earlier: "We figure out what a person might do by putting ourselves into his position" (Schelling 1984, 205). Paradoxically, the same author unabashedly admits that "this is cheap theory" (206).

The basic theoretical and empirical poverty of both schools explains why neither has produced any findings worth citing and worth using in business or public administration policy making. It may legitimately be asked why, if this is so, Max Weber, who is claimed by both schools, is rightly regarded as one of the founders of scientific (as opposed to armchair) sociology. The first point to be noted is that, as his only student hinted (von Schelting 1934, 370), Weber did not quite practice the methodology he preached. Indeed, he neither turned inwards nor practiced psychohistory. Instead, Weber studied social facts just as objectively as his archrivals Marx and Durkheim. (Ironically, both Marx and Weber declared that such study was impossible.) Moreover, far from focusing on individual action, he dealt mainly with impersonal entities and movements, such as feudalism, capitalism, religion, bureaucracy, and modernization. Moreover, he warned that, even if an account of human behavior in terms of its "signification" (goal) looks self-evident, it is just one more hypothesis that should be put to the test (Weber 1913, 437).

Besides, contrary to the idealist Dilthey, the Wittgensteinian Winch (1958), and the rationalist Popper (1974)—all of whom disowned the search for social relations in the external social world—Weber sought them right there. In particular, he looked for causal relations, such as the social causes of the decline of ancient culture, the close match between the caste system and Hinduism, and the stranglehold by the Prussian landowners on agriculture. (Even so, one should not exaggerate the importance of Weber's work. His major work, the massive *Wirtschaft and Gesellschaft* (1922), is bookish, nonquantitative, and almost purely descriptive. Consequently, it affords little understanding of the social processes described therein.)

In sum, neither interpretivism nor rational-choice modeling accounts for social matters. This is because both focus on the subjective sources of action, with total neglect of the fact that action is socially "significant" only to the extent that it affects the structure of some social system. Still, rational-choice theory has the virtue that it attempts to explain social facts in terms of precise if narrow reasons—namely interests—rather than in terms of either ad hoc motives to be disclosed by the somewhat mysterious *Verstehen*, or in terms of no less obscure social factors such as socialization, *Zeitgeist*, national destiny, collective memory, or historical necessity.

Moreover, the rational-choice approach can be expanded, as Boudon (1999) has suggested, by adding another three kinds of rationality to instrumental (or economic) rationality. These are (a) bounded rationality (satisficing, instead of maximizing, in the light of incomplete information and under the pressure of making decisions in real time); (b) cognitive rationality (sketching a semitheory of the situation, so as to come up with a system of strong reasons for taking action); and (c) axiological rationality: acting on principles rather than on expected consequences—e.g., voting because political participation is necessary for political democracy.

Such an enrichment is welcome but insufficient for it is still limited to individual behavior. Hence it cannot explain why certain rational actions succeed while others, no less rational, fail. The explanation of social facts requires some knowledge of the peculiar overall features of the social system in which action occurs, as well as of the mechanisms that such action triggers or blocks. For instance, a small band of revolutionaries can overthrow an unstable government, whereas it would be easily suppressed by a stable government. In sum, the transition from social psychology to sociology is still to be made. Such transition requires placing social structure and social mechanism, not individual mind, at the very center of the social-theory picture. The resulting social embedding of individual goals and choices suffices to show that, because they are severely constrained by social bonds, they are seldom (a) fully "rational," that is, in the individual's best interest; and (b) relevant to an adequate understanding of social facts.

In other words, the root trouble of the various versions of *Verstehen* we have been examining is their ontological assumption that there are no societies but only individuals—whence the belief that methodological individualism is the right approach to social facts. The recipe of methodological individualism is to focus on individuals and their circumstances. (When the relevance of the latter is stressed, one speaks of contextual or institutional rather than atomistic individualism.) This recipe works in dynamics to solve one-body problems: To find the orbit of a body subjected to an external force, plug the latter into the equation(s) of motion of the former, and solve for the position coordinate(s). (Example: a ball rolling down a ramp under the action of gravity.) But this recipe does not work if the force in question is an interaction between the bodies, for in this case each of them influences critically the behavior of the others.

(Example: a binary star.) As a result, the individual trajectories become hopelessly entangled, and consequently hard to calculate. To be sure, it is possible to write down the system of equation of motion for any number of bodies; but this system has no exact solution for more than two bodies.

If methodological individualism does not even work in dynamics except for the simplest cases, why should one expect it to work elsewhere, particularly in social science? In fact it does not work, as shown by the multitude of social events that were willed by no one in particular, such as the two world wars, the twenty million dead in the first, or the fifty in the second; the Great Depression or the immiseration of the peoples of the former Soviet empire after its fall; the current epidemics of obesity in the rich countries, or voter apathy in America; chronic unemployment in Europe, or the latest Wall Street crash; and the unsuccessful bombing raids on Iraq, Chechnya, Serbia, and Afghanistan. Rational choices indeed!

Methodological individualism is ineffective because it underrates interaction, which deflects the best calculated individual actions and is the marrow of social systems, and therefore of structures and mechanisms as well. For example, the well-being of the master derives from the misery of his slave, whereas the happiness of each spouse derives largely from that of the other. Alter drastically the bond in either case, and very different individual behaviors result along with different systems. Or add a third person, and the system may be either strengthened or weakened by the additional interactions—as Georg Simmel (1950 [1908]) vividly showed long ago. Thus, whereas the addition of a child to a married couple is likely to have the first effect, that of a lover is bound to have the second one. In sum, however important context and circumstance may be, interaction is even more important because it is the source of system and the fuel of mechanism, without which there is no social fact. And the rejection of the very idea of a social system endowed with emergent properties is the trademark of methodological individualism.

CONCLUSION

Social scientists, just like natural scientists, tackle cognitive problems: they are after knowledge for its own sake. The difference between the two groups is metatheoretical rather than theoretical. In the natural sciences there is a fairly long tradition of tackling well-posed problems and attempting to solve them by framing and trying out definite hypotheses or, even better, systems of hypotheses, that is, theories. This tradition is rather weak in social studies, where most problems are ill-posed, hypotheses are often disguised as either interpretations or inferences, theories are not well organized, or the fit-all hypotheses of class conflict and maximizing behavior are adopted uncritically.

The hermeneutic or interpretive school has the merit of shunning allegedly fit-all explanations, favoring instead particular or local "interpretations" (hypotheses) to account for each category of facts. But it goes too far in rejecting all general hypotheses. This is an objectionable strategy because, as Aristotle taught, there is no science but of the general. And in any case there are some widespread social patterns and rules of conduct, such as incest avoidance, territorial defense, cultural diffusion, and the invention of new institutions to cope with radically new situations.

Moreover, the hermeneutic school is dogmatic in putting forward particular "interpretations" just because they look plausible in the light of either preconceived notions or ordinary experience. (A point of intuitionism is that insight is infallible.) Tradition cannot cope with radical novelty; and ordinary experience is insufficient or even irrelevant with reference to large social systems, for these have suprapersonal features that often defy common sense (that is, received wisdom). For example, the legalization of abortion decreases criminality; the stock market drops when employment rises; the diffusion of higher education decreases the opportunities of social advancement; foreign investment is likely to impoverish an underdeveloped nation in the long run; and globalization introduces dangerous financial instabilities.

If common sense sufficed to understand social facts, social scientists would become redundant: journalists and writers could do the job. Ironically, this is just the point of the "humanistic" or literary camp: that the narrative mode of thought suffices, whereas the abstract and argumentative one—characteristic of mathematics, science, the law, engineering, and other intellectual achievements of civilization—is inadequate to account for social matters. What the hermeneuticists propose is no less than to remythologize (or reenchant) culture, thus turning the calendar back by a mere three millennia. (For the similar effect of holism, see Harrington 1996.)

It goes without saying that local circumstances have to be attended to. But surely, some individual motivations and social mechanisms are universal since all humans, and consequently their interactions and basic social organizations, resemble one another in many respects. That is, there are some universal or cross-cultural social patterns alongside many others that are system-specific and culture-specific, that is, place-and-time-bound. Yet, rational-choice models fail to distinguish families from clubs, armies from churches, schools from retail stores, and so on. We need then different social theories for social systems of different kinds. The same holds for social policies. There are no more panaceas in social matters than in medical ones.

To conclude, it is mistaken to oppose interpretation to explanation, or even to hold that the two are mutually complementary. This is mistaken because "interpretation" is just another name for "commonsensical ad hoc guessing," whereas every explanation proper is a deductive argument as far as logical form is concerned. The opposite of "interpretation" is "scientific hypothesizing," that is, making educated and testable guesses about imperceptible things and processes. In social science, such guesses may refer not only to facts but also to values and norms. Consequently, some of the premises in the explanation of a social fact are likely to be value judgments, whereas others are moral norms.

To advance our understanding of the social world, we must go beyond both intuitive understanding (*Verstehen*) and rational-choice modeling, because both strategies ignore social bonds, hence social systems, and do not care for empirical tests. The scientific study of social problems involves explicit hypothesizing—if possible of social mechanisms, such as imitation, division of labor, mutual help, and class struggle—and empirical testing, just as in natural science.

The main difference between the social and the natural sciences is not one of method but one of subject matter. In particular, humans satisfy what Merton (1968) has called the Thomas theorem, according to which people react not to social facts but rather to the way they "perceive" them. In other words, social relations, unlike physical relations, pass through people's heads. However, such intervention of subjective factors need not render the social studies subjective. Social science is, by definition, the scientific study of social reality. And social reality, though constructed and reconstructed by people, once made is out there, embedded in nature, just like rocks and rivers. More succinctly, social science is just as materialist and realist as natural science although it is not reducible to the latter. (More in Bunge 1996a, 1998b, 1999b.)

Something similar holds for the social technologies vis-à-vis the others. The vast majority of students in this field take it for granted that the social systems they study in order to exert control over them exist objectively and can be known to some extent. They too are realists: they distinguish the territory from our maps of it. They too make use of observations, hypotheses, and the occasional experiment. They too are fallibilists as well as meliorists. They too deal with agency-structure problems rather than with either individuals or wholes alone. They too learn—alas, not often enough—from adjoining disciplines. And they too are both blessed and plagued by a variety of approaches.

For example, the management scientists Mintzberg, Ahlstrand, and Lampel (1998) argue that there are nine different influential views of strategic management. Three of them are prescriptive: the design, planning, and positioning schools. The six remaining approaches are descriptive: the entrepreneurial, cognitive, learning, power, cultural, and environmental schools. Every one of these views accounts for one feature of strategic management—the proverbial elephant. Hence those management experts propose a tenth view, one that includes the previous views and more. They call it "configurational." I prefer to call it "systemic" because "configurational" suggests a gestalt or holistic view, whereas Mintzberg and his coworkers attempt to peep into the innards of the firm, to find out how individuals cooperate in some respects and compete in others, and how they adapt to their environment by altering it as well as by changing their own behavior and thus that of their firm.

In sum, social studies, whether descriptive or normative, call for hypotheses. But, for a hypothesis to qualify as scientific, it must be testable rather than being a wild "interpretation," however plausible at first sight. And, if the hypothesis concerns humans, it should not assume that all individuals are equally motivated and equally free to choose the course of action most likely to advance their interests. In fact, different individuals may have different motivations, and some are freer and better informed, and thus more powerful than others. In a nutshell: social studies must be scientific rather than literary if they are to attain truth or efficiency.

7

DOUBTS ABOUT SKEPTICISM

A skeptic is, of course, someone who, far from accepting everything he is told, or the first thing that comes to his mind, questions it. If what is at stake is a new datum, the skeptic looks at the way it was found, or even attempts to replicate it; if a new generalization, he looks for counterexamples (exceptions); if a novel procedure, he checks for its effectiveness; if a newly proposed norm of conduct, he checks for both its compatibility with other principles and the practical consequences of its application—and so on.

By contrast, the dogmatist holds on to what he regards as infallible received wisdom. But, like a character in one of Vladimir Nabokov's novels, he treats everything he does not know with skepticism. In short, the trademark of the skeptic is checking, whereas that of the dogmatist is blind acceptance and equally blind rejection.

Doubting does not come naturally. So much so that it appears to be all but unknown in primitive societies, where the most implausible myths go just as unchallenged as the most obvious pieces of solid knowledge. There are two good reasons for such gullibility and dogmatism particularly in earlier times. The first is that new ideas, particularly good ones, are hard to come by without methodical research and the backing of a substantial body of certified knowledge. The second is that people need to hold on to a bunch of shared beliefs if they are to cope with a restless and largely unknown and hostile environment. Most of them, whether primitive or modern, prefer to protect their belief systems by anchoring them. (Even Charles Sanders Peirce, an original proscientific philosopher, gave advice on how to fix belief.) But of course an anchored ship does not move. What we need to navigate safely is to equip the ship with a stabilizer. This stabilizer is the scientific method together with a ballast of well-confirmed laws and robust values, such as free inquiry, the free sharing of research findings, and criticism—particularly of the constructive type.

The habit of weighing reasons to believe or disbelieve is likely to have emerged as recently as about two and a half millennia ago. It appears that this habit emerged in the intellectual elite of a cosmopolitan society awash with conflicting views, torn by internal political strife, and rocked by international conflicts. This was Athens at the time of Pericles. It was there and then, some twenty-five centuries ago, that logic, mathematics, science, the law, and political democracy—all of which require doubt, critical discussion, and proof—flourished and interacted simultaneously for the first time. It was no coincidence that ancient Greece was also the cradle of skeptical philosophy, or the systematic doubting of everything.

Doubting has become so ingrained in practical affairs in the modern world that nobody, not even the religious fanatics, doubts the legitimacy of doubt at least in some circumstances. Thus, businessmen check goods before buying, and possible business partners before striking any deals. Better yet, consider the modern practice of law. The first task of the lawyer is to collect and sift the evidence for or against whatever data, guesses, or arguments the other party exhibits. A piece of evidence or an argument will not stand in court if it cannot satisfy the scrutiny of a persistent skeptic intent on discovering gaps, inconsistencies, or lies. And the jurors and judges are enjoined to pronounce their verdict only if the extant evidence is "beyond all reasonable doubt"—itself a doubtful concept that has been the subject of controversy for over two centuries. Skepticism is thus a bulwark of retributive justice: liberty, property, and life depend on the strength of the commitment of the legal system to the skeptical principle "Doubt before acquiescing; and, should any reasonable doubt remain, suspend judgment and delay action, or refrain from acting altogether."

In the philosophical domain things are even more complicated than in the practice of law. Indeed, the contemporary philosophical skeptics, just like the dogmatists, constitute a motley crowd. They only agree on the following five points: (1) abidance by the basic rules of logic, particularly the law of noncontradiction, that is, "not-(p and not-p)"; (2) demand of evidence for or against any statements concerning matters of fact—hence deep suspicion, if not out-right denial, of claims of the supernatural and the paranormal; (3) respect for intellectual honesty; (4) right to free inquiry and open rational debate; and (5) fallibilism, or the maxim "To err is human."

Other than this, skeptics differ on every conceivable point. For example, with regard to religion, whereas some are agnostics, others are atheists. Again, whereas some maintain, others dispute that it is pointless to conduct further experiments on telepathy, psychokinesis, palmistry, and the like. Whereas some skeptics criticize conventional morals—which involve a modicum of altruism—others claim that all moral judgments are culture-bound or even subjective. And, whereas some are skeptical about particular political programs or actions, others are suspicious of all politics. In sum, some skeptics are more tolerant of deviant opinions and practices than others.

Such diversity is understandable since different people have somewhat dif-ferent backgrounds, viewpoints, interests, and goals. And this diversity is to the credit of the skeptical movement. Indeed, such tolerance makes room for bold new ideas and stimulates their rational debate. It would be suicidal for a skep-tical movement to rule that only one school of thought should be tolerated on matters that are still under investigation. Just as suicidal is to rule that alchemists, flat-earthers, astrologers, creationists, homeopaths, and psychoana-lysts have as much claim to taxpayers' money as scientists.

The constructive skeptic has no more patience with zealots or charlatans than with salaried myth-mongers or professional impostors: he is too busy doing his bit to attain new truths, or debunk myths old and new, through painstaking research. After all, time is the scarcest and therefore the most valuable of all resources. However, in all epochs some skeptics have undertaken to shoulder the public burden of criticizing some of the delusions and fallacies passed off as sci-entific findings. The present chapter is one more effort in this direction. Anyone interested in more of the same should consult the journals *Free Inquiry* and the *Skeptical Inquirer*.

7.1 ❖ DOGMATISM AND SKEPTICISM COME IN DEGREES

Anyone naive enough never to doubt anything he has been taught, or he him-self has cooked up, deserves being called a dogmatist. The apriorist and intuitionist philosophers are dogmatic in the extreme, the former because they rely on allegedly general principles in no need of empirical testing, whereas the latter ask us to believe in their allegedly infallible insights. Typically, the writings of dogmatists are not chains of reasons buttressed by empirical evidence or logical inference, but rosaries of unjustified sentences. (See, e.g., any writings by Heidegger or Derrida.) A dogmatist does not feel the need to clarify, prove, or justify anything, except perhaps by recourse to either authority or analogy—neither of which cuts any ice with rationalists.

However, dogmatism comes in degrees. In addition to total or systematic dogmatism, there is partial (tactical or methodological) dogmatism—or bounded skepticism. Every reasonable person is only partially skeptical, and this for two reasons, one logical and the other practical. The first is that, in order to cast reasonable doubt on anything at all, we must take something for granted, if only for the time being. We may reasonably doubt an item only if it conflicts with the bulk of antecedent knowledge. For example, the telepathy hypothesis is inconsistent with cognitive neuroscience, according to which ideas cannot be detached from brains, any more than faces can broadcast smiles.

The practical justification for partial (or tactical) dogmatism is that nobody has the competence, resources, patience, or time required to check every idea that comes his way. For instance, nobody in his right mind doubts that two and two make four; that people must eat to survive; that cars need fuel to run; that knowledge is valuable; or that actions have consequences, whence we should inquire and deliberate before acting.

But it is one thing to be reasonably certain about ideas and procedures that have passed uncounted tests, and another to claim the existence of privileged propositions or procedures in no need of any testing because they have been revealed, or endorsed by some alleged authority, or because we find them self-evident. Skeptics of all varieties disbelieve in revelation and mistrust intuitions of all kinds, whether about the correctness of mathematical propositions, the grammaticality of sentences, the efficiency of cooking recipes, or even the morality of actions. Any self-respecting skeptic will demand grounds for believing or doing anything. Skeptics are grounders as well as grinders: constructive as well as destructive.

Now, bounded dogmatism is of course the same as bounded skepticism. Hence, like dogmatism, skepticism can be either total (radical, systematic), or tactical (moderate, methodological). Every reasonable person is partially skeptical, because life teaches us that anyone (particularly other people) can make mistakes. But it also teaches us that we have come to know quite a lot—for instance, that there are photons and atoms and genes and galaxies; that, whereas some infections are bacterial, others are viral; that institutions can become obsolete; and that extreme selfishness does not pay in the long run.

A few historical examples should help clarify the difference between the two varieties of skepticism. Pyrrho and Sextus Empiricus in antiquity were radical skeptics, for they claimed that nothing can be known with certainty. Francisco Sanches and Michel de Montaigne followed suit on the eve of the modern era, except that they admitted (very likely only to save their skins) that some truths can be known through revelation or faith. By contrast, Socrates and Descartes used doubt only as a means to attain ultimately what they regarded as certain knowledge. Their skepticism was then only tactical: doubt was just the first phase in their search for truth. This is why, by contrast to Pyrrho and Sanches, they succeeded in attaining some truths.

Few skeptics have doubted the power of reason to establish mathematical formulas beyond the shadow of a doubt. The reason is that mathematics is not given but made, whence it is thoroughly under human control. If the initial assumptions and rules of inference are posited, the consequences (theorems) follow necessarily. If for some reason we do not like a consequence, we are free to change some assumptions or even, within bounds, some of the rules of inference—as long as we keep the principle of noncontradiction. Hence certainty, at least in the long run, is always attainable in mathematics—barring the undecidable propositions that never pop up in mainstream mathematics anyway. However, mathematics is not a truth machine, for the choice of assumptions is in principle disputable. (For example, different set theories, hence different sets of proofs, result from admitting or rejecting the axiom of choice or the continuum hypothesis.)

By contrast, in matters of fact, only plausibility and partial (approximate) truth are attainable. That is, the statements made in physics, chemistry, biology, social science, technology, or moral philosophy can seldom be demonstrated conclusively. We regard some of them as true to some extent, only because they are consistent with other statements in the same field or in neighboring fields, or have been amply corroborated by empirical data. But we should be prepared to correct or even discard any of them if presented with unfavorable evidence, be it a counterexample or a better alternative theory. In sum, skepticism is inherent in factual science and technology. The only question is to find out whether such skepticism is moderate or radical.

A preliminary answer to this question can be obtained by comparing the two greatest skeptics in history: Sextus Empiricus, who flourished in the third century C.E., and David Hume, who wrote fifteen centuries later. At the time of Sextus, nobody could ascertain whether Earth circles the Sun or vice versa, whether light propagates instantaneously, whether there is spontaneous generation, whether blood circulates, whether alchemy works, or whether there are natural slaves. Asserting or denying either hypothesis did not lead to contradiction with the bulk of scientific knowledge, which was then exceedingly modest. Hence Sextus's radical skepticism was justified, particularly since he encouraged further investigation.

By contrast, when Hume wrote, all those questions and many more had already been resolved: science was in full swing. But Hume did not know any science: he might as well have written a couple of centuries earlier. This is why he could afford being a radical skeptic, repeating in 1758 Sextus's thesis that "the contrary of every matter of fact is still possible." As a matter of fact, this stand was no longer reasonably tenable. For example, in 1668 Francesco Redi had falsified experimentally the spontaneous-generation hypothesis; seven years later Olaus Roemer had shown the velocity of light to be finite; and in 1687 Newton gave the geocentric hypothesis the coup de grâce in the great treatise that expounded the earliest scientific theory proper—which Hume did not read for lack of scientific curiosity and for want of mathematical competence.

Now, two kinds of statement can be either asserted or doubted: particular and general. "Individual b has property P " is a particular statement, whereas "All individuals of kind P have property Q" is a general one. Empirical data are particular, whereas scientific laws are general. Empiricists are more interested in particulars than in generalities, whereas rationalists are more interested in general principles than in data. On the other hand, scientists and technologists are interested in both particulars and generalizations. They study sets of particulars hoping to discover patterns, and they check hypothesized patterns by contrasting them to data. Thus, whether or not they know it, they behave as ratio-empiricists (or empirio-rationalists) rather than as either empiricists or rationalists.

(In the philosophy of the social sciences, there is a standing debate between those who regard these disciplines as *idiographic*, or limited to recording episodes, and those who want them to be *nomothetic*, or pattern seeking. Actually no science proper, whether natural, social, or biosocial, can dispense with either component. Facts suggest and probe generalizations, and in turn these guide the search for further facts. We are born pattern-seekers as well as episode-recorders. So much so, that we have, among others, two distinct kinds of memory: procedural, or of general rules, and episodic, or of particular events. Each of them is in charge of a different part of the brain. Hence, a brain insult may destroy the one while sparing the other. Whether dogmatic adhesion to either the idiographic or the nomothetic party results from such a neurological disorder is yet to be investigated.)

Ptolemy, Bacon, Hume, Kant, Comte, Mach, Mill, and Popper trusted empirical data, but they were radical skeptics with regard to general hypotheses. In particular, Hume believed that the mind-body conundrum would never be solved; and Kant held that psychology would never become a science—a belief that effectively slowed down the advancement of this discipline.

As for Popper, although he did not doubt the existence of the external world, he held all scientific laws to be at best so far unfalsified guesses, no better than the untested pseudoscientific fantasies. At the same time, he argued for the vulgar view on the mind-body problem—namely psychoneural interactionism; he admitted the possibility of extrasensory perception; he was an agnostic rather than an atheist; and he did not accept any moral norms except for the Buddhist, Hippocratic, and Epicurean maxim "Do no harm." So Popper was a closet empiricist even though he called himself a critical rationalist; and he did not practice his own methodological injunction to put forward the boldest hypotheses. Moreover, Popper (1962, 2:246) claimed that nowadays "the problem cannot be the choice between knowledge and faith, but only between two kinds of faith." These would be the faith in reason and individuals, and "a faith in the mystical faculties of man by which he is united to a collective." So, the fundamental clash would still be a clash between two faiths. Thus, rationalism founders when attached to radical skepticism and closet empiricism.

And the postmoderns are total skeptics with regard to science—of which they know nothing. By contrast, they never doubt their own pronouncements, however inscrutable. Indeed, they state confidently, without any supporting evidence, that there is no objective truth: that every tribe and every epoch has its own set of truths, neither of which is superior to any other. That is, they are radical epistemological relativists when it comes to other people's beliefs. They are suspicious of every "discourse" to the point of seeing the claws of power even behind scientific statements and mathematical formulas. They also assure us that what passes for the search for truth is just making inscriptions and engaging in negotiations with competitors to gain power or legitimate the powers that be. Recall Michel Foucault's "Another knowledge, another power" and Bruno Latour's "Science is politics by other means." Their skepticism is pathological, and their epistemology paranoid. (For criticisms see Sokal and Bricmont 1998; Bunge 1999b; Koertge 1999.)

Where does contemporary science stand on this matter? Is it radically skeptical or only moderately so? And how effective can skepticism of either kind be in fighting superstition and dogmatism? These are the twin problems to be addressed in the present paper. Both problems will be handled in a strictly conceptual manner. No effort will be made to ask the empirical questions concerning the precise dosage of skepticism that individual scientists actually use, or the effectiveness of skeptical campaigns against such contemporary bunk as parapsychology, psychoanalysis, hermeneutic philosophy, or general economic equilibrium theory. All these matters of fact are interesting and worth pursuing, but they belong in the psychology and sociology of knowledge (and ignorance) rather than in philosophy.

7.2 ❖ IS ANYTHING POSSIBLE?

Although radical skepticism is a doctrine concerning knowledge, I submit that it is actually rooted in a view about the nature of the world. This is the hypothesis, still popular among open-minded people, that anything is possible. If everything were indeed possible, then no hypothesis, however implausible, should be discarded. In other words, if anything is really possible, then everything is equally plausible (or implausible). To state this more succinctly: There would be no degrees of plausibility (or implausibility).

For example, the radical skeptics must admit that scrambled eggs might unscramble spontaneously; that it is possible to receive telepathic signals to communicate with the dead, and to walk through a wall; or to be cured (not just given placebos) by incantations or homeopathic solutions. The radical skeptics will have to admit all of these possibilities because they do not believe in inflexible laws of nature. Indeed, if anything is possible, then no natural law can forbid anything. Equivalently: All impossibles are artifacts (human conventions).

There is a further reason that radical skeptics are prepared to believe that even the most trusted scientific laws are vulnerable. This is that they regard all such laws as mere inductive syntheses, that is, generalizations from empirical data—and all empirical knowledge is limited as well as fallible. (Hume's conception of laws as mere habits of nature comes to mind.) But this is not how scientists conceive of scientific laws. Indeed, they distinguish between a mere empirical generalization and a generalization embedded in a theory (hypothetico-deductive system). Only the latter deserves being called a scientific law because, unlike the former, it enjoys the support not only of the directly relevant data but also of other members of the same system. Think, e.g., of Newton's second law of motion, or of Faraday's law of electromagnetic induction, or of the second law of thermodynamics: every one of them is accompanied by uncounted well-corroborated hypotheses.

Now, science and technology do not countenance everything imaginable, because they are centered in laws, and every law allows certain facts while it disallows others. For example, pigs cannot fly on their own because they are wingless. So it is not a matter of waiting long enough to see whether an exceptional pig could take off by flapping its legs or ears. Nor is it necessary to make one more parapsychological experiment to check whether an extraordinary medium might send or receive messages without any physical channels: we know from biological psychology that thought is not a thing but a brain process, and as such is just as untransferable as digestion or pain. (Recall chapter 4.) Likewise, there is no point in designing a spacecraft to land on the Sun, for all solids necessarily evaporate as soon as they come within reach of the solar corona. A scientific law enables one to identify what is really impossible as well as what is really possible or really necessary. (Note the tacit distinction between real possibility on the one hand and logical or conceptual possibility on the other. To its discredit, modal logic ignores this elementary distinction. No wonder it is never used in science.)

Here is another random sample of impossibles: the annihilation of electric charge; the reabsorption of the radiation emitted by an antenna; human immortality; the metamorphoses invented by the ancients—e.g., of people into asses; biological evolution in reverse; thought without brains; wealth without work somewhere along the line; societies without norms; general market equilibrium; benevolent colonialism; the perfect institution.

To sum up, science and technology do not suspend judgment concerning miracles, the paranormal, and their kin. They have grounds to reject out of hand certain conceivable facts. These grounds are well-confirmed theories containing fairly solid law statements. For example, a patent office will refuse to even examine one more design for a machine for creating energy out of nothing because it is incompatible with the principle of conservation of energy. The same argument suffices to disqualify any claims to psychokinesis.

Likewise, there is no need to conduct clinical tests of homeopathic pseudoremedies: they cannot work except as placebos because a homeopathic dose contains at best only one molecule of the supposedly active substance, and no solitary molecule can affect an entire organ. Pharmacologists are too busy designing new drugs and trying out about half a million new compounds per year to waste their time testing for the alleged curative power of homeopathic merchandise.

In sum, skeptics have no obligation to engage in such wasteful activities as mind reading or voodoo to see whether they work. The radical skeptics are humble because they are not sure of anything. By contrast, the moderate skeptics should be modest but not humble: although they should admit their own limitations, they should also be confident that the scientific approach is the correct one, even if not every scientific finding is conclusive. Of course, they should be willing to examine the odd alleged anomaly, but only as part of their civic duty to educate the public and warn it against the claim that it undermines normal science.

7.3 ❖ ALL CONJECTURES ARE NOT EQUALLY PLAUSIBLE

If certain alleged facts are impossible, then the corresponding hypotheses, methods, or even data are radically implausible. How do we gauge the plausibility of a new hypothesis, datum, or technique? By comparing it with the relevant body of background knowledge. Why? By definition of "plausibility." Indeed, whatever is plausible is so not intrinsically but relative to some body of knowledge. For example, the hypothesis of the existence of gravitational waves, so far undetected, is plausible relative to the theory of general relativity, one of the most accurate of all theories. By contrast, the hypothesis that one can influence the reading of a measuring instrument by sheer willpower is inconsistent with both physics and cognitive neuroscience—unless of course one wires the brain to a servomechanism.

If a new item does not fit in with the system of background knowledge, there are two logical possibilities: either it conflicts with the pertinent basic general principles or it does not. In the first case we discard it, or at least push it to the back burner, without further ado. It is only in the second case, when the newcomer challenges just some component of the body of knowledge, that we suspend judgment and engage in further research, or at least encourage it.

In other words, reasonable doubt is always contextual or relative to some body of knowledge. Indeed, we doubt something in contrast with something else that is regarded as true or valid at least for the time being. For example, the hypothesis that all conceptual knowledge has to be learned is far more plausible than the innate-ideas fantasy. How do we know? Because (a) DNA is neither large nor complex enough to encode ideas—which engage whole systems of neurons anyway; (b) learning a new item does not alter the hereditary material (DNA), whence it cannot be passed off to the progeny; and (c) cognitive neuroscience shows that ideas grow in the brain, which is so immature at birth that it cannot conceive of any ideas.

Thus, some guesses are better educated than others, and some pieces of older knowledge are so firmly entrenched in the system of knowledge, that it would be foolish to challenge them without some reason. For instance, nobody has reason to doubt that there are electrons out there, and that Dirac's theory accounts for them to a very good approximation. Likewise, nobody can reasonably doubt that undernourishment stunts mental development; that too much TV watching favors obesity and passivity; that criminality increases with unemployment; that political instability and bureaucratic corruption discourage investment; that the concentration of wealth endangers democracy; or that organized religion inhibits freethinking. In such cases, the moderate skeptic observes the popular dictum "If it ain't broke, don't fix it."

In addition to dealing with unequally plausible conjectures, we face unequally likely facts. Indeed, some facts are more likely to occur than others, as a consequence of which they occur more often than others. Hence the corresponding forecasts are unequally plausible. For example, since earthquakes and stock-market crashes, though unavoidable, are infrequent, such forecasts as "San Francisco will be rocked by an earthquake tomorrow" and "The New York Stock Exchange will crash tomorrow" are implausible—unless of course ominous tremors are being recorded today. Still, since the losses from either event would be staggering, it would be foolish to ignore them altogether.

7.4 ❖ LIKELIHOOD AND PLAUSIBILITY: DIFFERENT THOUGH RELATED

Note the distinction between the *likelihood* of a fact and the *plausibility* (or verisimilitude) of a hypothesis. Whereas facts will happen regardless of whether we notice them, hypotheses are contextual in the sense that their meaning and truth depend on some body of knowledge or other. Consequently, whereas likelihood is context-free, plausibility is context-dependent. For example, whereas a placebo is likely to have some effect, some of the hypotheses concerning the placebo mechanism are more plausible than others.

It should also be noted that I am not using the common expression "probability of a hypothesis," for it makes as little sense as "temperature of a hypothesis." Indeed, probabilities can only be predicated of random events, which hypotheses are not. (A collection of facts can be said to be random if it is adequately represented by a probabilistic theory. Randomness can be primary, as is the case of quantum jumps. Or it can be a feature of a collection of nonrandom but mutually independent facts, such as the set of all car collisions in a city over a year. In the latter case randomness resides in our blind choice of a particular individual fact.) Moreover, whereas the concept of probability is quantitative, that of plausibility is qualitative—at least so far.

However, probability and plausibility are related, namely thus:

Let f_1 and f_2 be two random events of the same kind, and h_1 and h_2 the corresponding hypotheses about their occurrence at a given time or over a given period. Then h_1 is more *plausible* than h_2 if, and only if, f_1 is objectively more *probable* than f_2.

Plausibility must also be distinguished from credibility, intuitiveness (or familiarity), and truth (whether total or partial). Whereas the concept of plausibility is epistemological, that of credibility (or credence) is psychological, and that of truth is semantic. (Proposition X is *plausible* in the light of body of knowledge Y. Proposition X is *credible* to person Z. Proposition X is [exactly or approximately] *true* in the light of evidence Y.) A layperson may believe scientifically implausible theories while disbelieving scientifically plausible ones. So much so that counterintuitiveness (or epistemic unexpectedness) is the trademark of originality in mathematics, science, and technology. If you only care for well-established truths, shun original research and stick to routine.

The preceding suggests the following morals. First, incredibility is no argument against truth. Second, plausibility encourages tests for truth. Third, implausible ideas can safely be discarded, at least for the time being, provided their rivals have been satisfactorily justified. Fourth, only propositions that have passed truth tests deserve being believed. Fifth, only methods or artifacts that have passed effectiveness and efficiency tests deserve being adopted.

The following table exhibits the main traits of the five concepts distinguished so far.

Concept	Referents	Status
Likelihood	Facts (states or events)	Ontological
Probability	Facts (states or events)	Mathematical & ontological
Plausibility	Ideas (propositions, methods, plans, etc.)	Epistemological
Credibility	Facts or ideas	Psychological
Truth	Data or hypotheses	Semantical

Scientists and technologists are expected to justify their findings, whether they be data, hypotheses, methods, designs, or proposals. It is never enough to point out that something has not yet been falsified or invalidated: this consideration is only good for research projects. And no research project will be funded unless it is justified in terms of previous findings. For example, proposals to study life in the center of the Earth, the inheritability of beliefs, or emotion outside the brain will get no research grants, except from some private foundation that specializes in whacky ideas.

Authentic scientific findings are supported by arguments (e.g., computations) or empirical data (e.g., measurements). Certainly, further research may reveal that such support was weak or even illusory. But some preliminary support, or prior plausibility, is needed to motivate and support the very research that may end up undermining the initial idea. This rule is obvious to any practicing scientist. Yet, radical skeptics do not accept it, because they dismiss the very idea of justification: They are ready to accept reasons against but not reasons for. Their attitude is inquisitorial rather than reasonably adventurous.

In sum, not all scientific findings are equally conclusive or equally doubtful: some are more plausible than others. Certain reasons and certain empirical data are more compelling than others. Moreover, nothing is intrinsically (or absolutely) plausible or implausible. In other words, nothing is subject to reasonable doubt in a vacuum: Every time something is reasonably doubted, it is so by comparison with some benchmark. X is doubtful in the light of Y, which is incompatible with X and known, or taken to be, true; or, more succinctly: absolute doubt is unreasonable, hence unprofitable.

7.5 ❖ NEGATIVISM

The systematic or radical skeptic is more likely to utter negative sentences of the forms "I doubt X" and "It is not true that X" rather than positive ones of the forms "X looks plausible," "X is more plausible than Y," "It is true that X," and "X is truer than Y." In behaving in this way, the radical skeptic is on safer ground than the rest of us since negative truths come cheap. To collect them it suffices to deny obvious falsities. Thus, Earth is not flat, but the determination of the exact shape of our planet calls for a large geodetic project.

Moreover, a computer program might be designed to behave like a devil's advocate about any subject, asking automatically such standard questions as "How do you know?" "How can you be sure?" and "Will that finding hold?" By contrast, no computer program can be designed to act as a nonstandard passionate questioner and imaginative truth seeker. This is so not only because machines have no motivations other than electric pulses, but also because computer programs are designed to help answer questions, not to ask interesting new ones.

In particular, no computer program could question itself the way humans can question their own principles, motivations, or even existence. Doing this would require a metaprogram, itself protected from criticism. In short, computers are dogmatists. Hence, computer addiction can weaken the critical attitude by making a habit of applying rules without ever questioning their validity. However, this is not to endorse radical skepticism for it does not encourage constructive criticism. The philosophy of Karl Popper, the most famous skeptical philosopher of the twentieth century, is a case in point.

As argued elsewhere (Bunge 1996b), the bulk of Popper's philosophy is best understood as being signed by negation: Words do not matter; avoid ("like the plague") discussing the meaning of words; belief is unimportant; knowledge does not depend on the knower; never ask "What is" or "How do you know" questions; there are no essential properties; whenever possible refrain from making existential statements (for being "metaphysical"); we never confirm: we can only fail to falsify; never attempt to justify; we may know falsity but not truth; there is no inductive logic; in matters of knowledge the improbable is preferable to the probable; there is no scientific method aside from trial and error; shun normal science; determinism is false; evolutionary biology is not scientific; there are neither social wholes nor social laws; demand only negative liberty (freedom from); all ideology is pernicious; all revolution is bad; there is no summum bonum; do no harm—in particular, don't put philosophy in the service of oppression; do not engage in do-goodism: just refrain from evildoing—and so on. In short, Popper's philosophy may be dubbed *logical negativism*. In other words, Popper was essentially a skeptic—though, like Bertrand Russell, a passionate one. This is why his philosophy, though readable and interesting, is rather shallow and fragmentary (unsystematic). It is accordingly more helpful to spot errors and wrongs than to search for truth or fairness.

Popper was undoubtedly right in criticizing school philosophy and, in particular, what he called "oracular" philosophy. (I prefer to call it pseudophilosophy since the very least that a genuine philosophy can be is clear.) He was also right in emphasizing the role of rational criticism in the management of social conflicts as well as in the pursuit of knowledge. But surely statements and proposals must be made before they can be subjected to critical examination: creation precedes criticism, just as trees preexist logs and sawdust. Besides, to falsify a proposition is the same as to confirm its negation. In any case, all fields of learning are constantly pouring forth abundant justified yeas as well as nays and maybes. Hence, no philosophy of science and technology should underrate the former. Moreover, exaggerating the importance of criticism at the expense of theorizing and analysis, or of observation and experiment, comes dangerously close to both scholasticism and radical skepticism, as well as to the fashionable view that all research is just discussion. After all, negative truths are more plentiful and thus cheaper than positive ones: prefix "not" to any silly falsity and you get a truth.

Something similar holds for the realm of action. Constructive action, whether individual or social, calls for positive views and plans in addition to rational discussions of goals and means. In particular, the design, planning, and construction of a better social order requires more than a handful of danger signals to help avoid or fight tyranny: it also calls for a positive social philosophy including a clear vision of the open society—one capable of motivating and mobilizing people. (The warning "Here there be dragons" may be helpful, but it does not point to the right way.) And such a philosophy had better form a system rather than an aggregate of disjoint views for social issues—like any correct ideas about them—happen to come in bundles, not one at a time. One step at a time, yes; one thing at a time, no. In other words, social reform must be gradual but systemic. This is particularly true of societies in need of total reconstruction, such as the ex-Communist ones.

In short, negativism is no better than the positivism it criticizes: both are far too timid to help advance knowledge. Both border on know-nothingism. Worse, radical skepticism is hardly distinguishable from dogmatism since the two are only instances of X-ism. No wonder that David Miller (1999), a strict Popperian who calls himself an absolute skeptic, has denounced as dogmatic the physicists Sokal and Bricmont (1998) for defending science against its postmodernist critics. Once again, extremes meet.

7.6 ❖ THE SKEPTIC'S PARADOX

This is what I call the Skeptic's Paradox: *Whoever is radically and consistently skeptic must end up being just as gullible as the naive dogmatist because he cannot muster any arguments against the impossibility of anything.*

For example, if someone suspends judgment about magic, he will give magicians a break. If he suspends judgment about evolution, he will propose giving equal time in public schools to evolutionary biology and to creationism. If he suspends judgment about the possibility of telepathy or psychokinesis, he will support parapsychological research. If he suspends judgment over the efficiency of homeopathy, he may try it if disappointed by scientific medicine. And if he suspends judgment about the possibility of coming up with a creative computer, he may go bankrupt banking projects with this goal. In general, whoever rejects all scientific claims to scientific truth leaves room for myth. Indeed, radical skeptics do not and cannot avoid holding certain beliefs if they wish to go on living. In particular, in common with the rest of us, the radical skeptics believe their own mental states. They only doubt what scientists presuppose, namely the independent existence of the material world, and hypotheses that scientists have corroborated ad nauseam, such as that there is no mind outside the brain.

How should the supernatural and the paranormal be handled? That is, how are we to evaluate claims to the ghostly? Radical skeptics and empiricists are likely to respond in the same way: Give them a chance, keep trying to produce empirical evidence, and in the meantime suspend judgment. Radical skeptics and empiricists must abstain from pronouncing themselves on the ghostly because they lack an explicit and scientific worldview (or ontology) where the mind-body problem can be placed. They cannot afford holding any firm views on these matters, just as the innumerate cannot check sums, and the lay cannot say whether or not there can be Bose condensates, spontaneous neuron discharges, stateless societies, or price-inelastic goods.

Anyone who holds a scientific worldview will not wait for new arguments or new empirical evidence for the ghostly, and will regard research on these matters as a waste of time. He reasons as follows. In the first place, there is no scientific evidence for either the supernatural or the paranormal. Indeed, if either were detectable, it would be material rather than either supernatural or paranormal. The assumption of immateriality guarantees inscrutability.

Second, there *can be* no such evidence. For example, nobody can go to Hell and report back: by hypothesis, such a trip is one-way. As for disembodied ideas, they cannot exist according to cognitive neuroscience: all ideas are and remain in people's heads. How do we know this to be the case? Thanks to such scientific procedures as electrical and chemical stimulation of the brain, and everyday-life occurrences such as general anesthesia, drunkenness, and drug-induced "trips." (Recall chapter 4.)

Is this stand dogmatic and therefore an obstacle to research? Not at all. It only discourages groundless belief and wrongheaded and therefore wasteful research. It encourages concern for the justification of the hypotheses to be tested. It discourages wasting time with stray conjectures that are inconsistent with the bulk of the antecedent knowledge. And it encourages embedding hypotheses in hypothetico-deductive systems (theories), which make multiple contacts with empirical data.

The reasonable skeptic suspends belief only as long as the problem at hand warrants further research because the available evidence for or against the hypothesis in question is inconclusive. But if the hypothesis concerned is theoretically plausible, on top of having a strong empirical support, the researcher pronounces it true, at least to a good approximation and for the time being, and turns to some other problem.

Researchers cannot afford being permanently in a state of suspended belief. The search for truth presupposes that truth, or at least approximate truth, is attainable in real time. And, once a truth has been found, it can be used as a springboard in searching for further truths. This is how research projects proceed. Nobel Prizes are awarded for positive findings and not for criticisms, however justified.

7.7 ❖ RADICAL SKEPTICISM IS TIMID AND PARALYZING

The radical skeptic, if consistent, will shun new bold conjectures, particularly those concerning the unseen world—which, as the ancient atomists guessed, is by far the largest part of reality. He will then accept appearances, but will suspend judgment on, or even reject, any hypotheses concerning such unobservables as atoms and other people's minds. This is why the ancient skeptics and the nineteenth-century positivists rejected atomism, and one century later the behaviorist psychologists abstained from hypothesizing mental states. Luckily, science bypassed the skeptical objections: we now have atomic physics and a science of mind and much more.

Scientific research on matters of fact is realist: it presupposes the real existence of the external world and the possibility of knowing it. Moreover, it employs tacitly the ancient Greek concept of factual truth as adequacy of thought to fact, or correspondence between theory and world—a concept rejected by idealists and conventionalists, from Berkeley and Kant onwards. This idea of objective, hence cross-culturally valid truth, is rejected by the constructivist-relativist sociologists of science and the other postmoderns, starting with Kuhn and Feyerabend. (More on epistemological relativism in Gellner 1985; Boudon 1995; and Bunge 1996a, 1999b.)

Scientists may question any number of scientific findings in their own field. But they will not doubt their own ability to correct some of them, or even to come up with some new findings (truths). Least of all will they doubt the independent existence of the external world, the effectiveness of the scientific method, or even the truths they borrow from research fields other than their own. (For example, a biologist would be regarded as a crank if he were to question mathematics, physics, or chemistry.) So much for epistemic matters. Let us now turn to practical issues.

The consistent radical skeptic must also abstain from doing anything important because he is not sure about the issues, the options, or the possible outcomes of any actions. Being inordinately risk-averse, he can neither command confidently nor obey cheerfully, nor even participate conscientiously as a plain citizen. In short, he can be neither a leader nor a reliable team player. If thoroughly consistent with his own views, he must be passive and indecisive to the point of lethargy. And if forced to take action, he will be reactive and unlikely to ever take the lead. Hence, he will be at the mercy of his environment. To use Kantian terms, the radical skeptic is bound to be heteronomous rather than autonomous.

Such an indecisive animal is sometimes found in the worlds of business, academia, and politics. He is the manager who refuses to plan, and only reacts to day-to-day demands. He is the chairman or dean who, far from taking any decisions, let alone initiatives, refers every issue to a committee. He is the citizen so suspicious of government and politics in general that he opposes all kinds of government intervention, declines to participate in any political movement, or even refuses to vote. He is the proverbial café anarchist, long on big words and short on deeds.

By contrast, the moderate skeptic is neither a passive cynic nor a zealot. He is ready to act when necessary, provided he knows of better reasons for taking action than for refraining from doing so. Moreover, he will favor rational action over blind obedience, tradition, or momentary impulse. That is, he will attempt to design plans in the light of the best available social science and social technology. By contrast, the radical skeptic will abstain from using either, hence he will either refrain from acting or will act according to custom—a course of action that, in a fast-moving world and one demanding increasing knowledge, is likely to lead to disaster.

I submit that the maintenance and improvement of any social system calls for moderate skepticism on the part of its components. Indeed, only a moderate skeptic is likely to look for imperfections in a system and, at the same time, to propose or debate means to repair it. By contrast, a radical skeptic would at best bemoan imperfections and put up with them, whereas a dogmatist would either conserve the system or try to smash it.

This suggests that the good citizen of an open society—a democratic and progressive one, as Popper (1962 [1945]) defined it—is a constructive skeptic. By the same token, the docile subject of a dictatorship is either a radical skeptic resigned to suffer oppression or a fanatic intent on supporting the tyrant. Indeed, the radical skeptic is utterly pessimistic with regard to any social reform, while the zealot is blindly optimistic with regard to the status quo (or else the blueprint of his perfect utopia). The moderate skeptic, being a meliorist as much as a fallibilist, is a practical realist rather than either a pessimist or an optimist: He believes that some things can be changed for the better, but not that they will necessarily improve overnight.

In sum, progressive politics call for moderate skepticism. Likewise, sound business policies avoid the extremes of routine and mindless innovation, as well as those of total risk-aversion and gambling.

CONCLUSION

Just as a closed mind is impregnable to new knowledge, so a totally open mind is exposed to groundless fantasy or even superstition. Good scientific minds are porous: they let in new conjectures, methods, or plans, provided they are plausible. By the same token, they filter out the utterly implausible ones. In other words, scientists and technologists are expected to be skeptical, though only moderately so, because excessive *nescio* can be just as stifling as excessive *credo*. Likewise, total risk avoidance is just as unproductive as heedless action.

To be fruitful, fallibilism must be combined with meliorism. We do not yet know all we would like to know, but we may get to learn something through further scientific research. What holds for knowledge also holds, mutatis mutandis, for values and rational action. Although some values are time-bound, others are constant or, at least, they have a sound permanent core. And not everything that ought to be done can be done, but some of it can surely be carried out, and whatever good has been achieved deserves to be conserved or improved on.

To conclude. Radical skepticism is barren at best, and destructive at worst. By contrast, moderate skepticism is fruitful because it prefers the discovery of new truths and new values to the destruction of epistemic or axiological dogma. It is gradualist rather than saltationist: Every reasonable doubt is prompted by some reason that is not questioned for the time being because it has shown its conceptual or practical worth. There is no weighing of pros and cons in an epistemic and axiological vacuum. Both beliefs and doubts have got to be justified in the light of truths or values that have rendered distinguished service.

Unsurprisingly, science and technology are moderately skeptic: their practitioners do not doubt everything at all times, but only some ideas or procedures at a time. Even so, when they doubt they do so on the strength of other ideas or practices that are held to be firm until new notice. As Paul Kurtz (1992) would put it, their skepticism does not emphasize doubt and the impossibility of knowledge: instead, it is the skepticism that focuses on *inquiry* and the genuine possibility of knowledge.

Moreover, the skepticism of scientists and technologists is not individualist or anarchist like the philosopher's. Indeed, as Merton (1968) first noted, organized skepticism is part and parcel of the *ethos* of science: the individual researcher proposes, and his community debates, checks, and finally decides. This is why scientific findings are first discussed with associates, then in seminars, and finally submitted for publication, so that the entire community may evaluate and either validate or invalidate them.

A practical upshot for militant skeptics is this. They should be tolerant of new ideas, provided these are testable in principle and minimally plausible. And they should be willing to take part in dialogues with people beyond the fringe of science. However, such dialogues can only be fruitful if the other side too abides by the rules of rational debate—such as noncontradiction, sticking to the point, bearing the burden of proof, and avoiding arguments ad hominem. Yet, the only fruit to be reasonably expected from such dialogues is the conversion of the odd member on the other side. We have little if anything to learn from groundless speculation or magical ritual. We know that logic and the scientific method are superior, and we can exhibit an impressive catalogue of robust findings that no branch of illusory knowledge can match.

And the practical upshot for us all is that we should beware of the superstitions that are sometimes passed off as science, occasionally even by Nobel laureates. However, pseudoscience is so diverse, widespread, and influential that it deserves a separate chapter.

8

DIAGNOSING PSEUDOSCIENCE

Pseudoscience is just as typical of modern culture as science. It thrives everywhere, even within the scientific community. In fact, pseudoscience is far more popular and profitable than science; it confounds science policymakers and administrators; and it continues to mislead or challenge philosophers and sociologists of science. It is therefore necessary to try and characterize pseudoscience in a clear way vis-à-vis genuine science. This is the goal of the present chapter: to find out the peculiarities of pseudoscience and to discuss some specimens of it. The accent will not be on the most obvious cases, such as astrology and creation "science," but on some of the pseudoscientific bunkers scattered throughout the scientific landscape.

8.1 ❖ FAKING SCIENCE

Man, the supreme creator, is also the greatest faker. He can counterfeit almost anything, from dollar bills to love and art. Man can even fake science, and indeed in more ways than anything else: he can do so by plagiarizing, massaging data, and dispensing myth in wrappings that look scientific.

Plagiarism in science is no different from theft anywhere else: it consists in appropriating the fruits of someone else's honest toil—e.g., in lifting data, formulas, tables, or diagrams without giving proper credit. This kind of dishonesty is rather harmless, and it can be discovered quite easily. Moreover, if the original happens to be a good piece of research, the plagiarizer's petty crime contributes to broadcasting it, so it may have a social benefit. Its main negative effect is that it erodes the trust required to share knowledge to the point of inciting secrecy.

Massaging the truth is a different matter altogether. It consists in cheating about data or inferences—in fudging or even making up data, or in lying about the conclusions entailed by a set of premises. Like money counterfeiting, this is a serious crime, for it can be very harmful. (Remember Sir Cyril Burt's pseudo-data on the inheritance of intelligence accepted by most psychologists for three decades, and which led to discriminatory practices in British education.) Still, in most cases the harm is confined to a circle of specialists, and the crime is eventually discovered—or, better yet, forgotten.

Faking of the third kind, or mass-producing low-grade and hardly interesting scientific results, usually for the sole sake of the curriculum vitae, is far worse, even if committed in good faith. Indeed, it involves a betrayal of the ideal of knowing for the sake of understanding; it produces an annoying information overload; it strains human and material resources; and it makes people bored and disillusioned with science. (Think of the myriad of trivial experiments and routine calculations that, far from opening new vistas or posing new research problems, are dead ends deserving the humiliating comment "So what?") Yet that is the price we pay for upholding the slogan *Publish or perish*. Besides, the waste incurred in perpetrating fakes of the third kind is but a tiny fraction of what is being wasted in arms or drugs.

There is a fourth manner of faking science, and it is the most dangerous of all: it consists in presenting nonscience, and sometimes even antiscience, as science—and often also in presenting genuine science as unscientific. Popular examples of pseudoscience are parapsychology, psychoanalysis, creationist (as opposed to evolutionary) biology, neoclassical microeconomics, and scientific communism. Less popular but just as blatant examples of pseudoscience are creationist cosmology and talk of catastrophes or of chaos unaccompanied by mathematical formulas.

Pseudoscience is dangerous because (a) it passes wild speculation or uncontrolled data for results of scientific research; (b) it misrepresents the scientific attitude (the "spirit" of science); (c) it contaminates some fields of science, particularly the "soft" ones; (d) it is accessible to millions of people (whereas genuine science is hard and therefore intellectually elitist); (e) it has become a multibillion-dollar business preying on popular gullibility; and (f) it has the support of powerful pressure groups—sometimes entire churches and political parties—and the sympathy of the mass media. For all of these reasons, it behooves the philosopher to supply an accurate diagnosis of pseudoscience.

We pass over the fifth category: the pranks and spoofs of the *Journal of Irreproducible Results*, which are self-proclaimed fakes and therefore perfectly honest.

8.2 ❖ IMPORTANCE OF THE PROBLEM

Jonathan Swift (1965 [1726]) was perhaps the first to understand the gist of pseudoscience, although most critics believe that his intention was to make fun of science. In *Gulliver's Travels*, he tells us that Captain Gulliver, when in Balnibarbi, visited the grand Academy of Lagado. The majestic building of the academy contained more than five hundred rooms, every one of them occupied by one or more "projectors" and their assistants. One of them "had been eight years upon a project for extracting sun-beams out of cucumbers; which were to be put in vials, hermetically sealed, and let out to warm the air, in raw inclement summers" (p. 164). Another projector was engaged in "an operation to reduce human excrement to its original food; by separating the several parts; removing the tincture which it receives from the gall; making the odor exhale; and scumming off the saliva" (p. 165). Other projects pursued at the Academy were: a new method for building houses, starting at the roof and working downward to the foundation; a device of plowing the ground with hogs, to save the charges of plows, cattle, and labor; to employ spiders in the manufacture of silk; to compose books in philosophy, mathematics, etc., by mechanical means, namely by cranking a huge machine containing frames on which all the words were inscribed, until strings of words appeared that might look like sentences; a scheme for abolishing all words but nouns, and another for abolishing words altogether.

What makes all of these research plans ridiculous and so much like the pseudosciences of our time? First, they do not seek to find any laws: even the most speculative Lagado projects have narrow utilitarian goals. Second, they make no use of previously acquired knowledge; in fact they clash with our background knowledge. (For example, the first and second projects wanted to invert essentially irreversible processes, and the precursors of gigo computeering wanted to extract knowledge out of ignorance by means of a randomizer.)

Although Swift correctly identified two attributes of pseudoscience, we need a more detailed characterization if we are to cover the wide range of contemporary pseudosciences. However, before undertaking this task let us emphasize its practical and theoretical importance, lest anyone should suppose that ours is one more Byzantine puzzle occupying one of the projectors of the Academy of Lagado.

The practical importance of the problem of characterizing pseudoscience can be measured by the volume of the pseudoscience business, which is on the order of billions of dollars per year, and in a number of countries surpasses the R&D budget. Granted, philosophical and methodological criticism may do little—particularly if ignored by the mass media. But at least it may be expected to be of some use to decision makers and teachers concerned with promoting scientific research or with using it. A few examples should suffice to make this point.

(a) Parliament needs to know whether chiropractice, holistic medicine, homeopathy, or verbal psychotherapy is a scientific practice or sheer quackery before allowing Medicare to cover it.

(b) The National Science Foundation needs to find out whether parapsychology is a scientific field before funding research on telepathy, clairvoyance, psychokinesis, or precognition.

(c) Mining companies and public-works contractors, as well as developers, wish to know whether dowsing (water witching) is well-founded before they contract for ore, oil, or water prospecting.

(d) The Dean of Graduate Studies and Research wants to make sure that Lamarckian biology, soul psychology, psychohistory, cultural studies, and the like are scientifically respectable or rubbish before allotting research funds or approving courses on such subjects.

(e) Every science leader or administrator should like to be able to distinguish between immature but promising genuine science (that is, protoscience), on the one hand, and pseudoscience on the other—e.g., between political science and political ideology, between using computers as intellectual aids and using them as cloaks to cover intellectual destitution.

Now for the theoretical interest of the problem. The question of assessing the claims to scientific status of a given doctrine or practice is a typical and central problem in the philosophy of science and technology. Indeed, we can pass judgment on the scientific status of a doctrine or practice only on the strength of a precise characterization of science and technology in general. We can say that the field of knowledge X meets, or fails to meet, all of the necessary and sufficient conditions that define a science, just in case we have listed explicitly such conditions and have made sure that the list fits all the clear cases of genuine science (or technology), and does not fit all the clear cases of pseudoscience (or pseudotechnology).

Some philosophers have of course addressed the problem of demarcating science from nonscience, in particular pseudoscience. However, their efforts have not been successful. In some cases, entire sciences have been left out, whereas in others entire pseudosciences have been let in. The failure is so dismal that one well-known philosopher has claimed, though not argued, that there is no radical difference between science and nonscience, so that a democratic society should allot "equal time" to each in all schools (Feyerabend 1975). Thus, the "theory" of special creation of biospecies should be taught alongside evolutionary biology; psychoanalysis on the same footing as experimental psychology; faith healing alongside medicine; and so on.

This recommendation won't be accepted by most investigators, teachers, and administrators if only because, if adopted, it would entail a total collapse of academic standards and a frightful intellectual and administrative anarchy, as well as a waste of resources, particularly in developing countries. Just imagine a university establishing a School of Faith Healing across from its Medical School, a Department of Creationist Biology competing with its Department of Biology, a Pseudophilosophy of Pseudoscience and Pseudotechnology Unit rivaling its Philosophy of Science and Technology Unit, and the Dean of Pseudoarts and Pseudosciences fighting the Dean of Arts and Sciences over the soul of the student body. In sum, a Manichean university deserving of the Golden Fleece award.

I submit that the reason for the failure of philosophers to propose an adequate definition of science, which may be used as a criterion for telling pseudoscience from science, is that they have presupposed that a *single* attribute will do: this is what any simplistic view of science suggests. (Remember the tale about the five blind men intent on characterizing the elephant?) Let us review quickly the most popular characterizations of science proposed by philosophers.

(1) The *empirical content* doctrine maintains that science accepts only empirical data and inductive generalizations thereof, never hypotheses. Though still popular, particularly in science textbooks, this view was falsified long ago by the very emergence of theoretical physics, theoretical chemistry, theoretical biology, and other fields that teem with concepts representing entities—such as atoms, genes, and social classes—and properties, such as mass, field intensity, metabolic rate, and income distribution, that are not directly observable.

(2) The *consensus* view holds that, whereas the humanities are rife with

controversy, science is uncontroversial, or at least aims at attaining consensus. This characterization is inadequate for every field of active scientific research teems with controversy. What is true is that science has means for settling controversies in the long run and in a rational way. Consensus, when attained, is only a by-product of truth.

(3) The *success* view claims that for science only practical success counts. This pragmatist view does not fit basic science, which is after truth rather than success. Actually, it does not even fit technology, which makes intensive use of basic science and involves much designing and tinkering motivated primarily by curiosity rather than profit.

(4) The *formalist* doctrine holds that a body of knowledge is scientific just in case it has been mathematized. This characterization is too narrow: it disqualifies experimental science and young science, which is often premathematical. Moreover, it confers the title of scientific to theories which, like general equilibrium economics, are only mathematical exercises remote from the harsh realities of economic disequilibria. The truth is that science cannot advance beyond a certain point without the help of mathematics, which brings precision (whence clarity and enhanced testability) and systemicity (whence deductive power and growth).

(5) *Refutationism* maintains that the mark of science is falsifiability, that is, dealing exclusively with hypotheses that are conceivably falsifiable. But if science were in fact refutationist, we should accept as scientific all refuted beliefs, such as astrology and graphology, and reject instead the most general scientific theories for not being falsifiable without further ado. Besides, we need positive confirmation if we are to judge a hypothesis as true, at least partially so.

(6) *Methodolatry* holds that the sole requisite for science is adopting the scientific method. But if every application of the scientific method were indeed a piece of scientific research, then measuring the correlation between nose length and political opinion, testing the mental abilities of atoms, and trying to catch ghosts would pass for scientific activities provided certain precautions were observed.

Since neither of the above characterizations of science works, none of them is competent to identify any pseudoscience. Let us give up such simplistic approaches and face the fact that science, like any other human activity, is many-sided. One way of discovering the many sides of science is to study it as an ongoing research enterprise carried out in communities of researchers, instead of looking back at some philosophical tradition. Paradoxically enough, far from estranging us from philosophy, this procedure will make room for the ontological, epistemological, and ethical aspects of scientific research.

8.3 ❖ COGNITIVE FIELDS

We shall characterize a science, as well as a pseudoscience, as a particular kind of cognitive field. A *cognitive field* may be characterized as a sector of human activity aiming at gaining, diffusing, or utilizing knowledge of some kind, whether this knowledge be true or false. There are hundreds of cognitive fields in contemporary culture: logic and theology, mathematics and numerology, astronomy and astrology, chemistry and alchemy, psychology and psychoanalysis, social science and phenomenological sociology, and so on and so forth.

Whether or not a given cognitive field is successful in attaining truth or power, understanding or popularity, it shares a number of features with other cognitive fields. These features are encapsulated in the ten-tuple $\mathcal{F}$ = <C, S, G, D, F, B, P, K, A, M> where, at any given moment,

C = the *community* of knowers of $\mathcal{F}$;
S = the *society* that hosts C;
G = the *general outlook*, worldview, or philosophical presuppositions of $\mathcal{F}$;
D = the *domain* or universe of discourse of $\mathcal{F}$: the objects studied or handled by the Cs;
F = the *formal background*: the logical or mathematical tools employable in $\mathcal{F}$;
B = the *specific background*, or set of presuppositions of $\mathcal{F}$ borrowed from other fields;
P = the *problematics*, or set of problems, tackled in $\mathcal{F}$;
K = the *specific fund of knowledge* accumulated by C;
A = the *aims* or goals of the Cs;
M = the *methods* utilizable in $\mathcal{F}$.

Every one of the ten components or coordinates of $\mathcal{F}$ is taken at a given time, every one of them is a collection, and none of them need be consistent. (Every field of active research abounds with controversies, even if the disputants share a core of presuppositions, problems, objectives, and methods.) Note that a cognitive field is not a concrete system, such as a scientific community or a church, whose members are kept together by a network of information flows and social activities. The notion of a cognitive field is more abstract than that.

The family of cognitive fields is not homogeneous. In fact, it may be partitioned into two disjoint subsets: the family of *research fields* and that of *belief fields*. Whereas a research field changes all the time as a result of investigation, a belief field changes, if at all, as a result of controversy, brute force, or alleged revelation. (For example, Freud's original school has split into about two hundred schools, neither of which conducts any experimental research.) This, then, is the great divide:

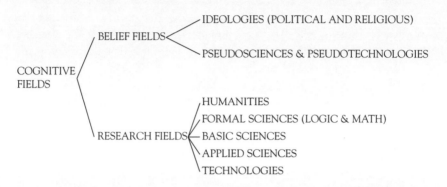

What characterizes a research field is, of course, active inquiry of some sort. This is the formulation and solution of problems, the invention of new hypotheses or techniques, and so on. Thus, a research field is composed, at any given time, by a number of research projects in the course of implementation. The notion of a research project or line can be elucidated as follows. Let $\mathcal{F} = <C, S, G, D, F, B, P, K, A, M>$ denote a research field at a given time. Then $\pi = (c, s, g, d, f, b, p, k, a, m)$ is a *research project* in $\mathcal{F}$ if (a) every component of π is a subset of the corresponding component of $\mathcal{F}$, and (b) g, f, b, k, a and m is each internally consistent or homogeneous.

Each researcher, or research team, works on one or more projects at a time. Two research projects may share problematics while differing in other respects, such as some items of general background, or formal background, or aims, or methods. Two research projects are said to *compete* with one another if they deal with the same set of problems in different ways, e.g., using different assumptions or special techniques. For example, at a given time physicists were divided into corpuscularians and continuists, and sociologists are still divided into holists and individualists.

Thomas Kuhn's vague notion of a paradigm, or rather his later one of an exemplar, can be elucidated thus: A *paradigm* (or *exemplar*) is a research project that, having proved successful in the past, is imitated (taken for a model) for the conduct of further research.

The above concepts help clarify another notion that Kuhn has exploited and popularized, namely that of a scientific (in general cognitive) revolution, similar to Gaston Bachelard's earlier *rupture épistémologique*. We shall say that a piece of research is *original* if it consists in (a) investigating old problems in new ways (e.g., employing alternative formal tools, or alternative measurement techniques), or (b) posing new problems, or (c) proposing new viable research projects.

In particular, a piece of original research can be said to be *revolutionary* just in case it (a) involves radical departures in some (not all) of the components of the usual general background G, or in the standard background B ; or (b) casts doubts on some (not all) long-established beliefs on fundamental general questions; or (c) opens up whole new research fields (without however cutting ties with all of the existing ones). The birth of science in antiquity, and its rebirth in the seventeenth century, were deep revolutions. All the other scientific novelties, however sensational, are best described as *breakthroughs*, because they do not involve a radical change in either general outlook or general method.

By contrast, an item of knowledge may be said to be *counterrevolutionary* if it involves (a) giving up, for no good reasons, substantial portions of the general background, the formal background, or the specific fund of knowledge; or (b) renouncing to investigating some problems that look promising on alternative approaches, without proposing other problems in their stead; or (c) returning to ideas or procedures that proved inadequate in the past, and moreover were superseded by later research. For example, neoclassical microeconomics was counterrevolutionary with regard to classical economics because it shifted natural resources and work to the background and revolved around the fuzzy notions of subjective utility and subjective probability. Likewise, psychoanalysis was counterrevolutionary relative to classical psychology because it revived the notion of immaterial soul, introduced plenty of wild fantasies, and rejected the experimental method.

Our definitions of cognitive (in particular scientific or technological) revolution and breakthrough do not involve a complete break with the past in such a way that the new ideas or procedures are wholly "incommensurable" with their predecessors—the way Kuhn (1962) and Feyerabend (1975) would like to have it. On the contrary, every genuine cognitive breakthrough is based on some past achievements and is evaluated relative to the latter—so that the new, no matter how novel, must be "commensurable" with the old. One concludes that a theory is truer than another, or a technique superior to another, only on the strength of comparisons regarding coverage, accuracy, or depth. For example, cognitive neuroscience is both broader and deeper than behaviorist psychology, just as molecular genetics is deeper and more accurate than Mendelian genetics.

169

The preceding definitions help avoid confusing research with research projects—a confusion that marks some of Kuhn's work. As is well known, Kuhn held that "normal" research does not consist in invention or discovery, but in puzzle solving: the outcome would be known beforehand except for details. Thus, all the scientists who had accepted Ben Franklin's ideas on electricity "knew" that "there had to be" a law of attraction and repulsion between electrically charged bodies. The actual discovery of such a law, according to Kuhn (1963), was just an example of "normal" science: it consisted in filling out the details of what was "known" beforehand. This is confusing a research project with actual research. The great American polymath may have conceived of the great lines of the research project, but only Coulomb stated and confirmed the law. This discovery was no less of a breakthrough than Franklin's. Likewise, Crick and Watson, working on a definite paradigm built by others, and on a problem posed by still others, made a monumental discovery when they guessed the basic structure of the DNA molecules. Yet, if we were to accept Kuhn's ideas, all four men were engaged in modest "normal" science pursuits—that is, in filling holes.

8.4 ❖ SCIENCE AND PSEUDOSCIENCE

We shall now proceed to define the concepts of science and of pseudoscience. To begin with, we stipulate that a *particular science*, such as biochemistry or sociology, is a cognitive field $\mathcal{F} = \;<C, S, G, D, F, B, P, K, A, M>$ such that

(1) the *general outlook* or philosophical background G consists of (a) an ontology of changing things (rather than, say, one of ghostly or unchanging entities); (b) a realist (but critical, not naive) epistemology (instead of, say, an idealist or a conventionalist one); and (c) the ethos of the free search for truth, depth, and system (rather than, say, the ethos of the bound quest for profit, power, or eternal salvation);

(2) the *domain* or universe of discourse D is composed exclusively of (certified or putatively) real entities (rather than, say, freely floating ideas) past, present, or future;

(3) the *formal background* F is a collection of up-to-date logical and mathematical theories (rather than being empty or formed by obsolete formal theories);

(4) The *specific background* B is a collection of up-to-date and reasonably well confirmed (yet not incorrigible) data, hypotheses, and theories obtained in other fields of inquiry relevant to F;

(5) The *problematics* P consists exclusively of cognitive (rather than practical) problems concerning the nature (in particular the laws) of the Ds as well as problems concerning other components of $\mathcal{F}$;

(6) the *fund of knowledge* K is a collection of up-to-date and testable (though not final) theories, hypotheses, and data, as well as scrutable methods, compatible with those in B and obtained in $\mathcal{F}$ at previous times;

(7) The *aims* or goals A of the members of C include discovering or using the laws of the Ds, systematizing (into theories) hypotheses about Ds, and refining methods in M;

(8) the *methodics* M consists exclusively of scrutable (checkable, analyzable, criticizable) and justifiable (explainable) procedures;

(9) $\mathcal{F}$ is a component of a wider cognitive field: that is, there is at least one other (contiguous) research field $\mathcal{F}' = <C', S', G,' D,' F', B,' P', K', A', M'>$, such that (a) the general outlooks, formal backgrounds, specific backgrounds, funds of knowledge, objectives, and methodics of the two fields have nonempty overlaps, and (b) either D is included in D' or conversely, or each member of D is a component of a system in D' or conversely;

(10) The membership of every one of the last eight components of $\mathcal{F}$ changes, however slowly at times, as a result of inquiry in the same field and in related fields (particularly those supplying the formal background F and the specific background B).

A cognitive field that fails to satisfy all ten above conditions will be said to be *nonscientific*. Classical examples of nonscientific research fields are theology and literary criticism. (Note the implicit distinction between theology, a research field, and religion, a body of belief.) However, scientificity comes in degrees. A cognitive field that satisfies approximately all ten above conditions, and is presumably moving toward the goal of full compliance with them, may be called a *protoscience* or *emerging science*. On the other hand, any cognitive field that is nonscientific and yet is advertised as scientific will be said to be *pseudoscientific*. The difference between science and protoscience is a matter of degree, whereas that between science and pseudoscience is one of kind. (Parallel: Some currencies are stronger than others, but they are all worth something, whereas counterfeit coin is not legal tender.) This is why it is mistaken to regard parapsychology and psychoanalysis as protosciences or even as failed sciences: they were pseudoscientific from the start.

We may finally define *science* in general, by contrast to a particular or special science, as the cognitive field every one of whose coordinates or com-

171

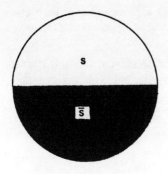

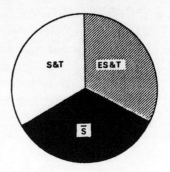

Fig. 8.1. The positivist map of intellectual culture: science (S) and nonscience (S̄).

Fig. 8.2. Adding technology (T) and the gray area of emergent science (protoscience) and emergent technology or prototechnology (ES&T).

ponents is the union (logical sum) of the coordinates peculiar to the various special sciences.

The preceding considerations will help us draw a map of present-day intellectual culture, that is, of the totality of cognitive fields. The simplest picture of the entire field is the one we have inherited from positivism. According to it, intellectual culture is composed of two disjoint regions: the luminous one composed of mathematics and the sciences, and the black one constituted by nonscience, often called "metaphysics" (see figure 8.1). This simplistic picture overlooks the technologies as well as the protosciences and prototechnologies, or cognitive fields in the process of becoming sciences or technologies respectively. A more accurate picture shows three sectors: the former black and white ones, where now the latter includes the technologies, and a third, gray region made up of the emerging sciences and technologies (figure 8.2). Yet, even this picture is incomplete in that it fails to include the humanities. This omission is corrected in figure 8.3. However, there are no homogeneous or pure sectors: All sciences have pockets of nonscience, and some nonscientific and protoscientific fields have pockets of science. This holds in particular for the social studies and technologies as well as for the humanities. But it also holds for such paradigmatic sciences as physics and astronomy, where unscientific procedures (such as the argument from authority) and even myths (such as the creation of the universe and

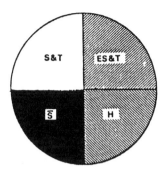

Fig. 8.3. Adding the
humanities (H)
to the map of intellectual
culture.

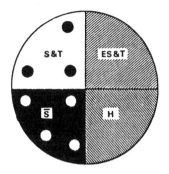

Fig. 8.4. Adding pockets of
nonscience to S, and of
science to S̄.
Pseudoscience and antiscience
are included in S.

the experimenter-dependence of all physical events) still raise their archaic
unkempt heads. (More on this in section 8.) Therefore, figure 8.4 is more correct, though perhaps still too simple to be completely faithful.

8.5 ❖ A CLOSER LOOK AT PSEUDOSCIENCE AND PSEUDOTECHNOLOGY

In case our negative definition of pseudoscience in the previous section is found
unsatisfactory, let us propose an alternative characterization of it in positive
terms. We stipulated that a pseudoscience is a cognitive field advertised as a science, though actually failing to be one. (Never mind the intentions of some of
the practitioners of pseudoscience: We all know that the road to hell is paved
with good intentions.)

We stipulate now that a *pseudoscience is* a cognitive field $\mathcal{F}$ = <C, S, G, D,
F, B, P, K, A, M>

such that

(1) C is a *community of believers* that do not conduct any rigorous research;

(2) the *host society* S either marginalizes C or tolerates it for practical reasons, such as being good business or ideological support;

(3) the *general outlook* or worldview G includes either (a) an ontology countenancing immaterial entities or processes, such as disembodied spirits and psychokinesis; or (b) an epistemology making room for arguments from authority, or for paranormal modes of cognition accessible only to the initiates or to those trained to interpret certain canonical texts; or (c) an ethos that, far from being that of the free search for truth, is that of the staunch defense of dogma, including deception and violence if need be;

(4) the *formal background* F is usually modest. Logic is not always respected, and mathematical modeling is the exception rather than the rule; moreover, the few mathematical models that have been proposed (e.g., for psi phenomena) are untestable, so they are phony;

(5) the *domain* or reference class D contains unreal or at least not certifiably real entities, such as astral influences, disembodied thoughts, superegos, collective consciousness, national will, destiny, UFOs, and the like;

(6) the *specific* background B is very small or even nil: a pseudoscience learns little or nothing from other cognitive fields; likewise, it contributes little or nothing to the development of other cognitive fields;

(7) the *problematics* P includes many more practical problems concerning human life (in particular how to feel better and influence other people) than cognitive problems; hence, most pseudosciences are better described as pseudotechnologies;

(8) The *fund of knowledge* K is practically stagnant and it contains numerous untestable or even false hypotheses in conflict with well-confirmed scientific hypotheses. And it contains no universal and well-confirmed hypotheses belonging to hypothetico-deductive systems, that is, law statements;

(9) the *aims* A are mainly practical rather than cognitive—in consonance with its problematics P; in particular, they do not include the typical goals of scientific research, namely the finding or application of laws and the understanding and prediction of facts in terms of laws;

(10) the *methods* in M are neither checkable by alternative (in particular scientific) procedures, nor are they justifiable by well-confirmed theories; in particular, criticism is not welcome in the pseudoscientific communities;

(11) there is no other cognitive field, except possibly another pseudoscience, that overlaps with the given pseudoscience and is thus in a position of enriching and controlling it: every pseudoscience is practically *isolated;* and

(12) the membership of every one of the last eight components of the tentuple changes but little in the course of time; and when it changes, it does so in

TABLE 8.1 COMPARISON OF ATTITUDES AND ACTIVITIES OF SCIENTISTS (S) AND PSEUDOSCIENTISTS (PS). 1 = YES, 0 = NO, ? = OPTIONAL.

TYPICAL ATTITUDES AND ACTIVITIES	S	PS
Undergoes long and rigorous apprenticeship	1	0
Admits own ignorance, hence need for more research	1	0
Finds own field hard and full of holes	1	0
Advances by posing and solving new problems	1	0
Welcomes new ideas and methods	1	0
Proposes or tries out new hypotheses	1	?
Attempts to find or apply laws	1	0
Relies on logic, shuns arguments ad hominem and from authority	1	?
Uses mathematics	1	?
Gathers or uses data	1	1
Bears the burden of proof	1	0
Looks for counterexamples	1	0
Invents or applies objective checking procedures	1	0
Is intent on minimizing systematic errors of observation	1	0
Favors close links with other fields	1	0
Admits fallibility of some pet ideas and procedures	1	0
Settles disputes by experiment or computation	1	0
Falls back consistently on authority	0	1
Suppresses or distorts unfavorable data	0	1
Updates information	1	0
Seeks critical comments from experts	1	0
Writes stuff that can be understood by anyone	0	1

very limited respects and as a result of controversy, turf competition, or external pressures rather than of scientific research.

It may be useful to supplement this general picture with a list of typical attitudes and activities of scientists and pseudoscientists (see table 8.1). (Admittedly, on occasion some scientists do not behave scientifically. But this is beside the point: we are concerned with norms.)

Let us next examine three specimens of pseudoscience: parapsychology, psychoanalysis, and computerist psychology.

8.6 ❖ PARAPSYCHOLOGY: CHASING GHOSTS

Pseudoscience is a body of beliefs and practices, but seldom a field of active inquiry: it is tradition-bound and dogmatic rather than forward-looking and exploratory. In particular, I have not heard of psychoanalytic or chiropractic laboratories; and the only homeopathic laboratory, that of a Doctor Benveniste in Paris, was closed down when its systematic frauds were discovered. Only parapsychology (or psychical research), which deals with so-called psychic, or spiritualistic, or extrasensory phenomena, is research-oriented. However, it fails to meet all ten conditions listed in section 4 for a cognitive field to be scientific. Let us check them, leaving the details to specialists (see, e.g., Alcock 1990; Kurtz 1985).

(1) *Scientific outlook.* Half a century ago, the distinguished philosopher C. D. Broad (1949) examined carefully the matter of the compatibility of parapsychology with the scientific worldview. He rightly regarded the latter as a set of "basic limiting principles." He found, as expected, that parapsychology violates these principles. Oddly, he concluded that, since parapsychology does not comply with them, the scientific worldview—not parapsychology—had to be given up. For example, precognition violates the principle of antecedence, according to which the effect does not happen before the cause. Psychokinesis, or PK, violates the principle that mind cannot act directly on matter. (If it did, no experimenter could trust his readings of measuring instruments.) It also violates the principles of conservation of energy and momentum. The claim that quantum mechanics allows for the possibility of mental power influencing randomizers—an alleged case of micro-PK—is ludicrous since that theory respects the said conservation principles, and it deals exclusively with physical things (recall chapter 3). Finally, telepathy and precognition are incompatible with the epistemological principle according to which gaining factual knowledge requires sense perception at some point. In short, parapsychology is inconsistent with some of the most robust and fertile of all principles of modern science.

(2) *Domain.* Parapsychology is about immaterial entities, such as disembodied spirits, whose existence has never been established. On the other hand, parapsychology ignores the very organ of thought, namely the brain. And it is inconsistent with the guiding principle of cognitive neuroscience, namely that mental processes are brain processes.

(3) *Formal background.* The typical parapsychologist is not very skillful at handling formal tools, in particular statistics. Thus, he consistently selects the

evidence ("optional stopping" of a sequence of trials); he does not distinguish a coincidence (accidental or spurious correlation) from a genuine correlation; and he is not fond of mathematical models or even of informal hypothetico-deductive systems: all of his hunches are stray.

(4) *Specific background*. Parapsychology makes no use of any knowledge gained in other fields, such as physics or psychology. In particular, the very idea of disembodied mental entities is incompatible with biological psychology (recall chapter 4); and the claim that ideas can be transmitted across space without fading with distance is inconsistent with physics. Worse, parapsychologists brush these anomalies aside, claiming that they deal with nonphysical phenomena, so that physicists and other scientists are not competent to study them.

(5) *Problematics*. Parapsychology is poor in problems: its entire problematics boil down to establishing that there are paranormal phenomena, that is, facts that cannot be explained by science. Nor is this problem formulated in clear terms, and this because of the appalling theoretical poverty of parapsychology.

(6) *Fund of knowledge*. Despite being several thousand years old, and of having attracted a large number of researchers over the past hundred years, we owe no single finding to parapsychology: no hard data on telepathy, clairvoyance, precognition, or psychokinesis, and no hypotheses to explain these alleged phenomena. All it tells us is that such and such alleged data are anomalous, that is, unexplained by the science of the day. It suggests no mechanisms, it proposes no theories. Compare this behavior with that of a scientist—an astronomer, say. If an astronomer were to announce that a certain celestial object does not seem to "obey" the laws of celestial mechanics or of astrophysics, he would feel it his duty to offer or invite some positive conjectures—e.g., that it is not an ordinary body but a quasar, a black hole, or some other physical thing. He might conjecture that this thing of a new kind "obeys" laws yet to be discovered—but not that it violates well-established physical principles such as that of the conservation of energy. (Which principle, incidentally, is violated by the psychokinesis hypothesis.) The parapsychologist does no such thing: he accepts apparently anomalous data as evidence for paranormal abilities, and takes no steps to explain them in terms of laws. Has anyone heard of the First Law of Clairvoyance, the Second Law of Telepathy, or the Third Law of Psychokinesis? And has anyone ever produced a mathematical theory of spooks capable of making definite testable predictions?

(7) *Aims*. Judging by the accomplishments of parapsychologists, their aim is not that of finding laws and systematizing them into theories in order to under-

stand and forecast. Rather, their aim is either to buttress ancient spiritualist myths or to serve as a surrogate for religion. (Recall that the Society for Psychical Research was founded in London in 1882 with the explicit aim of preserving the belief in the immortal soul that was being eroded by evolutionary biology. After all, belief in the efficacy of prayer presupposes telepathy, just as belief in the ability of supernatural beings to cause physical events at a distance presupposes psychokinesis.)

(8) *Methods.* The methods used by parapsychologists have been scrutinized by scientists and statisticians for more than one century and found invariably faulty. The most common defect is lack of strict controls. But deception, either unconscious as in the case of the ordinary experimental subject who wants the experiment to succeed, or deliberate as in the case of the famous Spoon Bender, has always plagued parapsychology. (For a great many examples see the journal the *Skeptical Inquirer*).

(9) *Systemicity.* Far from being a component of a cognitive system, parapsychology is an isolated field: it does not overlap with any other field of inquiry. This is why its practitioners ask that it be judged on its own merits: on the strength of the empirical evidence they claim to marshal. But this is impossible, quite aside from the fact that such "evidence" is quite suspicious for having been gathered with faulty methods—not to speak of old folk stories and other anecdotal "evidence" still going strong among parapsychologists. Indeed, facts can be "read" or "interpreted" in a number of ways (that is, explained by alternative hypotheses). This is one reason that only hypotheses harmonizing with several other hypotheses are worth being investigated in science. But this is not the case with the parapsychological hypotheses: they do not form a hypothetico-deductive system, and they do not jibe with ordinary science (recall point 1 above). Moreover, the parapsychologists themselves are proud of producing and studying phenomena that they regard as paranormal and as being beyond the reach of ordinary (that is, genuine) science.

(10) *Changeability* Parapsychology cannot be said to be moving fast, the way a genuine science does nowadays. In fact it is a collection of extremely old beliefs going back to primitive animism: parapsychologists keep retesting the same hunches over and over again without ever obtaining any conclusive results.

We conclude that parapsychology passes muster as a pseudoscience. If it is not always recognized as such, it may be because most philosophies of science are not about real science, or because the label "scientific" is attached without previous philosophical analysis.

8.7 ❖ PSYCHOANALYSIS: WILD FANTASIES

Many other pseudosciences besides parapsychology deserve the philosopher's attention, if only because they are even more popular and often more dangerous than belief in psi. Psychoanalysis is one of them. The emergence of psychoanalysis in 1900 has often been hailed as a scientific upheaval on a par with Galileo's, Newton's, Smith's, Darwin's, Marx's, and Einstein's. At first sight, psychoanalysis does look revolutionary in its hypotheses and methods. (See, e.g., Freud 1960.) Closer examination shows that these are not quite so new and that, far from constituting a revolutionary advancement, they constitute a counterrevolution. In fact, the original ideas of psychoanalysis are wild speculations rather than products of scientific research. That is, they are not supported by empirical data, and they do not jibe with experimental psychology or neuroscience. (See, e.g., Crews 1998; Loftus and Ketcham 1994; Macmillan 1997.) However, this does not worry Freud's followers, since he declared that psychoanalysis has nothing to learn from either experimental psychology or neuroscience.

From a methodological viewpoint, the psychoanalytic fantasies fall into two categories: testable and untestable. The latter, such as the thesis that all dreams have a sexual content, whether manifest or latent, are obviously unscientific. As for Freud's testable hypotheses, most of them (like recall of life in the womb, penis envy, fear of castration, the intellectual and moral inferiority of women, and the cathartic effect of watching violent episodes) have been refuted by experimental psychology and serious clinical observation.

The only true psychoanalytic hypothesis is that there are unconscious mental processes. But Freud did not discover the unconscious. Socrates knew about tacit knowledge; Hume mentioned the unconscious in 1739; Eduard von Hartmann devoted it an influential book in 1870—when Freud was fourteen years old; and both Helmholtz and Wundt wrote about unconscious inferences before Freud. Besides, psychoanalysts do not investigate scientifically any unconscious mental processes, although they claim that the free association they invite their clients to engage in is "the royal road" to the unconscious. They just write stories about it. By contrast, implicit (or tacit) knowledge, as in blindvision, word memory, and know-how, is being investigated experimentally by nonpsychoanalysts (see, e.g., Köhler and Moscowitch 1997).

Another pivotal and influential conjecture of Freud's is the claim that infancy is destiny: that the first five years of life shape irreversibly all the remaining years, with no possibility of recuperation from early traumatic experiences. But the massive and long-term follow-up study of Sir Michael Rutter and coworkers (1993) has falsified this dogma: it has shown that people are resilient and continue to develop throughout life.

An even more important Freudian myth is that of the Oedipus complex. Here is the story: (1) We are all born with a sex drive; (2) our parents and siblings are the nearest and therefore the earliest objects of our sexual desire; (3) the incest taboo is a social construction; (4) when incestual desires are repressed, they are stored in the Unconscious; (5) repression shows up deviously in father-hatred (Oedipus) in boys, and in mother-hatred (Electra) in girls. Let us check this popular story.

The hypothesis (1) of infantile sexuality is false: the sex center is the hypothalamus, which is underdeveloped in infants. Hence hypothesis (2) is false too. But hypothesis (3) is independent of (1) and (2), and therefore it ought to be investigated. Should research falsify the hypothesis that incest avoidance is a social construction rather than natural, hypotheses (4) and (5) would prove to be false, and the entire psychoanalytic building would crumble. Let us see what the facts of the matter are.

The Swedish-Finnish anthropologist, sociologist, and philosopher Edward Westermarck (1862–1939) was the earliest evolutionary social anthropologist. And he was also the first to gather empirical evidence relevant to the question whether the incest taboo—and by extension the exogamy rule—is natural or artificial. In his *History of Human Marriage* (1891), he concluded that "there is a remarkable absence of erotic feelings between persons living closely together from childhood." Consequently, the incest taboo only consecrates a natural disposition. Freud and other famous contemporaries dismissed this thesis out of hand: they behaved as dogmatic skeptics. However, later research fully vindicated what has become known as Westermarck's hypothesis.

In fact, it has been well known for four decades that kibbutz children, reared together from infancy, and free to choose their mates later in life, never marry their erstwhile playmates. A more recent finding is that of the Stanford anthropologist Arthur P. Wolf, who devoted most of his academic life to testing Westermarck's hypothesis in a sort of natural laboratory, namely northern Taiwanese society. This is, or rather was, a laboratory of sorts because arranged marriages used to proceed in either of two different ways. Whereas some girls stayed with their parents until the wedding day ("major" marriage type), others were moved to their future in-laws' home as nursing infants to be raised together with their future husbands ("minor" marriage type). Comparison between the two groups qualifies as a "natural experiment" because a representative sample of marriages of the major kind acts as the control group, whereas an equivalent sample of the minor kind acts as the experimental group.

Wolf (1995) studied the history of 14,402 marriages of both kinds, using government statistics in the years 1905 to 1945 in addition to his own data about a number of living individuals. He found that those of the minor type—involving early intimate association—were significantly less successful than those of the major type, as measured by low fertility, adultery, and divorce. Thus, "far from conceiving a sexual attraction for members of the same family, children develop an active sexual aversion as a result of unavoidable association. I therefore conclude that the first premise of Oedipal theory is mistaken, and that all the conclusions reached on the basis of the presumed existence of an Oedipus complex are also mistaken" (Wolf 1995, 491).

Among these failed conclusions are Freud's claim that the Oedipus complex is the main source of intellectual and artistic activity (through "sublimation"), religion, the law, and ethics, as well as of social conflict and war. And, since the Oedipal "theory" is false, there is no need for psychoanalytic therapy—except as a profitable occupation.

So, as the old chestnut goes, what is true about psychoanalysis is old, and what is new is either untestable or false. To make things easier for us, psychoanalysts eschew experiment, alleging that their doctrine is being tested daily on the couch. They also avoid statistics, with the excuse that no two individuals are the same—a lame excuse because biology, medicine, and psychology are in the same boat, and yet they find regularities. In short, psychoanalysts, like homeopaths and chiropractors, are not researchers but practitioners of a groundless body of beliefs.

Despite its lack of scientific credentials—or perhaps because of this—psychoanalysis has had a tremendous impact on contemporary culture. In fact, it has generated a whole movement (see Gellner 1993). During several decades this movement slowed down the pace of scientific psychology and contaminated social studies; it transformed psychiatry into quackery, and supplied literary critics and half-baked intellectuals a cheap and all-purpose doctrine (see Torrey 1992). It was, in sum, not just a scientific counterrevolution but a major cultural disaster.

The sensational cultural and commercial success of psychoanalysis is largely due to five facts. It demands no scientific background; it addresses topics that had been neglected by classical psychology—mainly feelings and sex; it provides a cheap explanation for everything personal and social; it debunks religion—in an unscientific way, though; and, above all, it is entertaining.

The technology associated with psychoanalysis is of course psychoanalytic therapy, a variety of verbal psychotherapy. However, the treatment of mental ailments by purely verbal means has been around for thousands of years in all human societies. Until the advent of psychoanalysis it was usually bound with animistic or religious beliefs and groundless rituals performed by shamans or priests. Since then, logotherapy has become a booming industry, though one now showing signs of recession. There are about two hundred logotherapy schools bickering among themselves, most of them alien to experimental psychology and biological psychiatry. Few of them have been subjected to rigorous tests: they are usually adopted and practiced on faith or authority. Food items, pharmaceutical drugs, and even cars are subjected to close scrutiny—not so verbal psychotherapies. When the U.S. National Institute for Mental Health proposed in 1980 to undertake rigorous tests for safety and efficiency of just two varieties of psychotherapy, the psychoanalytic community raised hell. How dare they challenge a deep-seated belief and profitable practice in the name of public mental health?

8.8 ❖ COMPUTERIST PSYCHOLOGY: CONFUSING BRAINS WITH MACHINES

Psychoanalysis and the sundry verbal psychotherapies are not the only pseudoscientific approaches to the study of the mind. Another such approach, and one that has been gaining popularity alongside the computer, is the computer model of mind. Although it looks scientific, or better technologically, because it uses the computer-science language, it is pseudoscientific for the following reasons.

The computer model of mind

(1) is at variance with post-Aristotelian physics in that it postulates that every state transition is caused by some external stimulus—an axiom of the theory of Turing machines, which underlies the whole of computer science;

(2) bypasses the brain and thus ignores the whole of neuroscience; in particular, it has no use for typical properties of the nervous tissue, such as lateral inhibition, synaptic plasticity, spontaneous neuronal discharge, and spontaneous self-asssembly;

(3) ignores developmental and evolutionary biology, neither of which can be accounted for in terms of such artifacts as communication channels and algorithms;

(4) is at odds with psychology, in that it regards the brain as an information-

182

processing device incapable of posing problems, doubting, having emotions, and creating original concepts and hypotheses;

(5) consecrates the mythical mind-body duality by distinguishing and detaching the (inborn) material hardware from the (learned) software, which it regards as stuff-free;

(6) admits the dichotomy between "organic" and "psychological" dysfunction—which has blocked the progress of psychiatry—by claiming that, whereas the former are wiring defects, the latter are information errors;

(7) makes no precise predictions, hence it cannot be subjected to empirical tests;

(8) is limited to algorithmic operations: it ignores such nonalgorithmic processes as emotion, perception, and the invention of new concepts, theories, methods, plans—and algorithms;

(9) overrates computers to the point of crediting them with the abilities of their designers and programmers, as was the case of the sensational match, in 1998, between Deep Blue, an IBM machine, and the chess grand master Boris Kasparov;

(10) discourages artificial intelligence experts form studying natural intelligence, and thus stunts the growth of knowledge engineering.

In sum, the computational model of the mind is pseudoscientific and pseudotechnological. It produces only an illusion of knowledge by replacing the honest "We don't know yet how we perform mental task X" with the high-sounding but hollow "The computation of X." Its root is the idealistic, and ultimately magical, view of the mind as detachable from matter. To be sure, computer science and artificial intelligence (in particular robotics) are admirable branches of applied mathematics and engineering respectively. But they are no substitutes for the study of the mental functions of live brains.

We could go on hunting for more specimens of pseudoscience, as they abound not only in folk culture but also in the scientific literature—not excluding high-level journals in physics, biology, psychology, and social science. Suffice it to mention a random assortment of such beasts: (a) the quantum theory of measurement, supposedly applicable to every possible measurement device, yet never put to the experimental test; (b) string theory, which postulates that space-time has actually ten dimensions, not four, but that we have no access to the six extra ones; (c) the sensational but groundless prophecies issued from time to time by certain "think tanks"; (d) the "general systems" models criticized by Berlinski (1976); (e) the applications of catastrophe theory to biological and social problems criticized by Zahler and Sussman (1977); (f) the artificial (or dry) life project, that identifies computer simulations of biological processes with living processes (see Mahner and Bunge 1997); (g) Dawkins's fantasies about the selfish gene and the autocratic genome—soundly trounced by the geneticists Lewontin (2000) and Dover (2000); (h) pseudo-Darwinian medicine, or the doctrine that every sickness is an adaptation—no doubt a great comfort to AIDS patients; (i) the sociobiological account of human cognitive abilities that passes for evolutionary psychology, one of whose theses is that the human brain was "designed" to deal with human life as it was 100,000 years ago—but then why talk of mental evolution? (j) psychohistory, or the psychoanalysis of historical and even mythical characters; (k) many of the sociological theories ridiculed by Sorokin (1956), Andreski (1972), and Bunge (1996a, 1998a, 1999b); (l) the use, in psychology and social studies, of the language but not concepts of probability theory, information theory, catastrophe theory, and chaos theory; (m) the post-Mertonian constructivist-relativist sociology of science (see chapter 5); (n) the rational-choice models that are neither mathematically precise nor empirically supported (Bunge 1998a); and (o) the health quackeries denounced once in a while by Consumer's Union.

The pseudosciences abound for several reasons: because they have ancient roots, handle questions neglected by science, make wild claims, promise effective results at low cost, and are far easier to understand and practice than science. So, they are likely to pop up everywhere at all times.

8.9 ❖ DISTINGUISHING PSEUDOSCIENCE FROM PROTOSCIENCE AND HETERODOXY

We have drawn the line between science and pseudoscience, but have said almost nothing about science fiction, protoscience, scientific unorthodoxy, and antiscience. A few words about all four are in order because they are sometimes confused with pseudoscience.

The difference between science fiction and pseudoscience is of course that the former makes no truth claims: it is just a branch of fantastic literature. However, there are two kinds of science fiction: plausible and implausible. The former is an imaginative extrapolation of current science. For instance, it may imagine superluminal signals, superhuman beings, mind-reading devices implanted in the brain, or genetically engineered organisms. By contrast, implausible science fiction violates well-entrenched scientific laws. For instance, it may invent spaceships traveling at superluminal speeds, immortal humans, telepathic communication, galactic societies, or creative and self-programming robots. In short, there is honest science fiction, which demands a great deal of scientific imagination because it works within the limits of real possibility; and there is pseudoscience fiction—a double cheat.

As for the difference between pseudoscience and science, there is always the fear that some gold nuggets may lie hidden in the former: that it may be nothing but protoscience, or emerging science. Such fear is quite justified at the infancy of a research field, particularly since an extremely original view or technique—an unorthodoxy—may smack of pseudoscience just because of its novelty. But caution must be replaced with skepticism, and skepticism with denunciation if, at the end of some decades, the novelty fails to evolve into a full-fledged component of science. Indeed, whereas the genuine protosciences advance and mature into sciences propelled by rigorous research, the pseudosciences are stagnant pools on the side of the swift scientific mainstream. And no caution at all is called for even at the beginning if the new idea or procedure collides head-on with the scientific outlook, the scientific method, or the best-established (yet of course fallible) scientific findings. The conceivable objection that such intolerance would have nipped modern science in the bud is beside the point, for in 1600—which is roughly when modern science began—there was hardly a scientific outlook, a scientific method, or well-established scientific theories outside pure mathematics.

That "there may be something" in certain claims of pseudoscience is true but another matter. Thus, the alchemists were right in holding that lead could be transmuted into gold. But they were wrong in believing that they would eventually bring about such transmutation, for they lacked (a) the necessary theory (of nuclear structure); (b) the necessary tool (particle accelerators); and (c) the possibility of acquiring either theory or tool because they were hooked to tradition (in particular the four-elements theory), and put their faith in trial and error (rather than in well-designed experiment) combined with magical incantation. So, the modern discovery of (genuine) transmutation of the elements was just a coincidence—the more so since the alchemists rejected atomism.

Likewise, the phrenologists were onto something when, in 1810, they first revealed the circumvolutions of the cerebral cortex, and revived Galen's hypothesis of the cerebral localization of mental abilities. But their claim that such modules could be identified by just stroking the scalp in search of bumps was ludicrous, and their appearance at country fairs finished by discrediting the valuable hypothesis of localization.

Again, telepathy may be for real after all—though not clairvoyance, precognition, or psychokinesis, all of which contradict basic physical laws. However, if thought transmission does occur, it must be through a physical field. After all, the human brain emits electromagnetic radiation. True, this radiation is a hundred thousand times weaker than would be required for effective transmission—not to speak of the absence of known detection and decoding mechanisms in the brain (Taylor and Balanovski 1979). Still, telepathy cannot be excluded through some as yet undiscovered physical field. So, its unlikely discovery would not confirm parapsychology, which claims that the effect is nonphysical, hence undetectable by measuring instruments. If it were proved to exist, telepathy would become a subject of normal scientific research—like the effective transmutation of lead into gold in a high-energy laboratory. Hence, such discovery would kill parapsychology, just as chemistry and nuclear physics finished off alchemy.

Scientific unorthodoxy is a different kettle of fish altogether: it is just unconventional or unpopular science. Field physics was radically unorthodox when it was first proposed in mid-nineteenth century, for it disagreed with the then-dominant action-at-a-distance theories. But it was a genuine scientific field, rife with testable hypotheses, stunning new experiments, and pregnant with undreamed of powerful technologies: electric power, radio, television, and electronic mail. The same can be said of all the scientific unorthodoxies that followed, such as Darwin's theory of evolution, Marx's analysis of classical capitalism, statistical mechanics, genetics, the two relativities, the synthetic theory of evolution, quantum theory, molecular biology, cognitive neuroscience, economic sociology, and so on.

All of these were, to borrow Isaac Asimov's apt expression, endoheresies—deviations within science—to be distinguished from *exoheresies* or deviations from science. Whether proposed by members of a given discipline or by outsiders, a new item of knowledge that satisfies the definition proposed in section 4, but happens to conflict with some (though not all) items in the standard specific background, or in the agreed-on fund of knowledge, qualifies as endoheresy. Endoheresy should be welcome in science, exoheresy not. Tolerance, yes, but only within science. To paraphrase Saint Paul, there is no (intellectual) salvation outside science.

It does not follow that science has no internal enemies or fifth columns. It does have them, but they are easily identifiable because they are nonscientific fragments. I submit that the most dreadful such internal enemies are (a) excessive tolerance for ideas or practices than run against the grain of science; (b) unwillingness to refine coarse ideas; and (c) refusal to discuss matters of principle. Let us examine a few instances of each.

An example of excessive tolerance for unscientific ideas is the anthropic hypothesis. According to it, the universe was carefully designed so that humans could appear when and where they did. This hypothesis is ambiguous: it may be interpreted either as a tautology or as a theological principle. In either case, it is empirically untestable, and therefore unscientific (Bunge 1985). Another case of excessive open-mindedness is the old myth of the immaterial mind hovering above the brain. Since immaterial items can be neither recorded nor controlled in the laboratory, this is an unscientific hypothesis (recall chapter 3). Worse, both hypotheses block scientific research: the former stands in the way of evolutionary biology, and the latter in that of cognitive neuroscience.

Examples of blindness to the fuzziness of certain key ideas are the use of such stock phrases as "DNA molecules *specify* proteins" and "the animal's nervous system *computes* its motions." The italicized words only mask our ignorance of the mechanisms at stake. Worse, they give the false impression that there are adequate theories to account for protein synthesis and the control of bodily motion respectively, whereas in fact so far only descriptions of such processes are available.

Finally, an example of dogmatism concerning successful theories is the (currently waning) rigidity concerning the physical interpretation of the mathematical formalism of the quantum theory—a marvelously accurate construction somewhat spoiled by a wrong obsolete antirealist philosophy (recall chapter 3). The moral of all three batches of examples is: The scientific mind should be neither too closed nor too open (recall chapter 7).

Students of pseudoscience are currently divided as to which of the two, pseudoscience or scientific dogma, is the more harmful. In my view this question is ill-formulated, and the usual way of handling it unscientific. Indeed, the appropriate question is not just "Which is worse?" but rather "Which is the most harmful to whom in what respect?" And the latter question should be investigated scientifically rather than being discussed in an empirical vacuum for it concerns factual matters. Indeed, the problem is one for the psychology, sociology, and even economics of knowledge and ignorance. Let me explain.

Presumably, pseudoscience can do little harm to the scientific specialist, who is on the other hand constantly in danger of yielding to dogma, which in turn blocks research along new lines. (Caution: Since every scientist is a layman in fields other than his own, he is named twice in the preceding hypothesis.) By contrast, the layman, knowing little or nothing about the scientific orthodoxies of the day, is at the mercy of a number of superstitions, both those he learned as a child and those he sees touted as scientific. Not being competent to tell the fake from the genuine article, the layman is presumably more likely to buy the former, if only because he sees far more of it at a far lower price. Besides the greater exposure, there is what William James called the will to believe: Many who embrace superstitions, old or new, do so because they feel the need for some extra support to cope with adversity.

In short, it would seem that, whereas dogmatism concerning scientific ideas is more harmful to scientists than to laymen, the latter have more to fear from pseudoscience. But this is just an untested conjecture. What is hardly in doubt is the economics of pseudoscience. We know that it has become a multibillion-dollar industry. And we know that, whereas belief in extrasensory perception comes rather cheap, belief in psychoanalysis can be ruinous. However, this again is a matter for empirical investigation.

Antiscience is an entirely different matter again. By definition, an *antiscience* is a belief system that is openly hostile to science and struggles to displace science. Examples include all the occult "sciences"; homeopathy (as opposed to allopathy or "official" medicine); humanistic psychology (opposed to experimental psychology); and humanistic sociology (opposed to empirical sociology). Antiscience is not just hostile to a given body of scientific knowledge: it militates against the scientific outlook and the scientific method.

However, the difference between antiscience and pseudoscience is only one of marketing: although both are equally nonscientific, pseudoscientists claim to be doing science, whereas antiscientists openly deprecate the latter. Aside from this, both groups are exoheresiarchs, and both exert a pernicious influence on the unwary public. Yet, they are not equally pernicious. Indeed, whereas some antisciences may be comparatively harmless, others—in particular humanistic psychology and humanistic sociology—are definitely noxious, possibly more so than parapsychology. Indeed, they attempt to destroy what little has been won in one century of hard scientific sailing against the prevailing philosophical winds. Nevertheless, let us not exaggerate the differences between antiscience and pseudoscience, for neither is scientific, and both attempt to dislodge science.

CONCLUSION

Scientists and philosophers tend to treat pseudoscience and antiscience as harmless rubbish: they are far too busy with their own research to be bothered by such nonsense. This attitude is unfortunate for the following reasons. Firstly, pseudoscience and antiscience are not ordinary rubbish—misplaced stuff—that could be recycled into something useful. They are intellectual germs that can attack anybody, layman or scientist, to the point of sickening a whole culture and turning it against science. Secondly, the emergence and diffusion of pseudoscience and antiscience are important psychosocial phenomena worth investigating scientifically. They might even be used as indicators of the state of health of a culture. Thirdly, pseudoscience and antiscience are good test cases for any philosophy of science. Indeed, the worth of such a philosophy can be gauged by its sensitivity to the differences between science and nonscience, high-grade and low-grade science, and living and dead science. What would you think of an art historian who is consistently taken in by gross artistic fakes, or of an art critic who consistently overlooks great art and overrates artistic impostures, or who turns his back to the entire art of his time?

Given the intrinsic interest and the cultural importance of pseudoscience and antiscience, it is surprising that they should receive so little attention on the part of philosophers, particularly in our times of crisis of public confidence in science. It must be admitted that the philosopher has forsaken the scientist at this hour of trial. Worse, some philosophers have sided with the enemy, in claiming that science is no better than pseudoscience, religion, magic, faith healing, or witchcraft, all of which ought to be given "equal time" in schools—without of course offering any arguments for such claims. This should be a clear indication that there is something basically wrong with contemporary philosophy. Could it be that some magician or alchemist is turning it into pseudophilosophy?

9

VALUES AND MORALS IN A MATERIALIST AND REALIST PERSPECTIVE

Where are values and morals located: is their abode worldly or other-worldly? If worldly, are they rooted in nature, society, the self, or all three? And if unworldly, are they self-existing Platonic ideas, or else divine gifts (or curses)? Whether worldly or unworldly, what are the functions of values and morals: to please the divinity, gratify the individual, strengthen social cohesion, entrench vested interests, or help live?

Again, how do we ascertain that something is valuable, or that a moral norm is valid: through revelation, intuition, pure reason, trial and error, or science and technology? And can science and technology help validate or invalidate value judgments and moral norms, or are all of these subjective (in particular emotive), utilitarian, or just local and time-bound customs on a par with wearing tattoos?

These are only a few of the many conceptual and empirical questions raised by any claims that something is (or is not) valuable, and that a moral rule should (or should not) be observed. Some of these questions have been pondered and debated for over three millennia by religionists, philosophers, and social scientists. And yet, they are still to be answered in a satisfactory manner as well as in harmony with a materialist ontology, a realist epistemology, and a progressive political philosophy. In the following one such answer will be sketched. This answer may be called axiological and ethical realism. It is also ratio-empiricist in claiming that correct valuation and right action rest on both reason and fact rather than feeling, intuition, or convention.

Any inquiry into the nature, source, and function of values and morals belongs in what used to be called practical philosophy. This discipline may nowadays be regarded as philosophical technology, or the art and science of the good and the right. More precisely, I submit that *philosophical technology* is composed of axiology (value theory), praxiology (action theory), ethics (moral philosophy or the theory of morals), political philosophy, and methodology (or normative epistemology). These five normative disciplines may be regarded as technologies because they are ultimately concerned with doing rather than with either being or knowing—and moreover with doing what is good and right in the light of the best available factual knowledge.

9.1 ❖ FACT AND VALUE

A landslide is a physical fact. Hence, the statement "That was a landslide" is a factual statement and, as such, either true or false. By contrast, "The victims of the landslide were rescued at great risk" is a moral statement as well as a factual one, and perhaps a true one to boot because the rescue workers put their own lives on the line to save others. Hence, the second statement can be said to faithfully represent a moral fact, namely that the landslide raised the moral problem: To rescue or not to rescue?

The preceding constitutes a tacit endorsement of axiological and moral realism, or the view that some facts are moral, and that some value judgments and some moral norms are just as objective—hence capable of being true or false—as factual statements. I have also made tacit use of the definition of a moral fact as one that raises a moral problem, which in turn may be defined as one that invites, though does not command, a supererogatory action—and moreover a good action, not just a useful one. As will be seen in section 9.6, axiological and moral realism are at variance with emotivism, intuitionism, deontologism, utilitarianism, and contractualism.

However, axiological and moral realists do not deny the difference between facts on the one hand, and values and norms on the other. For one thing, moral facts constitute a very special kind of fact: there would be none in the absence of moral agents. Think of Robinson Crusoe before meeting Friday: he was not a moral agent because, being all by himself, he faced no moral problems. Moral problems only arise in connection with other people.

Secondly, it is well known that ought-statements are not deducible from is-statements. For example, "He is doing it" neither implies nor is implied by "He ought to do it." (However, I will argue below that ought-statements ought to be grounded in is-statements.) In short, as Hume and others have noted, there is a gap between ought-statement and is-statements.

Still, a gap can be either ditch or abyss. And ditches are not chasms: we may be able to jump over the former though not over the latter. As a matter of fact, we bridge the fact-value gap every time we take action to attain a desirable goal. In other words, action—particularly if well planned—may lead from what is the case to what ought to be the case. In short, action can bridge the logical gap between *is* and *ought*, in particular between the real and the rational. This platitude has eluded most if not all value theorists, moral philosophers, and even action theorists—which is witness to their indifference to the real world of action.

(Let us put this in systems-theoretic terms. Call S the state space of an agent-patient supersystem, that is, the set of all the really possible states of it. Further, call D the subset of desirable states of that supersystem. A deliberate action may then be construed as a function $\alpha: S \to D$ from a possible situation to a desirable one. Since first shots are seldom successful, and their outcomes can in principle be improved upon by ulterior actions, we add the condition that there is a finite sequence of successive actions that reduce progressively the subset of desirable outcomes until the optimal one is attained—that is, until the box D is projected onto a designated point inside D.)

Idealists deal with values in themselves, such as truth and justice. To them, a valuable item is an instance or embodiment of a value, which would be an ideal and therefore eternal object. By contrast, materialists and pragmatists deal with *valuations* performed by live animals, in particular humans. To them, there are only items—things, events, ideas, etc.—that we attribute a value to for certain goals and under certain circumstances. That is, values are not individuals but relational properties, as suggested by the schema "Item u has value v for social unit (person or social system) w in respect x for goal y under circumstance z." However, in the interest of brevity one can still speak of values rather than of valuations, provided one remembers that there are no values without animals (in particular people) capable of evaluating.

One can further say of an item that it is valuable to an individual or a social system when it meets some needs or some wants (desires) of the person or system in question. In our axiology, objective needs take precedence over mere wishes, which are often fanciful. However, some human needs, such as the needs to attain consistency and avoid ugliness, are not directly related to survival. As with needs, so with values: there is a broad gamut of them.

In fact, values can be grouped in several mutually consistent ways. For our purpose, the most interesting types are the following:

(a) objective, like nutritional value and peace of mind; and subjective, like acquired taste and beauty;

(b) individual, like love and dignity; and social, like fairness and peace;

(c) environmental, like biodiversity and minimal contamination; biological, like health and the ability to enjoy good things; economic, like productivity and marketability; political, like liberty and democracy; and cultural, like creativity and knowledge.

The above are typologies rather than classifications because the classes in question are not mutually disjoint. For example, an item may be valuable to someone both objectively and subjectively: it may be a desirable must, such as a beautiful tool or an elegant mathematical proof. Likewise, genuine social values, like good will, loyalty, liberty, security, and justice, are valuable to individuals. And environmental values are also biological and economic values—even if shortsighted politicians, businessmen, and mainstream economists seldom realize it. Such blindness to collective values is endangering not only the individual well-being of billions of people, but also the very social order championed by the apostles of the market values—as Gray (1998) and Soros (1998) have eloquently argued.

How are values—or rather valuable items—realized, attained, protected, or altered? More precisely, are there any rules for handling values, other than those handed down by tradition? This will be our next problem. Let me anticipate the answer: Yes, there are such rules, and they are similar to the technological rules from which they differ only in their explicit moral ingredient.

9.2 ❖ LAW AND RULE

An objective law is a pattern of events in the real (natural or social) world. In contradistinction, a law statement is a more or less true conceptual representation of such objective pattern. *Example 1*: Under perfect competition, supply increases, whereas demand decreases with price. A simple possible conceptualization (law statement) is: "PQ = constant," where "P" stands for price and "Q" for quantity. *Example 2*: The volume C of contaminants produced by an industry is proportional to the production P of the latter. Possible law statement: "$C = c \cdot P$," where the parameter c is characteristic of the industry in question. *Example 3*: In urban communities, criminality C increases with unemployment U. Possible law statement: "$C = a + bU$," where a is the "natural" crime rate (under full employment), whereas b is the rate of change of criminality due to unemployment.

No doubt, all three law statements are in principle both fallible and perfectible in the light of empirical and theoretical research. That is, in principle one and the same objective pattern can be represented in various alternative ways: one pattern-many law statements. In other words, although the world is one, it can be modeled variously. Moreover, alternative models of real things are not necessarily mutually equivalent: some may be more accurate or deeper than others. In fact, it is a philosophical principle tacitly admitted by all scientists that, given any partially true statement, there must be a way to improve on it, that is, to find a better approximation. This principle of successive approximations distinguishes scientific realism from naive realism. Besides, it disposes of the odd claim that the laws of science "lie" whenever they are not fully accurate. I submit that the same principle holds also for rules, in particular moral norms: these too are just as perfectible as they are fallible.

A well-known characteristic of modern technology, by contrast to traditional craftsmanship, is that it is based on science. In particular, technological rules are grounded on scientific law statements—or, more precisely, law statements reasonably close to the experiential plane. This proviso excludes such high-level law statements as the principles of electrodynamics and quantum mechanics.

More precisely, in principle any given law statement reasonably close to the empirical plane can serve as the foundation for two technological rules: one for doing something and the other for either doing the opposite, or for abstaining from doing something. For example, a law statement of the form "C causes E" is the common basis of the rules "To get E, do C," and "To avoid E, refrain from doing C." Similarly, the law "C is likely to cause E" serves as the common basis for the rules "To make E likely to happen, do C," and "To make E unlikely to happen, refrain from doing C." (The probabilistic restatement of the law statement and the corresponding rules are left to the reader.) In short, every law statement L justifies two mutually dual technological rules, that will be called R^+ and R^-.

Let us examine the three scientific examples given at the beginning of this section in the light of this philosophical result.

Example 1: The so-called law of the markets is the basis for two rules:

R^+: To increase sales, lower price. R^-: To increase price, lower supply.

Note the moral difference between these two rules: Whereas the application of R^+ is likely to benefit sellers and buyers alike, that of R^- is likely to hurt consumers, to the point of being punishable by law in times of natural shortages. In this case, the application of this technological law calls for the implementation of a moral rule to the effect that it is antisocial, hence morally objectionable, to hoard food in times of food shortages.

Example 2: The law relating the amount of contamination to the volume of industrial production is the ground for the dual rules: "To increase contamination, increase production," and "To decrease contamination, decrease production." Since neither an increase in environmental contamination nor the dismantling of a useful industry is likely to benefit anyone, we are faced with a typical techno-ethical problem: that of determining the level of contamination acceptable to both industry and the public. The solution to this problem requires the cooperation of all the stakeholders, as well as the expertise of specialists in health and engineering. (Mathematically, the problem boils down to transforming the given law statement, namely "$C = c \cdot P$," into the technological rule "$C = (1\text{-}b) \cdot c \cdot P$," where the new parameter b is the strategic variable to be determined by the team in question. The value of b must be greater than 0—maximal contamination resulting from no regulation—and smaller than 1—no contamination at all resulting from banning the industry.) Since the given problem has a technically and socially feasible solution, the only moral problem is the one raised by the willful ignorance of the contamination issue.

Example 3: The sociological law that the crime rate is a linear function of the unemployment rate is the basis for two rules. One of them states that, to reduce crime, one ought to promote jobs creation. Its dual states that, to increase crime, one should favor policies that destroy jobs. Whereas the first rule benefits nearly everyone, the second rule only benefits those who live by crime, such as handgun manufacturers and dealers, criminal lawyers, prison wardens, parole officers, locksmiths, jail constructors and suppliers, politicians who wage Wars on Crime, and their ilk. Common decency dictates that only the first rule be implemented: that attention be focused on a major source of crime rather than on its product. But why do we object to crime? At first sight, from fear of becoming a victim of it. However, this cannot be the major concern since crime is unpopular even in low crime-rate countries. The major concern is principled rather than prudential: We object naturally to murder and all other kinds of violence because we empathize with the victim and we respect the integrity of the person; we object to theft because we respect toil as a source of wealth; and we object to crime of all kinds because we cherish security and social cohesion, even under an imperfect social order.

The above examples illustrate the following principles. First, values and morals have both biological and social roots (Bergson 1932; Bunge 1989; Boudon 1995). Second and consequently, many important values and moral norms are objective and moreover cross-cultural—cultural relativism notwithstanding. Third, deliberate action is not the automatic outcome of either instinct or social convention: it is taken on the strength of more or less well-grounded and well-argued reasons—albeit usually under severe constraints rather than freely. Fourth and consequently, science and technology can help tackle practical issues, whether or not they have a moral component. Fifth and consequently, although axiology and ethics are distinct from science and technology, all four fields are linked to one another.

Now, the typical practical issues with a moral component involve conflicts between rights, between duties, or between rights and duties. Such problems constitute the very heart of the moral life and therefore the focus of the problematics of moral philosophy. Let us turn to them.

9.3 ❖ RIGHT AND DUTY

If no one had any rights, there would be no moral problems because nobody would be called upon to help anyone else meet his rights. Likewise, there would be no moral problems if no one had any duties, for failing to do one's duty might inconvenience someone but should not elicit any moral censorship. But of course every able person, in any sustainable society, is given some rights and assigned duties of various kinds. The question is then not whether there are rights and duties, but which ones are legitimate, and which ones among the latter are primary and which ones secondary. For instance, are all property rights inalienable? Are we compelled to kill the enemy in war? Are the rights to procreation and free speech boundless?

The amoral person does not pose himself such questions, but just looks up a conventional list of do's and don'ts. For example, if a religious fundamentalist consults his sacred scriptures, he will know what to do with unbelievers, blasphemers, adulteresses, homosexuals, and abortionists: kill them.

By contrast, the moral person will examine the moral questions that concern him or his community, and he will do so not in the light of a tradition but in that of the best available knowledge. For example, he will oppose the death penalty on the strength of (a) the empirical findings that capital punishment is not an effective deterrent, that it has made many innocent victims, and that it sets a bad example; and (b) the humanistic moral and political principles that one's life belongs only to oneself, and that in a good society it is everyone's duty to help protect other people's lives.

That is, the moral person will be neither the prisoner of his passions nor that of his society: he will fit neither the naturalistic nor the culturalist model of man. He will, instead, seek to ground his choices and decisions on "strong reasons" (Boudon 1999)—which, depending on the problem, may be prudential considerations, empirical data, well-confirmed scientific hypotheses, or universal moral principles that have proved to promote individual welfare and social values. In particular, the moral person will start by finding out the moral rights and duties to be invoked in deliberating over the social action in question. Let us then proceed to proposing characterizations of such rights and duties.

A right is a permission, and a legal right is a permission entrenched in the legal code of the land. For example, in all civilized countries but the United States, ordinary citizens do not have the right to bear arms for the simple reason that they do not have the right to take lives. By contrast, a moral right is a permission that may or may not be guaranteed by the law of the land. For example, according to Locke, Stuart Mill, and the socialists, everyone has the right to enjoy the fruits of his labors, although so far no society has transformed this moral right into a legal one—except perhaps on paper.

Just as a legal right is one entrenched in some code of law, so a moral right is one that occurs in, or is based on, some moral code. Moral codes are neither natural nor God-given: they are just as artificial (man-made) as the legal codes. The difference is that the moral rights, unlike most legal rights, are anchored in basic human needs. For instance, the right to work derives from the needs to make a living and feeling useful and therefore wanted. An ideal legal code would be one wherein legal and moral rights coincide. As a matter of fact, such convergence has been at work since the mid-eighteenth century. That is, by and large, legal progress has matched moral progress—albeit discontinuously.

Two kinds of moral right may be distinguished: basic (or primary), and secondary. A moral right is *basic* if its practice contributes to the agent's welfare without jeopardizing other individuals' ability to exercise the same right. By contrast, a moral right is *secondary* if its practice contributes to someone's reasonable happiness without interfering with other persons' basic rights. For instance, everyone has a basic right to education, but the right to study philosophy at the taxpayer's expense is secondary, or perhaps a privilege rather than a right.

Duties are parallel. If a person has a basic moral right to something, then another person has the *primary* duty to help her exercise it if no one else can do it better in his place. (For example, if I see someone suffering an accident, and nobody else is capable of helping her, I have the basic moral duty to lend her a helping hand.) And if a person has a secondary right, then another has the *secondary* moral duty to help her practice it if no one else is in a position to do it better. For example, I have the secondary moral duty of helping my neighbor's child to study for her philosophy exam, since nobody else is at hand.

The preceding elucidations invite the following moral rules.

Norm 1 All basic rights and duties are inalienable, unless they are the subject of a negotiation leading to a fair (equitable) contract among able adults under the supervision of a third party capable of enforcing the contract.

Norm 2 (1) The basic moral rights and duties have precedence over the corresponding secondary ones. (2) The basic moral duties have precedence over the secondary moral rights. (3) In case of conflict between a right and a duty, the agent has the right to choose either, subject to condition (2). (4) In case of conflict between two rights, the agent has the right to choose the one that suits him best, provided it does not infringe upon anyone else's basic rights. (5) In case of conflict between two duties, the agent has the duty to choose the one that suits best the beneficiary's interests, provided it does not infringe on any of the agent's own basic rights.

Norm 3 The conventional and legal norms should be consistent with the moral norms.

These three postulates have a number of logical consequences. One of them is the following

Theorem 1 Every right implies a duty.

Proof Consider a toy universe composed of two persons, to be called 1 and 2. Further, call N_i a basic need and R_i the corresponding right, with i = 1, 2. Analogously, call D_{12} the duty of person 1 to person 2 with regard to her need N_2, and D_{21} the duty of person 2 to person 1 with respect to her need N_1. The gist of the first two norms may now be symbolized as follows:

Norm 1 $(N_1 \Rightarrow R_1)$ & $(N_2 \Rightarrow R_2.)$
Norm 2 $[R_1 \Rightarrow (R_1 \Rightarrow D_{21})]$ & $[R_2 \Rightarrow (R_2 \Rightarrow D_{12})]$.

By the principle of the hypothetical syllogism, it follows that

$[N_1 \Rightarrow (R_1 \Rightarrow D_{21})]$ & $[N_2 \Rightarrow (R_2 \Rightarrow D_{12})]$.

We now introduce as a lemma the platitude that we all have basic needs. We conjoin it with the last formula, and use the modus ponens rule of inference to obtain the desired conclusion:

Theorem 1 $(R_1 \Rightarrow D_{21})$ & $(R_2 \Rightarrow D_{12})$.

Finally, this theorem, jointly with Norm 1, implies the

Corollary Everyone has some duties.

I apologize to the reader unfamiliar with logical symbols. But I wanted to make the point that exactness is better than sloppiness: it brings clarity, and thus facilitates systemicity, which in turn enhances consistency and deductive power. Consequently, exactness minimizes endless barren debates over what exactly did author so and so really mean. More on the virtues of exactness in the next chapter.

9.4 ❖ AGATHONISM: A HUMANIST ETHICS

What is good? Anything valuable or that helps attain something valuable is good. What is right? Anything that helps exercise moral rights or moral duties is right—even if it involves infringing upon the law of the land. So much for a formal characterization of the good and the right. Let us now put these definitions to work.

Postulate 1 Whatever contributes to the welfare of an individual without jeopardizing the basic rights of any others, is both good and right.

Postulate 2 Everyone has the right to enjoy life and the duty to help others enjoy life.

These two principles, like any others in any field, are justifiable in two ways: by their consequences, and by their compatibility with other formulas in the same field and in neighboring fields. (The former kind of consistency is internal, the latter external.) Let us see how they fare in both ways.

Clearly, both principles promote the pursuit of happiness within reasonable bounds—that is, not at the expense of physical or mental health, or at the expense of others. Both synthesize selfishness, which we need to survive, with altruism, which we need to feel good and live in the company of others. So much for considerations of utility or prudence.

The above principles are consistent with at least two humanistic principles. One is the principle of moral equality, according to which everyone has the same basic rights and duties as everyone else. (This principle is of course far broader than the isonomy principle, of equality under the law.) The other is the principle of fairness, according to which the exercise of rights is only fair if accompanied by that of the concomitant duties—and conversely. (This includes the principle that rewards should match contributions.)

So much for the moral philosophy that I call *agathonism* (from *agathon*, Greek for "good"). It is broader than both Kant's deontologism and Bentham's utilitarianism because it places duties and rights on a par. It is also broader than contractualism because it concerns not only people capable of signing on the dotted line, but also infants, the disabled, and generally people unable to understand explicit contracts—or unwilling to let morality collapse onto the law of the land. And, more importantly, agathonism is explicitly realist and materialist (in the ontological, not moral sense). Therefore it holds a promise of practicality.

9.5 ❖ TECHNOHOLODEMOCRACY: A HUMANIST SOCIAL PHILOSOPHY

Social (or political) philosophy is a branch of practical philosophy (or philosophical technology). It is concerned with analyzing, evaluating, and sketching political projects aimed at maintaining, reforming, or replacing a social order. This task is usually accomplished by legislators, statesmen, and political analysts with little if any help of either moral principles or social-science findings. I claim that the tasks of social philosophy are to examine and evaluate the various known social orders, and to propose reforming them on the strength of both scientific social studies and a realistic moral philosophy such as agathonism. Only such double foundation can avoid unfeasible utopias, particularly those that presume to attain the perfect social order through regulating every aspect of life.

I suggest that it is worthwhile contemplating a social and political philosophy summarized into the following hexagon centered in agathonism: Equality, liberty, solidarity, self-government, justice, and technical expertise. (The first three components constitute of course the slogan of the French Revolution.) Let me explain briefly.

Equality is here conceived in a broad sense: as the absence of gender and race discrimination, and as equal opportunity of access to wealth, culture, and political power. Liberty is the freedom to be what one wishes to be, as long as such an attempt does not entail a burden on society and does not infringe on other people's basic values: My liberty ends where yours begins. Solidarity (or fraternity, or better yet siblinghood) is the readiness to help and the freedom to ask for help. Self-government is democracy in every social system above the family level: in the workplace and the voluntary association, as well as on all levels of government. It is, in Lincoln's words, government of the people, by the people, for the people. It, together with equality, implies that cooperatives are socially superior to corporations—a point made long ago by Mill (1965 [1871]), but ignored by other socialists. Justice is a corollary of equality, but it can only be enforced by solidarity. Finally, technical expertise is necessary in any complex society, if only to avoid waste.

The basis of the hexagon is equality. This is the main feature because it is nec-essary for liberty, solidarity, self-government, justice, and impartial technical expertise. Indeed, without equality some people are bound to dominate others and thus jeopardize the liberty of the greater number. Without equality there can be no solidarity, which consists in reciprocity or mutual help, not in charity. Without equality there can be no self-government (democracy) because the powerful will rule over the rest. Without equality there can be no justice either, because the rulers will be able to bend in their own favor the laws or their implementation. Finally, without equality technical expertise is likely to favor the powerful because technologists, as has been aptly said, are always on tap, never on top.

As for liberty, it is necessary not only for self-realization but also to defend equality and justice by word or deed, as well as to run for office and cast consci-entious ballots. Solidarity is necessary to promote trust, decrease social stress, resolve conflicts, and reduce government to a minimum. Self-government (democracy) is necessary to implement equality: to give everyone a chance to participate in the affairs that may concern them. Justice is necessary to protect equality, freedom, and self-government. And technical expertise—particularly in law, management, normative economics, and politology—is necessary to opti-mize governance. Nothing is more ineffective and therefore costly and time-consuming than an assembly of ill-informed people. And nothing is more dan-gerous than a charismatic but ignorant ruler with enormous power.

In sum, equality supports liberty, solidarity, democracy, justice, and impar-tial technical expertise. However, egalitarianism need not be construed literally, as actual equality of all. Were it possible, a society of nearly identical individuals would be boring, stagnant, and even unsustainable. We should cherish indi-vidual diversity along with moral equality. Moreover, only the latter, jointly with liberty, can safeguard and favor the diversity of individuals. For, without equality and the liberty required to defend it, there might be intolerance to the deviant—in particular the talented and the nonconformist. Hence, gray unifor-mity will be enforced in the name of tradition, common sense, or even decency.

Now, if diversity is tolerated, then some individuals will stand out, and will therefore be regarded, rightly or wrongly, as being more meritorious than others.

In particular, some persons will render more valuable services than others. And, of course, merit should be rewarded because—as Durkheim (1950) and Rawls (1971) have argued—it is in the interest of everyone that competent people render distinguished service to others. However, recognition of merit does not imply meritocracy, or the rule of the more enlightened or more useful members of society, for the very notion of self-government is inconsistent with that of a ruling class. The role of the leader in a democratic society is not to rule but rather to inspire and set the good example, to teach and criticize, to propose and organize, to elicit debate and moderate it, as well as to make accountable, technically competent, and morally right decisions.

The ideal social order that has just been sketched may be called *techno-holodemocracy*, for it involves both integral democracy (biological, economic, political, and cultural) and the use of the social technologies to tackle social issues. However, this social order would be neither attained nor sustained without a minimal moral code. This code would have to be acceptable to everyone because, far from being arbitrary or conventional, it fits the universal craving for the good life in the good society. I submit that agathonism (section 9.4) fills the bill. In short, agathonism lies at the center of the equality-liberty-solidarity-democracy-justice-competence hexagon.

CONCLUSION

There are two main rival schools in modern moral philosophy, namely deontologism and utilitarianism. The pivot of deontologism is duty, whereas that of utilitarianism is right. Whereas deontologism enjoins us to sacrifice pleasure to obligation, utilitarianism invites us to take pleasure. Neither contemplates the desirability or even possibility of joining duties with rights. Hence neither fits real life, which is a tissue of selfish and altruistic actions. Consequently, neither deontologism nor utilitarianism can be an efficient compass to navigate in society. We need an alternative to them. The alternative I propose is agathonism, or the striving for the good of self and others. I claim that, unlike its rivals, agathonism has deep biological and social roots.

All animals are selfish, but gregarious animals are also altruistic in some regards. The reasons, or rather causes, are survival and social coexistence. Indeed, individual survival requires some selfishness, just as sociality—which is necessary for individual well-being—calls for solidarity. In the case of humans, such objective causes are conceptualized and turned into principles that guide choice, planning, and action. Hence these principles can be argued about in the light of their practical consequences as well as of other principles. As a matter of fact, few things are more hotly debated than value judgments and moral norms. The reason is that they guide or misguide action, which is the wellspring of individual and social life.

Axiological and moral principles with neither biological nor social roots will not work. Hence, they are unlikely to last, let alone be observed in all societies. This has been the fate of most ideological (in particular religious) commandments, as well as of most of the moral maxims concocted by philosophers. By contrast, the value judgments and moral norms that help enjoy life—such as those of equality, reciprocity, and loyalty—are objectively valid. This is why they end up by commanding the assent of all reasonable agents. To be sure, the application of any such universal principles will depend on the particular circumstances—just like the principles of physics. But this only proves their universality, not their cultural relativity. Parallel: The general laws of physics must be enriched with subsidiary assumptions and data every time they are used to solve particular problems. Likewise, the legal codes have to supplemented with data and ad hoc considerations every time they are used to pass sentences.

However, a common human nature and the features common to all societies are not enough to justify value judgments and moral norms. We must also be able to argue cogently about them. This is particularly important when judging the worth of new values, new moral rules, or new government policies: We need to know whether they constitute real advances rather than commercial or political gimmicks. For example, the citizens of a democracy are entitled to know why fighting inflation at all costs should be preferable to tolerating a modest rate of inflation as long as it allows for a decent level of employment and the maintenance of basic social services. Another example: We need solid reasons to advocate secular public education, universal medicare, transparent (accountable) public administration, or the conditioning of foreign aid to the observance of human rights. The "reasons" in question should be solid social science findings, effective sociotechnological rules, firm empirical data, and universal moral principles, rather than untried traditional beliefs or ideological slogans.

That is, our axiology and ethics must be realist, cognitivist, and ratio-empiricist, rather than authoritarian, emotivist, intuitionist, utilitarian, or relativist. And, if they are to be geared to individual well-being and are to promote social values, axiology and ethics should also be systemist rather than either individualist or holist. The reason is that humans are cognizant and active components of social systems rather than either self-reliant loners or nondescript drops in an uncontrollable ocean.

To conclude, because they are expected to guide social action, values and morals thrive better on solid materialist and realist soil than in the idealist sky. And, far from being beyond the reach of the scientific method, they are being studied by psychologists and social scientists precisely because they are facts of life rather than denizens of Plato's Realm of Ideas, Dilthey's "objective mind," or Popper's "world 3." This makes it possible to protect or perfect them with deeds, not just words.

10

CRISIS AND RECONSTRUCTION IN PHILOSOPHY

There seems to be consensus that philosophy is currently at a low ebb. Some even claim that it is dead. This idea is not new: it was stated by Comte and repeated by Nietzsche, later on by Wittgenstein, and nowadays by Richard Rorty and others. Moreover, there is a whole Death of Philosophy industry. In particular, there are ever more studies on three notorious enemies of philosophy: Nietzsche, Wittgenstein, and Heidegger. Ironically, some professors make a living from burying, exhuming, and reburying philosophy: their activity is more necrophilic than philosophical.

The claim that philosophy is dead is false, and its propagation is immoral. The idea is false because all humans philosophize from the moment they become conscious. That is, we all ask and debate general questions, some of them profound, that trespass the disciplinary frontiers. And the professional broadcasting of the idea that philosophy is dead is immoral because one ought not to cultivate what one regards as a graveyard.

Philosophy is far from being dead but, in my opinion, it is stagnant. In fact, few if any radically new and correct philosophical ideas, let alone systems, are being proposed. Gone are the days of exciting new and grand philosophical ideas that spilled over other disciplines or even the public—for better or for worse. Today most philosophers teach, analyze, comment on, or embellish other scholars' ideas. (For instance, a comment on Cicero's discussion of Clitomachus's account of Carneades' views is likely to be regarded as the summit of serious scholarship.) Others play frivolous if ingenious academic games. Few philosophers think on a large scale: most are schoolmen without a school. However, if the philosophy looks barren, the genuine philosopher will attempt to cultivate it instead of just lamenting its decay.

In this chapter I will start by attempting to justify my claim that philosophy is in crisis. I will then proceed to try and find the causes of this crisis. Finally, the options of whoever endeavors to reconstruct philosophy will be explored.

10.1 ❖ THE CRISIS

A simple experiment should suffice to check whether philosophy is indeed in crisis. Compare what you learn sampling the recent philosophical production with what you learn reading the same number of recent scientific papers. After one day of reading philosophy and another of reading science, you are likely to have learned quite a bit of science and hardly any new philosophy. It is not only that very few new ideas are coming from the philosophical workshop, but that most of them are either false or uninteresting.

The following examples are drawn from recent issues of prestigious philosophical journals. They belong in the main branches of our discipline: logic (L), semantics (S), epistemology (E), ontology (O), and practical philosophy (P). In each case I will exhibit an example of a crass error or useless toy, and another of a lacuna.

L1 Predicate. Every statement involves some predicate (or attribute). For example, the predicate in the previous statement is the relation "involves." The general concept of a predicate is usually either taken as a primitive (undefined) in predicate logic, or it is defined in the manner of Frege. According to Frege, a unary (or monadic) predicate, such as "is peopled," is analyzed as a function from a domain of individuals to the set of truth values. That is, $P: D \to \{0,1\}$, where P stands for the predicate, D for its domain, and 0 and 1 symbolize falsity and truth respectively. According to this, the value of the predicate "is long-nosed," for the individual Cyrano would be 1, that is, truth. But this is absurd: the value in question ought to be the proposition "Cyrano is long-nosed." That is, the value of P at c, where c is in D, ought to be Pc, which is a proposition.

I submit then that the correct analysis of a predicate is $P: D \to Q$, where Q is the set of all the propositions containing P. (The generalization to n-ary predicates is $P: A \times B \times \ldots \times N \to Q$, where $\times$ designates the cartesian product.) If we wish to rope in truth, we shall have to introduce a truth-valuation function V from Q to the set of truth values, that is, $V: Q \to \{0,1\}$. The composition of the functions V and P yields what may be called the corresponding Frege predicate $F = V \circ P: D \to \{0,1\}$. However, F is only good to form a commutative diagram with P and V.

L2 Modal logic. The logic of possibility and necessity, or modal logic, is still fashionable. It was crafted seven decades ago to solve two problems at once: those of defining the relation of entailment (as different from that of implication), and the ontological concept of possibility. But in fact it has solved neither problem. Indeed, the syntactic concept of entailment ($\vdash$) has been elucidated by ordinary logic, and the semantic concept ($\vDash$) by model theory. The mathematicians, who are nowadays in charge of logic, are unlikely to have even heard about the concept of strict implication that was expected to do the job of entailment. As for the ontological concept of possibility, modal logicians have approached it the wrong way, since the operands of the modal operator $\Diamond$ (possibly) and its compounds, such as $\neg\Diamond\neg$ (necessarily) are propositions, whereas they ought to be facts since only facts can be really possible. Propositions can only be more or less plausible (relative to some body of knowledge) and more or less true. If ever the need for a qualitative theory of real possibility is felt, its modal operators will have to bear on facts. In short, modal logic—which was originally a serious if ill-conceived enterprise—has not delivered the goods: it is but a jeu d'esprit. So much for a first error.

S1 "Semantic" conception of scientific theories. The word "model" does not mean the same in logic and mathematics than in the factual sciences and technologies. In the former, particularly in model theory, every model is one of an abstract (uninterpreted) theory, such as set theory or group theory. And the model of an abstract theory is but an example of it. For example, the set of all plane rotations around a point is a model of group theory, because any two rotations combine forming a third, and every rotation can be undone when combined with its inverse. By contrast, in the factual sciences and technology, a theoretical model is a theory of concrete things of a restricted kind, such as the class of helium atoms or the collection of supermarkets. Hence, the theoretical models have real referents and are true or false to some extent. However, the philosophy of science initiated by Patrick Suppes, and elaborated by Joseph Sneed, Wolfgang Stegmüller, Ulises Moulines, and others rests on the confusion between the two concepts of a model. This confusion is just as blatant as the confusion between algebraic rings with wedding rings. As a consequence, the view in question misses the marrow of the semantics of scientific theories, which is their reference to the real world—on which more anon.

S2 Reference. None of the well-known semantic theories in either philosophy or linguistics contains the concept of reference or aboutness. This is not surprising given the lack of interest of grammarians and linguistic philosophers in the external world: theirs is a world of words. Worse, the concept of reference is often confused with that extension or coverage. Yet, the extension of a predicate is not necessarily the same as its reference. For example, the predicate "is ghostly" has an empty extension even though its referents inhabit mythology and parapsychology. To find out the reference class of a predicate we must start by analyzing the way we did in *L2*.

I postulate that the reference class of a unary predicate $P: A \rightarrow Q$ is its domain A. That is, $\mathcal{R}(P) = A$. On the other hand, the extension of the same predicate is $\mathcal{E}(P) = \{x \mid Px\}$. The difference between reference and extension becomes even clearer in the case of an n-ary predicate $P: A \times B \times \ldots \times N \rightarrow Q$. Whereas its reference class is a "flat" set, its extension is a "spiked" one, that is, a cartesian product. Indeed, in this case $\mathcal{R}(P) = A \cup B \cup \ldots \cup N$, whereas $\mathcal{E}(P) = \{<a, b, c, \ldots, n> \mid Pab \ldots n\}$. This closes a scandalous hole in philosophical semantics.

Moreover, my proposal allows one to find out what theories are about. This is particularly useful in such controversial cases as the relativistic and quantum theories, the theory of evolution, and economic theories. For instance, instead of stating dogmatically that quantum mechanics refers to experiments or even to experimenters, one analyzes its key predicates, such as the Hamiltonian operator. The outcome is that these predicates refer to physical things such as atoms, whether or not they are under observation. Thus, philosophical semantics ceases to be a formal game to become a useful tool for analyzing scientific theories and resolving some philosophico-scientific controversies. In this capacity it is even a spear to slay the constructivist-relativist dragon—of which more follows.

E1 Constructivism-relativism. This is the epistemology inherent in the sociology, anthropology, and philosophy of science inspired by Thomas S. Kuhn and Paul K. Feyerabend, and made fashionable by David Bloor, Bruno Latour, Karen D. Knorr-Cetina, Thomas J. Pinch, Harry Collins, Steven Woolgar, and other contributors to the journal *Social Studies of Science*. According to them, scientists construct reality instead of studying it; and they do not cooperate to understand reality, but struggle for power. (Thus, they turn Robert K. Merton's classical analysis upside down.) And, since they regard facts as conventional constructions, they claim that there are as many truths as social groups. That is, the validity of any piece of knowledge would be relative to group, society, or circumstance: there would be no universal or cross-cultural truths.

This cartoon of science does not explain why scientists perform observations, measurements, experiments, or statistical analyses; it explains neither the progress of science, nor its universality, nor its practical success in technology. Yet, despite this total failure, constructivism-relativism is in fashion, at least in the faculties of arts in the industrialized countries and their imitators. A sociological explanation of this fact is overdue. However, I surmise that it has three main causes. One is that attacking science is easier than learning it; a second is that the doctrine jibes with the current revival of the Counter-Enlightenment philosophies, in particular intuitionism, vitalism, phenomenology, and existentialism; a third is that it appears to attack the powers that be. The facts that some philosophers have jumped on this wagon, and that most have remained silent, indicate that the rationalist and realist parties are weak.

E2 Reduction and fusion. Everyone talks about reductionism, whether for or against, but few seem to know exactly what it is. Indeed, most of the many studies on reduction are inadequate: no detailed study of particular cases of authentic or putative reduction has been performed. (In particular, there is no satisfactory study of the oldest and most cited cases of reduction, namely those of classical thermodynamics to statistical mechanics, and of classical mechanics to quantum mechanics.) No wonder that such philosophical studies have been ineffective to evaluate the most popular reduction projects of the day: geneticism ("Biology is reducible to genetics, and the latter to chemistry"), cognitive neuroscience ("Mental states are brain states"), sociobiology ("Everything social is traceable to a biological root"), and "economic imperialism" ("Everything social is economic, and everything economic boils down to exchange relations ruled by rational choices").

A closer study of reduction shows that the actual cases of radical reduction, such as those of statics to dynamics, optics to electromagnetism, and thermodynamics to statistical mechanics, are rare. Most reductions, such as those of chemistry to physics, or genetics to molecular biology, are moderate or weak in the sense that they require the addition of auxiliary hypotheses. Besides, even the best-known studies of reduction have only taken into account the logical side of the question, overlooking the ontological and epistemological aspects. As a consequence, it has not been understood that one may have ontological reduction without a concomitant epistemological reduction. This is the case with the psychoneural identity project. Indeed, it involves an ontological reduction ("Everything mental is neurophysiological"), but it has not eliminated some typically psychological concepts and methods, such as the idea of visual illusion and the measurement of reaction times.

Besides, reduction is less common than fusion, or the formation of an interdiscipline, such as biophysics, biochemistry, neurolinguistics, social psychology, sociolinguistics, socioeconomics, and anthropological archaeology. To make two disciplines coalesce it is necessary and sufficient that their respective reference classes have a nonempty overlap; that they share some specific (or "technical") concepts; and that there be some "glue formulas" where concepts of the two disciplines occur, such as "Speech is the specific activity of the Wernicke and Broca areas" in the case of neurolinguistics, and "All market transactions are embedded in social networks" in the case of socioeconomics. So much for the project of covering a third hole in the philosophical field.

O1 Supervenience. It is said of properties of certain kinds that they supervene on properties of a different type, when the possession of the former "depends" on that of the latter. For example, the psychological properties supervene upon certain biological properties, which in turn supervene on certain physicochemical properties. But the precise form of such dependence has never been specified in a precise manner. Hence, the concept of supervenience remains just as vague as when G. E. Moore introduced it nearly a century ago, or when Donald Davidson popularized it three decades ago.

Indeed, the standard analysis of the concept, due to Jaegwon Kim, is basically flawed because it overlooks the things possessing the properties, it is static, and it involves negative and disjunctive properties. In short, it confuses, in a Platonic vein, properties with attributes. (The set of predicates with the same domain constitutes a Boolean algebra, whereas the set of properties of concrete things of a given species is only a semigroup.) Moreover, talk of supervenience skirts the far tougher and more interesting problem of emergence, which is linked to the questions of novelty, evolution, levels, and reduction. For example, one would like to know how life emerged from abiotic materials; how speech may have evolved from grunts, calls, and gestures; and how the state emerged from the council of elders in the first urban societies. To be sure, these problems are beyond the philosopher's ken. But the philosopher can elucidate the concept of emergence, namely thus: "A property of systems of a given kind is emergent if it is not possessed by any of the components of the system." For instance, temperature, specific heat, and viscosity are emergent properties of liquid bodies, not of their constituent molecules. Similarly, the mental faculties are properties of numerous systems of neurons, not of individual cells, and they have emerged in the course of evolution, and also emerge in the course of individual development. Unsurprisingly, whereas the notion of supervenience is unknown to scientists, that of emergence occurs with increasing frequency in the scientific literature.

O2 Existence. Everyone, save perhaps some logicians and mathematicians, believes that existence is a property and, moreover, the most important of all properties. The reason for the exception is that the mathematical objects do not exist by themselves, but only by postulation or proof. Moreover, the "existential" quantifier can usually be interpreted as "some," and it is definable in terms of the universal quantifier, namely thus: "Some are *F*" is equivalent to "Not all are not-*F*." In sum, logical and mathematical existence are noncommittal. Hence, talk of their ontological commitment via the "existential" quantifier is mistaken. If we want to exactify the concept of real existence, as it occurs outside logic and mathematics, we must turn to ontology.

The intuitive concept of existence can be rendered exactly as follows. Let U be an arbitrary universe of discourse or reference class, and χ_U the characteristic function of U. [$\chi_U(x) = 1$ if $x \in U$, and 0 if $x \notin U$.] We stipulate that " $\chi_U(x) = 1$" is the same as "$E_U x$," to be interpreted as "x exists en U." In other words, the (contextual) existence predicate is the function $E_U: U \to P$, where P designates the set of all the existential propositions, such that, if $x \in U$, then $E_U(x) = [\chi_U(x) = 1]$. If U is a set C of conceptual objects, such as numbers, then E_C designates the concept of ideal (or formal) existence. On the other hand, if U is a collection M of concrete objects, such as photons, then E_M designates the concept of material or real existence. In this way we can formalize the following statement, which would be ill-formed if "exists" were confused with "some": "Some objects exist really," or $\exists x(Ox \ \& \ E_M x)$. (In turn, the philosophical concept of materiality, which is broader than its physical counterpart, may be defined thus: "x is material $=_{df} x$ is changeable." In words: To be is to become.) We have just filled a fourth embarrassing hole.

P1 Instrumental rationality. Utilitarianism and the vast majority of rational-choice models employ a hazy notion of value, namely that of subjective value, or utility. This concept is conceptually fuzzy, empirically vacuous, or both. It is fuzzy unless defined in mathematical terms, and it is empirically vacuous unless checked against empirical data about the way real people attribute values to goods and bads of various kinds. Now, most authors place only two necessary conditions on a utility function: that it increases with the quantity of the good concerned, and that its increase be decelerated—which of course is the law of decreasing returns. Since both conditions are satisfied by infinitely many functions, they do not define the concept of subjective value, any more than "biped and cruel" do not define humanity. Obviously, any theory containing that concept is imprecise and, for this reason, it is not empirically testable with any precision. Hence such a theory cannot be proclaimed to be true.

This criticism holds, in particular, for the so-called principle of instrumental rationality, which states that we act, or at least ought to act, so as to maximize the expected value of the outcome of any of our actions. Worse, the expected value equals, by definition, the product of the subjective value by the subjective probability—another ghostly concept. The fantasy becomes delirious when the expected utility of an entire society is calculated by adding the individual utilities, as if the satisfaction of the desires of one person did not interfere with that of other individuals—and as if utilities were additive like lengths. In short, instrumental rationality is not altogether rational and it enjoys no empirical support. Only a far more modest norm can be upheld, such as "Rational people estimate costs and benefits and prefer to take the actions that are likely to be the more cost-beneficial to self or others."

P2 Objective value. An object can be assigned a subjective value, it can possess an objective value, or it may have both an objective and a subjective value, though not necessarily in the same respect. We still do not know how to exactify adequately the former—and, in any event, that is a task for psychology. As for the objective value of a good, it may be estimated in various ways, according to its kind: by its usefulness, price, efficiency, durability, popularity, or what have you. However, in value theory and ethics we are only interested in a general concept of objective value, if only to serve in discussions involving the concepts of moral fact and moral truth, and of the possible relevance of science and technology to valuation and moral norm.

To exactify the notion of objective value we may start with the intuitive idea that a thing is useful or beneficial to the extent that it satisfies some needs or desires. Using the last two concepts as primitives, we stipulate that the *objective utility* of an object a to an animal or social group b equals the set of needs (N) or desires (D) of b that a meets. (Note that relativity to a subject is not the same as subjectivity. We know our desires but we may take some of them for needs, and may not know all our real needs.) That is, we stipulate that $U(a,b) = \{c \in N \cup D \mid Sacb\}$, where $Sacb$ abbreviates "object a satisfies need or desire c of individual b." This qualitative concept of objective utility allows one to define the corresponding comparative concept. We shall say that object a is *objectively preferable* to object b for subject c (that is, $a \geq_c b$) if the utility of b for c is included in that of a. That is, $a \geq_c b =_{df} U(b,c) \subseteq U(a,c)$. Obviously, the relation $\geq_c$ inherits the antisymmetry and transitivity of the relation $\subseteq$ of inclusion.

In short, we have identified five big blunders and as many large lacunae in contemporary philosophy. I believe that these ten examples show the confusion and irrelevance of a good chunk of fashionable philosophy. And I have not undertaken the easy task of pointing out the mountain of existentialist, phenomenological, hermeneutic, or deconstructivist nonsense. I have restricted my examination to a few if important blunders, and another of embarrassing silences in sober philosophy. Along the way I have indicated how to correct those mistakes and fill those lacunae. I shall return to the constructive task in section 10.3.

10.2 ❖ CAUSES OF THE CRISIS

I submit that current philosophy suffers from the following ten ailments.

(1) *Excessive professionalization.* In the old times philosophy was a calling: it only attracted amateurs enamored of general problems and bold if often vague or even wacky ideas. From Kant on, philosophy has become one more profession. (Science has suffered the same process since the end of World War II.) Technical competence, and the attendant caution, often replace passion. The philosophy chairs have become so numerous that many of them are held by persons with neither avocation nor vision. Worse, since employment and promotion depend on publication, far too many philosophical productions are potboilers, hence boring or irritating. The profession has thus been filled with functionaries that are neither advancing philosophy nor transmitting an enthusiasm they lack, and without which no great enterprise can be undertaken.

(2) *Confusion between philosophizing and chronicling.* Doubtless, a knowledge of the past of his discipline is more important to a philosopher than to a scientist or a technologist. Whereas the latter are unlikely to consult any papers published twenty years earlier, philosophers are bound to consult books written twenty centuries ago. This is because many important philosophical problems have ancient roots and are still open. The history of philosophy is therefore a guide that sometimes inspires new ideas, and at other times spares the repetition of old mistakes. This is why it is regrettable that so many contemporary philosophers, under the influence of linguistic philosophy, hermeneutics, phenome-

nology, or existentialism, are disconnected from the past. This severance is just as pernicious as taking the history of philosophy, a valuable tool, for a goal. After all, the historian of philosophy studies original philosophers, not fellow historians. Yet, most doctoral dissertations in philosophy deal with other philosophers' opinions rather than with philosophical problems of current interest. The historicist distortion is such that the most popular philosophical dictionaries of the day—unlike the classical ones such as Lalande's—look more like cemeteries than workshops: they include biographies of long-forgotten philosophers, and discuss concepts and theories that are useless to tackle the philosophical problematics posed by contemporary developments in mathematics, science, technology, or society at large.

(3) *Mistaking obscurity for profundity*. Deep thought is hard to understand, but it can be grasped with some effort. In philosophy, obscure writing is sometimes just a cloak to pass off platitude or nonsense for depth. This is how Heidegger won his reputation as a deep thinker: by writing such sentences as "Time is the ripening of temporality." Had he not been a German professor and the star pupil of another professor famous for his hermetism—namely Husserl—Heidegger might have been taken for a madman or an impostor.

(4) *Obsession with language*. No doubt, philosophers must be careful with words. But they share this responsibility with all other intellectuals, whether they be journalists or mathematicians, lawyers or demographers. Only poets can afford to write about lucky winds or drunken ships. Besides, it is one thing to write correctly and another to turn language into the central theme of philosophy—without, however, paying any attention to the experts, namely linguists. Philosophers are not equipped to find out how certain words are used in a given linguistic community: this is a task for field linguists and anthropologists. Nor should they decree that grammar rules over content. Authentic philosophers work on ontological, epistemological, semantical, or ethical problems.

Certainly, philosophers can be interested in the general concept of a language, but only as one of many general ideas, on a par with those of matter, chance, life, mind, knowledge, morals, culture, or history. If they restrict their attention to language, they are bound to irritate linguists and bore everyone else. In this way they will enrich neither linguistics nor philosophy. Nor has the "linguistic turn" in social studies—inspired by Dilthey, Wittgenstein, Heidegger, and the deconstructionists—resulted in any new social findings. It could not have done so because social facts are not texts or discourses: they lack syntactic, semantic, and phonological properties. Moreover, the linguistic approach does not even help analyze social documents such as economic statistics and legal codes because they refer to extralinguistic facts. In sum, glossocentrism is mistaken and barren. But it is easy, since it only requires familiarity with one language. This explains its popularity.

(5) *Idealism.* Although idealism is one of the dominant academic philosophies, it is just as exhausted as Marxism: it has produced no new ideas in recent times. Objective idealism, from Plato to Leibniz, and from Bolzano to Frege, is only viable in the philosophy of mathematics—and even so on condition that live mathematicians and active mathematical communities are overlooked. All the other disciplines, whether scientific or technological, are tacitly materialist since they deal with concrete objects. (Recall chapter 3.) True, the hermeneutic thesis that social facts are "texts or like texts" has been well received in the shantytowns that surround the social sciences. But it is barren because it neither describes nor explains any social facts and, a fortiori, it cannot guide social-policy making. (Recall chapter 5.)

As for subjective idealism, from Berkeley to Kant, and from Mach to Goodman, it only inheres in some action theories and in the social studies centered on subjective probabilities and utilities. This approach is unscientific because it involves no empirical tests. Nor is it deep because, in ignoring material things and processes, such as natural resources and work, it does not help understand what happens around us. To understand or alter reality, whether natural, social, or mixed, we must start by assuming that it is concrete rather than a subjective experience. We must also adopt a realist epistemology, one helping explore both reality and the ways to alter it. Focusing on inner life can only lead to some forms of art.

(6) *Exaggerate attention to miniproblems and fashionable academic games.* Examples: Possible worlds metaphysics, the *grue* paradox, Newcomb's problem, and asking whether Plato would retain his name in alternative worlds. Why kill time thinking of a handful of artificial miniproblems when knowledge and action pose so many authentic and urgent problems? For example, why do not moral philosophers devote more attention to the problems affecting billions of people—such as those of poverty and unemployment—than to those that touch only a few, such as those of abortion and euthanasia? Just because religionists are more upset by the latter than by the former?

(7) *Insubstantial formalism and formless insubstantiality.* William James famously classed philosophers into tough-minded and tender-minded. Regrettably, nowadays the tough-minded, if skillful in the handling of formal tools,

seldom tackle bulky problems. They usually work under the delusion that logic suffices to reveal the secrets of the universe—something that actually only science can do. By contrast, some of the tender-minded brave tough problems but without making use of formal tools. The result of combining hard methods with bland problems is triviality. That of combining soft methods with tough problems is disappointment. And handling bland problems with soft methods, in the manner of the linguistic (Wittgensteinian) philosophers, only elicits yawns.

Formal tools serve not only to clarify concepts but also to debunk any number of foggy received ideas. Let us examine two cases: the utilitarian maxim and Pareto's optimality condition. The former, proposed by Helvétius, copied by Priestley, and adopted by Bentham, is "the greatest happiness of the greatest number of people." To examine this idea, imagine the total available happiness to be like a pie to be divided among n people in equal slices of size h, where this is the slice angle in radians. Since the size of the whole pie is 2π, the budget constraint is $nh \leq 2\pi$. Obviously, an increase in n entails a decrease in h and conversely. Hence n and h cannot be maximized at the same time. In sum, the nice-sounding utilitarian maxim is absurd.

Pareto's optimality, widely used in ethics as well as in economics, is the condition of a society in which "no one can be made better off without someone else being made worse off." However, any distribution, whether equitable or not, satisfies this condition. Indeed, consider the simplest case, of a total quantity c of goods to be divided among two people. If x and y are the quantities assigned to the first and the second person respectively, they are subject to the condition "$x + y = c$." Obviously, any increase in x entails a decrease in y and conversely. (That is, $\Delta x = -\Delta y$.) Thus, Pareto's condition is satisfied regardless of the amounts x and y. In short, Pareto's optimality has nothing to do with either economic efficiency or fairness: it is just empty.

(8) *Fragmentarism and aphorism.* We have paid dearly for the failure of the "grand" philosophical systems, such as those of Aristotle, Aquinas, Leibniz, Wolff, Kant, Hegel, or Lotze. The price has been diffidence for any attempts to build philosophical systems, and the concomitant preference for the brief essay or even the aphorism. Nowadays the expression *esprit de système* is used in a pejorative sense. But this diffidence is as unreasonable as it would be to mistrust physics or engineering because sometimes they fail. What is wrong is not to systematize (organize) ideas, but to cling dogmatically to this or that product of such effort. It is wrong because all things and all ideas come in systems.

We ought to systematize ideas because stray ideas are unintelligible; because we need logical consistency; because deductive power is desirable; and because the world is not a pile of unrelated facts but a system of interrelated things and processes. In context, every idea drags other ideas. For example, every concept of truth involves the concepts of proposition and meaning. Second example: Relativistic physics has taught us that the notion of time must be treated in combination with the ideas of space, matter, and event. Third: The idea of human action relates the concepts of person, intention, value, goal, norm, outcome, social environment, and circumstance. In short, we need systems of ideas in all fields of learning and all walks of life, because the world is a system, our knowledge another system, and living involves interacting with systems. Why should philosophy be the exception? Just because the puny and ephemeral is easier than the great and durable?

(9) *Detachment from the intellectual engines of modern civilization.* These engines are science, technology, and ideology. Detachment from them expedites wild and anachronistic speculation. Examples: The philosophies of mind that ignore the very existence of cognitive neuroscience; the philosophies of language that ignore that language is primarily a tool of cognition and social action; the action theories that ignore the most important types of action, namely work and social interaction, as well as the disciplines that deal with action, such as management science and political science; the philosophies of history that ignore the systemic, realist, and materialist approach of the *Annales* school.

(10) *Ivory tower.* Most philosophers live in the proverbial tower. They do not care to know what goes on in other departments or in the society that feeds them. They only read other philosophers and write exclusively for colleagues. They behave as if they were theologians or pure mathematicians. Consequently, their work is seldom of interest to those who work in other fields. Fortunately there are exceptions, namely, the epistemologists who try to understand technology, and the ethicians who tackle such real social issues as overpopulation, environmental degradation, poverty, oppression, and war. But, of course, by definition of "exception" there are few such philosophers. Most contemporary philosophers have neither their feet on the ground nor their eyes fixed on the stars.

So much for a diagnosis of the ailments of contemporary philosophy. Every one of them ought to suffice sending the dear old lady to the emergency wing. All ten necessitate sending her to the intensive care unit. The adequate treatment of the patient is obvious: A transfusion of new and tough problems whose solution would advance knowledge; intensive exercises in conceptual rigor resulting in the elimination of pseudophilosophical toxics; selected morsels of mathematics, science, and technology; training in the detection and inactivation of ideological minefields; and renewal of contacts with the best philosophical tradition. Unless the patient follows this treatment, or a similar one, it will die of hunger and boredom. If this were to happen, its place would be taken by amateur philosophers, which would not be tragic because the best among them would eventually discipline themselves. After all, none of the fathers of philosophy held a philosophy chair, or even a doctorate in philosophy.

10.3 ❖ OPTIONS AND DESIDERATA FOR RECONSTRUCTION

Whoever wishes to wake up the philosophers who dream of possible (or rather impossible) worlds, converse only with the dead, or play academic games can do either of two things. One is to raise hell, the other is to undertake the reconstruction of philosophy—knowing that, though unending, this task is not necessarily Sisyphean. I expect and fear to have accomplished the first task in the preceding pages. Now I proceed to listing some of the options at the disposal of whoever wishes to reconstruct philosophy. They will be listed alphabetically. However, the features in question are interrelated. For example, a closed philosophy, one that owes nothing to the rest of knowledge, is born behind the times; and an anachronistic philosophy is as useless as tedious.

Authentic / fake. Whoever writes hermetic texts like Heidegger's *Sein und Zeit* perpetrates a philosophical imposture. He incurs the same sin as someone who, writing clearly, tackles pseudoproblems or digresses without contributing anything new, as is the case with Wittgenstein's *Philosophical Investigations.* Authentic philosophizing contributes new knowledge, however modest. One can do so in many ways: by restating old problems in a more adequate manner, pointing out new problems, inventing ideas, analyzing concepts or theories, exhibiting previously unnoticed relations, etc.

Clear / obscure. Obscurity is an indicator of incompetence, confusion, or imposture. If we wish competence and authenticity, let us follow Descartes's injunction: let us try to craft clear and distinct ideas—neither obscure nor confused ones. There are two recipes to attain clarity: To analyze with the requisite formal tools, and to systematize—that is, to find or posit relations with other ideas. In sum, let us attempt to do exact and systematic philosophy.

Critical / dogmatic. Original philosophizing is not repetition but opening to question or attempting to solve problems, new or old, on one's own. Nor is it to restrict oneself to criticizing ideas: Criticism is a means to eliminate error, not to invent new ideas. Besides, there are two kinds of criticism: destructive and constructive. The former is unavoidable when the object of criticism has no redeeming features—as are the cases of pseudoscience and pseudophilosophy. But when the object of criticism is mistaken in some regard but not wrongheaded, constructive criticism is called for—that is, a criticism that aims at repairing instead of demolishing. This is the type of criticism characteristic of moderate or tactical skepticism, in contradistinction to radical or systematic skepticism. (See chapter 7.) Regrettably, though standard in mathematics and science, constructive criticism is seldom practiced by philosophers.

Deep / shallow. All good philosophies are radical: that is, they look for the roots of things and the presuppositions (tacit assumptions) behind the explicit assumptions. For example, the radical philosopher does not bother to criticize this or that detail of a probabilistic theory of meaning or truth. Instead, he attacks the very idea that it is possible to attribute probabilities to propositions; he does not call "indeterministic" the probabilistic theories but makes room for them in a broadened concept of determinism as lawfulness; he does not spend time with special models of rational choice but attacks their presupposition that it is possible to assign a probability to any event. The radical philosopher rejects phenomenalism—whether Kantian or positivist—because phenomena (appearances) are mere manifestations, to some observer, of processes inaccessible to the senses. He criticizes value-theoretical absolutism for overlooking local and subjective values just as strongly as he criticizes value-theoretical relativism for overlooking such objective and universal values as life, solidarity, peace, reason, and truth. And he rejects ethical deontologism for ignoring rights, and utilitarianism for underrating duties. The radical philosopher is not distracted by details but is a generalist: he looks for patterns in all fields—or at least he does not discourage such a search.

Enlightened / obscurantist. Enlightened philosophers honor the Enlightenment even while criticizing its limitations, whereas obscurantists follow in the footsteps of the Romantic Counter-Enlightenment. The enlightened philosophies are naturalistic, humanistic, rationalist, empiricist, or both, pro-science, and progressive.

Interesting / boring. There is no stronger deterrent of intellectual work than boredom. Philosophizing should be as exhilarating and pleasant an experience as falling in love. Doing philosophy is exciting when it involves tackling new problems or seeing old problems in a novel way. And studying philosophy is a pleasant task when something new is learned in the process: something that elucidates an idea, solves an open problem, stimulates the imagination, or awakens a new intellectual restlessness. Doing philosophy without ever having the *aha!* or the *eureka!* experiences is just doing one more chore.

Materialism / idealism. An idealist philosophy is of course one that posits the autonomous existence of ideas. Idealism is inconsistent with the factual (or empirical) sciences and the technologies, all of which study, design, or alter concrete things—which are changeable rather than unalterable. Hence, a philosophy that matches science and technology must be materialist—though not vulgar (e.g., physicalist) but emergentist, since many concrete things, such as organisms, social systems, and artifacts have supraphysical (emergent) properties. Materialism denies neither the existence of ideas (in brains) nor the importance of some of them. It only involves regarding ideas as brain processes or as "embodied" in artifacts. To be sure, when analyzing the logical or semantical properties of an idea we feign that it exists independently of biological or social contingencies. This fiction is convenient, even necessary, in mathematics and elsewhere. But it is inadmissible in any ontology that claims to be consistent with science and technology.

Noble / vile. Any doctrine that degrades the human condition and discourages attempts at enhancing human dignity deserves being called vile. Examples: racism and the dogmas of original sin, predestination, and the noble lie; Freud's dogma that infancy is destiny: that no one can fully recover from infantile traumas; the theses that poverty is the punishment for sins incurred in an earlier life, or the price for inferior genetic endowment; that humans are only sophisticated automata; that individuals are like leaves swept by the hurricane of history; that social progress is impossible: that "the poor will always be with us"; that we live mainly to die (Heidegger's *Sein zum Tode*); that the masses are herds that deserve being led by inscrutable and unaccountable supermen; that the truth is or ought to be accessible only to a social elite; that reason is useless or pernicious; and that we need two morals: one for the rulers and another for the ruled. By contrast, a noble philosophy is one that helps improve the human condition. It does so by promoting research, rational debate, grounded valuation, generous action, good will, liberty, equality, and solidarity.

Open / closed. A philosophy can be either open or closed to the world and to the rest of knowledge. If closed, it commits the sin of willful ignorance. A philosophy can also be open or closed in another sense: according as it be conceived of as a *philosophia perennis* or as an ongoing research program, always ready to correct errors, tackle new problems, incorporate new views, or shift focus. If one remembers that the cemetery of ideas is full of perennial philosophies, one will prefer a philosophy open in both senses, that is, welcoming and on the go.

Realist / fantastic. A realist philosophy is one that tackles "real" problems rather than artificial ones; that adopts the epistemological realism inherent in the factual sciences and the technologies; and that subjects its theses to "reality checks." It is fantastic if it plays with ingenious but insubstantial problems, ignores all the relevant findings in other departments, and spins untestable or utterly false fantasies about the world, knowledge, or action.

Systemic / fragmentary. A philosophy can be systemic in either of two senses: in constituting a coherent whole, or in regarding everything as either a system or a component of one. And a philosophy may be fragmentary in similar ways: in being a heap of disconnected theses or arguments, or in failing to see the forest for the trees. Of course, it is not mandatory to opt for either style. There have been brilliant fragmentarians and dismal systemists. The important thing is to do some good philosophy. However, to paraphrase Baltasar Gracián, good philosophy, if systemic, is twice as good. As mentioned earlier, the reasons for such preference are internal consistency, deductive power, and matching the systemicity of both the world and human knowledge.

Topical / anachronistic. The philosophers who do not renew their problematics or their information lag behind. In so doing they become obstacles to progress because they deviate the attention from topical problems and recent findings. Caution: To be up-to-date is not the same as to imitate what is fashionable in Cambridge, Massachusetts, Oxford, or Paris. To be up-to-date means to be informed about contemporary physics when speculating about being or becoming, space or time, causation or chance; about chemistry, biochemistry, and cellular biology when thinking about emergence or self-organization; about cognitive neuroscience when doing philosophy of mind; about neurolinguistics, sociolinguistics, and historical linguistics when working on the philosophy of language; about economic sociology and history when analyzing social applications of game theory, and so on. In short, a topical philosophy is original to some extent rather than mimetic, and in touch with other fields of inquiry rather than isolated.

Useful / useless. A philosophy is useful if it helps nonphilosophers notice or state new problems; design viable strategies to investigate them; elucidate general ideas by analyzing or interrelating them; debate rationally the merits and flaws of rival approaches or doctrines; detect impostures, in particular pseudophilosophies and pseudosciences; or analyze and evaluate moral norms. By contrast, a useless philosophy detects no interesting new problems and fails to suggest any solutions to old problems. Let me hasten to add that I am not proposing that we always search for immediate applications. Utilitarianism, whether in the humanities, basic sciences, or the arts, clips the wings of imagination and only yields short-lived articles. In those fields we ought to look for long-run usefulness. This is the product of the features listed above: Authenticity, clarity, criticism, depth, enlightenment, interest, materialism, nobility, openness, realism, systemism, and topicality.

The preceding covers another two dichotomies: tender-minded/tough-minded, and lumpers/splitters. It appears that most tender-minded philosophers are lumpers rather than splitters, but this is because they confuse ideas rather than because they bridge them. Good philosophers split what is complex, and lump what belong together: they are analysts as well as synthesizers. The reason is simply that they deal with systems rather than with isolated items. And they split or lump, as the case requires, because they wish to understand. All good philosophy brings some enlightenment.

There may be further alternatives to reconstruct philosophy—or for allowing it to disintegrate even further. However, the ones listed above may suffice to craft projects of either maintenance or reconstruction rather than demolition.

CONCLUSION

Philosophy is rather stagnant. All the philosophical schools—in particular Aristotelianism, Thomism, Kantianism, Hegelianism, dialectical materialism, positivism, pragmatism, intuitionism, phenomenology, and linguistic philosophy—are in ruins. No new broad and deep philosophies have been proposed in recent times, and none of the extant ideas has been of much help to understand the sea changes that have signed the twentieth century. If we wish philosophy to become again a knowledge of knowledge, a midwife of science, a judge of values, and a beacon for action, we must try and reconstruct it. We must rethink it not only correctly but also on a large scale. And we must never settle for the so-called weak thinking and the concomitant crippled writing characteristic of postmodernity, which is a betrayal of twenty-five centuries of efforts to crawl out of the cave.

We should face this great task the way the architects of the great medieval cathedrals proceeded, namely using some fragments of ruins as well as inventing new ideas. This is an endeavor for generations of curious, fearless, and industrious philosophers willing to listen to people in other departments and even in the street. At the entrance of this construction site let us hang a sign saying "Building under permanent reconstruction." This should dissuade the professionals without avocation, while attracting the lovers of original philosophizing.

NOTE ON THE SOURCES

Half of the chapters in this book, namely 5, 6, 7, 9, and 10, are new. The others are thoroughly revised versions of previous publications. An earlier version of chapter 1 was read at the Congress of the International Humanist and Ethical Association held in México City, and published in *Free Inquiry* 17, no. 2 (1997): 24–28. Chapter 2 was read at the symposium on cosmology held at the Lateran University, Vatican City, and published in *Aquinas* 35: 219–35. Chapter 3 owes a lot to my book *Scientific Materialism* (Dordrecht, Boston: Reidel, 1981). An ancestor of chapter 4 was read at the neuroscience symposium held in Galveston and published in *Information Processing in the Nervous System*, edited by H. M. Pinsker and W. D. Williams (New York: Raven, 1980), pp. 1–16, and reprinted in *Perspectives: News in Physiological Sciences* 4 (1989): 206–209. A precursor of chapter 8 appeared in *Fundamenta scientiae* 3 (1982): 369–88, and was read at the CSICOP (Committee for the Scientific Investigation of Claims of the Paranormal) conference in 1984. And the Spanish parent of chapter 10 was circulated at the I Congreso Iberoamericano de Filosofía (Cáceres-Madrid, 1998).

REFERENCES

Agassi, J. 1975. *Science in flux*. Dordrecht and Boston: Reidel.

Alcock, J. 1990. *Science and supernature: A critical appraisal of parapsychology*. Amherst, N.Y.: Prometheus Books.

Allman, J. M. 1999. *Evolving brains*. New York: Scientific American Library.

Andreski, S. 1972. *Social science as sorcery*. London: André Deutsch.

Aspect, A., J. Dalibard, and G. Roger. 1982. Experimental test of Bell's inequalities using time-varying analyzers. *Physical Review Letters* 47: 1804–1807.

Bales, R. F. 1999. *Social interaction systems: Theory and measurement*. New Brunswick, N.J.: Transaction Publishers.

Beaumont, J. G., P. M. Kennedy, and M. J. C. Rogers, eds. 1996. *The Blackwell dictionary of neuropsychology*. Oxford: Blackwells.

Becker, G. S. 1976. *The economic approach to human behavior*. Chicago: University of Chicago Press.

Bergson, H. 1932. *Les deux sources de la morale et de la religion*. Paris: Presses Universitaires de France.

Berlinski, D. 1976. *On systems analysis*. Cambridge, Mass.: MIT Press.

Bianco, F. 1981. Comprensione, spiegazione, interpretazione. In *Max Weber e l'analisi del mondo moderno*, edited by P. Rossi, 53–81. Torino: Einaudi.

Blitz, D. 1992. *Emergent evolution: Qualitative novelty and the levels of reality*. Dordrecht and Boston: Reidel.

Bochenski, J. M. 1990. On the system. In *Studies on Mario Bunge's treatise*, edited by P. Weingartner and G. J. W. Dorn, 99–104. Amsterdam and Atlanta: Rodopi.

Boring, E. G. 1950. *A history of experimental psychology*, 2d ed. New York: Appleton-Century-Crofts.

Boudon, R. 1995. *Le juste et le vrai: Etudes sur l'objectivité des valeurs et de la connaissance*. Paris: Fayard.

———. 1999. *Le sens des valeurs*. Paris: Presses Universitaires de France.

Broad, C. D. 1949. The relevance of psychical research to philosophy. *Philosophy* 24: 291–309.

Bunge, M. 1959. *Metascientific queries*. Springfield, Ill.: Charles Thomas.

———. 1973. *Philosophy of physics*. Dordrecht and Boston: D. Reidel.

———. 1974. The concept of social structure. In *Developments in the methodology of social science*, edited by W. Leinfellner and E. Köhler, 175–215. Dordrecht and Boston: Reidel.

———. 1974–89. *Treatise on basic philosophy*, 8 volumes. Dordrecht and Boston: Reidel (Kluwer).

———. 1979. *Treatise on basic philosophy*, vol. 4, *A world of systems*. Dordrecht and Boston: Reidel.

———. 1980.*The mind-body problem*. Oxford and New York: Pergamon Press.

———. 1981. *Scientific materialism*. Dordrecht and Boston: Reidel.

———. 1983. *Treatise on basic philosophy*, vol. 6, *Understanding the world*. Dordrecht and Boston: Reidel.

———. 1985.*Treatise on basic philosophy*, vol. 7, *Philosophy of science and technology*, pt. 1: *Formal and physical sciences*. Dordrecht and Boston: Reidel.

———. 1988. Three faces and two masks of probability. In *Probability in the sciences*, edited by E. Agazzi, 27–50. Dordrecht and Boston: Reidel.

———. 1989.*Treatise on basic philosophy*, vol. 8, *Ethics*. Dordrecht and Boston: Reidel.

———. 1991a.The power and limits of reduction. In *The problem of reductionism in science*, edited by Evandro Agazzi, 31–49. Dordrecht and Boston: Kluwer.

———. 1991b. A skeptic's beliefs and disbeliefs. *New Ideas in Psychology* 9:131–49.

———. 1992. Systems everywhere. In *Cybernetics and applied systems*, edited by Constantin Negoita, 23–41. New York: Marcel Dekker.

———. 1995. *Sistemas sociales y filosofía*. Buenos Aires: Sudamericana.

———. 1996a. *Finding philosophy in social science*. New Haven, Conn.: Yale University Press.

———. 1996b. The seven pillars of Popper's social philosophy. *Philosophy of the Social Sciences* 26: 528–56. Repr. in Bunge 1999b.

———. 1997. A new look at moral realism. In *Normative systems in legal and moral theory*, edited by E. Garzón Valdés, W. Krawietz, G. H. von Wright, and R. Zimmerling, 17–26. Berlin: Duncker & Humblot.

———. 1998a. *Social science under debate*. Toronto: University of Toronto Press.

———. 1998b [1967]. *Philosophy of science*, 2 vols. New Brunswick, N.J.: Transaction Publishers.

———. 1999a. *Dictionary of philosophy*. Amherst, N.Y.: Prometheus Books.

————. 1999b.*The sociology-philosophy connection*. New Brunswick, N.J.: Transaction Publishers.

————. 2000a. Systemism: The alternative to individualism and holism. *Journal of Socio-Economics* 29: 147–57.

————. 2000b. Ten modes of individualism—none of which works—and their alternatives. *Philosophy of the Social Sciences* 30: 384–406.

————. 2000c. Energy: Between physics and metaphysics. *Science and Education* 9: 457–61.

Bunge, M., and R. Ardila. 1987. *Philosophy of psychology*. New York: Springer-Verlag.

Calvo Martínez, T. 1978. Introduction to Aristóteles, *Acerca del alma*. Madrid: Gredos.

Carnap, R. 1950. *Logical foundations of probability*. London: Routledge and Kegan Paul.

Castells, M. 1996. *The rise of the network society*. Cambridge, Mass.: Blackwell.

Changeux, J.-P. 1988. *Neuronal man*. New York: Pantheon Books.

Churchland, P. M. 1984. *Matter and consciousness: A contemporary introduction to the philosophy of mind*. Cambridge, Mass.: MIT Press.

Clark, A. 1997. *Being there*. Cambridge, Mass.: MIT Press.

Cohen, A. 1974. *Two-dimensional man*. Los Angeles: University of California Press.

Coleman, J. S. 1990. *Foundations of social theory*. Cambridge, Mass.: Belknap Press of Harvard University Press.

Cornman, J. W. 1971. *Materialism and sensations*. New Haven, Conn.: Yale University Press.

Crapanzano, V. 1992. *Hermes' dilemma and Hamlet's desire: On the epistemology of interpretation*. Cambridge, Mass.: Harvard University Press.

Crews, F., ed. 1998. *Unauthorized Freud: Doubters confront a legend*. New York: Penguin Books.

D'Abro, A. 1939. *The decline of mechanism (in modern physics)*. New York: Van Nostrand.

Dahrendorf, R. 1987. Max Weber and modern social science. In *Max Weber and his contemporaries*, edited by W. J. Mommsen and J. Osterhammel, 574–80. London: Unwin Hyman.

Dallmayr, F. R., and T. A. McCarthy, eds. 1977. *Understanding and social inquiry*. Notre Dame, Ind.: University of Notre Dame Press.

Deutsch, K. 1966. *Nationalism and social communication*, 2d ed. Cambridge, Mass.: Harvard University Press.

Dilthey, W. 1959 [1883]. *Einleitung in die Geisteswissenschaften*. In *Gesammelte Schriften*, vol. 1. Stuttgart: Teubner; Göttingen: Vandenhoeck & Ruprecht.

————. 1961 [1900]. *Die Entstehung der Hermeneutik*. In *Gesammelte Schriften*, vol. 5, pp. 318–31. Stuttgart: Teubner; Göttingen: Vandenhoeck & Ruprecht.

Dixon, W. J., and T. Boswell. 1996. Dependency, disarticulation, and denominator effects: Another look at foreign capital penetration. *American Journal of Sociology* 102: 543–62.

Donald, M. 1991. *Origins of the modern mind*. Cambridge, Mass.: Harvard University Press.

Dover, G. 2000. *Dear Mr. Darwin*. London: Widenfield and Nicholson.

Durkheim, E. 1950. *Leçons de sociologie*. Paris: Presses Universitaires de France.

———. 1988 [1894]. *Les règles de la méthode sociologique*. Paris: Flammarion.

Einstein, A. 1949. Autobiographical notes. In *Albert Einstein: Philosopher-scientist*, edited by P. A. Schilpp, 1–95. Evanston, Ill.: The Library of Living Philosophers.

———. 1951 [1944]. Remarks on Bertrand Russell's theory of knowledge. In *The philosophy of Bertrand Russell*, 3d ed., edited by P. A. Schilpp, 177–291. Evanston, Ill.: Tudor Pub. Co.

Engels, F. 1978. *Anti-Dühring*. London: Lawrence & Wishart.

Feyerabend, P. K. 1975. *Against method*. London: New Left Books.

Fischer, C. S., M. Sánchez Jankowski, S. R. Lucas, A. Swidler, and K. Voss. 1996. *Inequality by design: Cracking the bell curve*. Princeton, N.J.: Princeton University Press.

Flew, A., ed. 1987. *Readings in the philosophical problems of parapsychology*. Amherst, N.Y.: Prometheus Books.

Fogel, R. W. 1994. Economic growth, population theory, and physiology: The bearing of long-term processes on the making of economic policy. *American Economic Review* 84: 369–95.

Fotheringhame, D. K., and M. P. Young. 1997. Neural coding schemes for sensory representation: Theoretical proposals and empirical evidence. In Rugg 1997, 47–76.

Freud, S. 1960 [1924]. *A general introduction to psychoanalysis*. New York: Washington Square.

Gardner, M. 1983. *Science: Good, bad and bogus*. Oxford: Oxford University Press.

Garfinkel, H. 1967. *Studies in ethnomethodology*. Englewood Cliffs, N.J.: Prentice-Hall.

Gazzaniga, M., ed. 2000. *The new cognitive neurosciences*, 2d ed. Cambridge, Mass.: MIT Press.

Gazzaniga, M., R. B. Ivry, and G. R. Mangun. 1998. *Cognitive neuroscience*. New York: W. W. Norton.

Geertz, C. 1973. *The interpretation of cultures*. New York: BasicBooks.

———. 1983. *Local knowledge: Further essays in interpretive anthropology*. New York: Basic-Books.

Gellner, E. 1985. *Relativism and the social sciences*. Cambridge: Cambridge University Press.

———. 1993. *The psychoanalytic movement*, 2d ed. London: Fontana Press.

Goldstone, J. A., and B. Useem. 1999. Prison riots as microrevolutions: An extension of state-centered theories of revolution. *American Journal of Sociology* 104: 985–1029.

Gould, S. J. 1999. Non-overlapping magisteria. *Skeptical Inquirer* 23 (4): 55–61.

Gray, J. 1998. *False dawn: The delusion of global capitalism*. New York: New Press.

Harrington, A. 1996. *Reenchanted science: Holism in German culture from Wilhelm II to Hitler*. Princeton, N.J.: Princeton University Press.

Harris, M. 1979. *Cultural materialism*. New York: Random House.

Hebb, D. O. 1980. *Essay on mind*. Hillsdale, N.J.: Lawrence Erlbaum.

Heidegger, M. 1987 [1953]. *Einführung in die Metaphysik*, 5th. ed. Tübingen: Max Niemeyer.

Herrnstein, R. J., and C. Murray. 1994. *The bell curve: Intelligence and class structure in American life*. New York: Free Press.

Herschel, J. F. W. 1830. *Preliminary discourse on the study of natural philosophy*. London: Longmans.

Hurwitz, R. 1999. Who needs politics? Who needs people? The ironies of democracy in cyberspace. *Contemporary Sociology* 28: 655–61.

Jeans, J. H. 1930. *The mysterious universe*. Cambridge: Cambridge University Press.

Kentor, J. 1998. The long-term effect of foreign investment dependence on economic growth, 1940–1990. *American Journal of Sociology* 103: 1024–48.

Koertge, N., ed. 1999. *A house built on sand: Exposing postmodernist myths about science*. New York: Oxford University Press.

Köhler, S., and M. Moscovitch. 1997. Unconscious visual processing in neuropsychological syndromes: A survey of the literature and evaluation of models of consciousness. In Rugg 1997, 305–73.

Kosslyn, S. M., and O. Koenig. 1995. *Wet mind: The new cognitive neuroscience*. New York: Free Press.

Kuhn, T. S. 1962. *The structure of scientific revolutions*. Chicago: University of Chicago Press.

———. 1963. The function of dogma in scientific research. In *Scientific change*, edited by A. C. Crombie, 347–69. London: Heinemann.

Kurtz, P. 1988. *Forbidden fruit: The ethics of humanism*. Amherst, N.Y.: Prometheus Books.

———. 1992. *The new skepticism: Inquiry and reliable knowledge*. Amherst, N.Y.: Prometheus Books.

Kurtz, P., ed. 1973. *Humanist manifestos I and II*. Amherst, N.Y.: Prometheus Books.

———. 1985. *A skeptic's handbook of parapsychology*. Amherst, N.Y.: Prometheus Books.

Lamont, C. 1982. *The philosophy of humanism*, 6th ed. New York: Frederick Ungar.

Latour, B., and S. Woolgar. 1979. *Laboratory life: The social construction of scientific facts*. London and Beverly Hills: Sage.

Lewontin, R. 2000. *It ain't necessarily so: The dream of the human genome and other illusions*. New York: New York Review of Books.

Loftus, E., and K. Ketcham. 1994. *The myth of repressed memory: False memories and allegations of sexual abuse*. New York: St. Martin's Press.

Lovejoy, A. O. 1953. *The great chain of being: A study of the history of an idea*. Cambridge, Mass.: Harvard University Press.

Luhmann, N. 1984. *Soziale systeme*. Frankfurt: Suhrkamp.

Macmillan, M. 1997. *Freud evaluated: The completed arc*, 2d ed. Cambridge, Mass.: MIT Press.

Mahner, M., ed. 2001. *Scientific realism: Selected essays of Mario Bunge*. Amherst, N.Y.: Prometheus Books.

Mahner, M., and M. Bunge. 1996a. Is religious education compatible with science education? *Science & Education* 5:101–23.

Mahner, M., and M. Bunge. 1996b. The incompatibility of science and religion sustained: A reply to our critics. *Science & Education* 5: 189–99.

———. 1997. *Foundations of biophilosophy*. Berlin, Heidelberg, and New York: Springer.

McMullin, E., ed. 1964. *The concept of matter*. Notre Dame, Ill.: University of Notre Dame Press.

Menzies, H. 1995. *Whose brave new world?* Toronto: Between the Lines.

Merton, R. K. 1968. *Social theory and social structure*, enlarged ed. New York: Free Press.

———. 1973. *Sociology of science*. Chicago: University of Chicago Press.

Mill, J. S. 1965 [1871]. *Principles of political economy*, 7th ed. In *Collected works*, vol. 3. Toronto: University of Toronto Press.

Miller, D. 1999. Being an absolute skeptic. *Science* 284: 1625–26.

Mintzberg, H., B. Ahlstrand, and J. Lampel. 1998. *Strategy safari: A guided tour through the wilds of strategic management*. New York: Free Press.

Mountcastle, V. 1998. *Perceptual neuroscience: The cerebral cortex*. Cambridge, Mass.: Harvard University Press.

Mueller-Vollmer, K., ed. 1989. *The hermeneutics reader*. New York: Continuum.

Naville, E. 1880. *La logique de l'hypothèse*. Paris: Alcan.

Negroponte, N. 1996. *Being digital*. New York: Vintage Books.

Peirce, C. S. 1958 [1902]. *Scientific method*. In *Collected papers*, vol. 7, edited by A. W. Burks. Cambridge, Mass.: Harvard University Press.

Pinker, S. 1997. *How the mind works*. New York: W. W. Norton.

Poincaré, H. 1903. *La science et l'hypothèse*. Paris: Ernest Flammarion.

Popper, K. R. 1959 [1935]. *The logic of scientific discovery*. London: Hutchinson.

———. 1962 [1945]. *The open society and its enemies*, vol. 2. London: Routledge & Kegan Paul.

———. 1967. Quantum mechanics without "the observer." In *Quantum theory and reality*, edited by M. Bunge, pp. 7–44. Berlin, Heidelberg, and New York: Springer-Verlag.

———. 1974. Intellectual autobiography. In *The philosophy of Karl Popper*, vol. 1, edited by P. A. Schilpp, 3–181. La Salle, Ill.: Open Court.

Randi, J. 1982. *Flim-flam!* Amherst, N.Y.: Prometheus Books.

Rawls, J. 1971. *A theory of justice*. Cambridge, Mass.: Harvard University Press.

Renfrew, C., and E. B. W. Zubrow, eds. 1994. *The ancient mind: Elements of cognitive archaeology*. Cambridge: Cambridge University Press.

Reyna, S. P. 1994. Literary anthropology and the case against science. *Man (N.S.)* 29: 555–81.

Ricoeur, P. 1975. *La métaphore vive*. Paris: Seuil.

Rohrlich, F. 1983. Facing quantum-mechanical reality. *Science* 221: 1251–55.

Rugg, M. D., ed. 1997. *Cognitive neuroscience*. Hove East Sussex: Psychology Press.

Rutter, M., and M. Rutter. 1993. *Developing minds: Challenge and continuity across the life span*. New York: BasicBooks.

Schelling, T. C. 1984. *Choice and consequence: Perspectives of an errant economist*. Cambridge, Mass.: Harvard University Press.

Sellars, R. W. 1922. *Evolutionary naturalism*. Chicago: Open Court.

Simmel, G. 1950 [1908]. *Soziologie: Untersuchungen über die Formen der Vergesellschaftung*. Partial translation in *The sociology of Georg Simmel*, edited by K. H. Wolff. Glencoe, Ill.: Free Press.

Smart, J. J. C. 1963. *Philosophy and scientific realism*. London: Routledge & Kegan Paul.

Smelser, N. J., and R. Swedberg, eds. 1994. *Handbook of economic sociology*. Princeton, N.J.: Princeton University Press; New York: Russell Sage Foundation.

Sokal, A., and J. Bricmont. 1998. *Fashionable nonsense: Postmodern intellectual's abuse of science*. New York: Picador.

Sorokin, P. 1956. *Fads and foibles in modern sociology and related sciences*. Chicago: Henry Regnery.

Soros, G. 1998. *The crisis of global capitalism (Open society endangered)*. New York: Public Affairs.

Squire, L. R., and S. M. Kosslyn, eds. 1998. *Findings and current opinion in cognitive neuroscience*. Cambridge, Mass.: MIT Press.

Stoll, C. 1995. *Silicon snake oil: Second thoughts on the information highway*. New York: Anchor Books.

Storer, M. B., ed. 1980. *Humanist ethics*. Amherst, N.Y.: Prometheus Books.

Swift, J. 1965 [1726]. *Gulliver's travels*. London: Folio Society.

Taylor, C. 1971. Interpretation and the sciences of man. *Review of Metaphysics* 25: 3–34, 45–51.

Taylor, J. G., and E. Balanovski. 1979. Are there any scientific explanations of the paranormal? *Nature* 279: 631–33.

Tilly, C. 1998. *Durable inequality*. Berkeley: University of California Press.

Tocqueville, A. de. 1998 [1856]. *The old regime and the French Revolution*, vol. 1, translated by A. S. Kahan. Chicago: University of Chicago Press.

Torrey, E. F. 1992. *Freudian fraud: The malignant effect of Freud's theory on American thought and culture*. New York: Harper Collins.

Von Schelting, A. 1934. *Max Weber's Wissenschaftslehre*. Tübingen: J. C. B. Mohr.

Wallerstein, I. 1976. *The modern world-system*, 3 vols. New York: Academic Press.

Weber, M. 1976 [1922]. *Wirtschaft und Gesellschaft. Grundriss der verstehenden Soziologie*, 5th ed. Tübingen: J. C. B. Mohr.

———. 1988 [1913]. Ueber einige Kategorien der verstehende Soziologie. In *Gesammelte Aufsätze zur Wissenschaftslehre*, 427–74. Tübingen: J. C. B. Mohr.

Whewell, W. 1967 [1847]. *The philosophy of the inductive sciences*, 2 vols. Reprint, London: Frank Cass.

Wilson, R. A., and F. C. Keil, eds. 1999. *The MIT encyclopedia of the cognitive sciences*. Cambridge, Mass.: MIT Press.

Winch, P. 1958. *The idea of a social science*. London: Routledge & Kegan Paul.

Wolf, A. P. 1995. *Sexual attraction and childhood association*. Stanford, Calif.: Stanford University Press.

Wolpert, L. 1992. *The unnatural nature of science*. London: Faber and Faber.

Woolgar, S. 1986. On the alleged distinction between discourse and praxis. *Social Studies of Science* 16: 309–17.

Zahler, R. R., and H. J. Sussmann. 1977. Claims and accomplishments of applied catastrophe theory. *Nature* 269: 759–63.

NAME INDEX

Alcock, J., 176
Allman, J. M., 92
Andreski, S., 184
Aquinas, T., 9, 218
Aristotle, 30, 35, 50, 109, 135, 218
Asimov, I., 186
Aspect, A., 55

Bachelard, G., 169
Bacon, F., 117
Balanovski, E., 186
Bales, R. F., 129
Beaumont, J. G., 80
Becker, G. S., 114
Bentham, J., 201, 218
Bergson, H., 197
Berkeley, G., 217
Berlinski, D., 183
Bianco, F., 123
Blitz, D., 76
Bloor, D., 210
Bochenski, J. M., 43

Bolzano, B., 217
Bonnet, C., 31
Borges, J. L., 38
Boring, E. G., 35
Boswell, T., 104
Boudon, R., 133, 156, 197, 198
Bricmont, J., 146, 154
Broad, C. D., 176
Broca, P., 98
Buffon, G. L. L., 31
Burt, C., 162

Calvino, I., 38
Calvo Martínez, T., 50
Carnap, R., 66, 124
Castells, M., 22
Changeaux, J.-P., 80
Churchland, P. M., 74
Clark, A., 74
Cohen, A., 121
Coleman, J. S., 44, 125
Comte, A., 30, 207

SUBJECT INDEX

244